Views
from the
Conning Tower

To: RYAN

HOPE YOU ENJOY THE BOOK!

Rich Slate

2016

"What a great book! It was wonderful to read of your adventures and tribulations. Thanks for the great rides."

Daniel F. Belknap, Professor of Earth Sci., Univ. of Maine

"Your book is a treasure. It should be mandatory reading for all potential and existing geologists/oceanographers of any age."

Clark Lambert, St. Petersburg, Florida

"I found your book in our mail box and have been reading it ever since. Many of us in the geosciences have had an adventure or two in the field but your many expeditions and exploits are truly astounding. You clearly have a gift for writing and in a manner that provides both the sense of adventure surrounding your work as well as very clear explanations of technical details understandable to all readers. What an amazing record of accomplishment."

James Ingle, Professor Emeritus Geology, Stanford University

"Not since my Navy days when I purchased Cousteau's "Silent World", in a Hong Kong bookstore, in 1954, has a book forced me to read it cover to cover-non-stop. Your book did just that."

Harold Hudson, President of Reef Tech Inc., Miami, Florida

"Your book arrived and I must say I thoroughly enjoyed reading it. Of all the different subs I have been privileged to use over the years, the Nekton *series were by far the best for functionality and ruggedness. I have very fond memories of my dives with you."*

Pat Colin, Director "Coral Reef Research Foundation", Palau

Views
from the
Conning Tower

The Adventures of a Deep-Sea Explorer

Richard A. Slater

ISBN: 978-0-9849105-2-6
Library of Congress Catalog Number: 2011962152

Cover design by Robert Aulicino

Cover: Pilot's view of the southern Alaskan coast, from the *Delta* submersible conning tower, while diving in the Gulf of Alaska during 1997. The black post is the compass support bar with digital compass on top. (photo by David Slater)

Conning tower: A raised enclosed observation post on top of a submersible, with view ports, used by the pilot. Entrance to the submersible is through a hatch on top of the conning tower.

Title page photo: *Nekton Gamma* submersible in action off Southern California coast in 1975.

All photographs are from the author's collection unless otherwise indicated.

For my children: David, Melinda, Kylie, and Stephen—all very happy and doing well in life, despite growing up with a wandering father who was not always there to guide them.

Also for Ryan, Logan, Mallory, Hayden, Natalie, Riley, and Addisyn so they will know what their grandfather was up to all those years.

CONTENTS

FIGURES

vi

Preface

Growing Up

There's a race of men that don't fit in,
A race that can't stay still;
So they break the hearts of kith and kin,
And roam the world at will.

—Robert Service, *The Spell of the Yukon and
other Verses* (1911)

IT WAS A BEAUTIFUL sunny day. The ocean was sparkling and clear off Catalina Island twenty-two miles south-southwest of Los Angeles. I was piloting *Nekton Beta,* a deep-diving submersible when, at a depth of about 150 feet, there was a tremendous CRASH and a violent shaking—I instantly blacked out. The rapidly sinking submersible carried my partner and me into the depths. When I regained consciousness, I was slumped over in a dark tube of cold steel rapidly filling with icy water on the sea floor 240 feet below the surface. How did I get into this predicament? What did I do to deserve this? Let me start from the beginning;

My mother saved a horoscope from a newspaper the day I was born. It read:

> A child born on this day may have excellent abilities,
> being constructive, versatile, energetic, and bold, but
> at the same time it may be too adventurous, impulsive,
> or foolhardy unless it is given proper discipline and
> direction.

This, as it turned out, was a fairly accurate prediction for my future, as many of my adventures were probably impulsive and several could even be called foolhardy.

I never thought of becoming a scientist, especially one who would spend much of his career under the ocean. There were no scientists in my family and except for a few of my maternal grandfather's ancestors, whalers from Nantucket, no one had ventured out onto the sea. My only contact with the ocean was an occasional day at the beach or a rare fishing trip to one of the Southern California offshore islands.

Searching for adventure

With my sister

BE A FROGMAN!

Frogman Club

My father died in 1946 so my mother raised two small children, my sister and me, in the small Ventura County town of Santa Paula, about fifty miles northwest of Los Angeles. At night we could see the glow of the big city lights over the nearby mountains. Santa Paula was an idyllic place to grow up in the 1940s and 1950s and I have many fond memories of living there. I attended a two-room country school between Ojai and Santa Paula where five students in one class was considered an overload. It was the only school I know of that closed for the opening day of fishing season. We moved into town when I was in the sixth grade and I lived only one block from the high school. I continued being an average student, more interested in sports than studying.

My first interest in the ocean began in the sixth grade when I joined the Freddy Frogman Club, for a dollar, after seeing an advertisement in a *Boy's Life* magazine. Soon I was the proud owner of my first mask, flippers, and a snorkel with a Ping-Pong ball stopper. In the late 1940s, a sympathetic neighbor drove me to Morro Bay for my first ocean snorkel dive. We swam around the big rock located just offshore, while making shallow free dives to gather abalone with a tire iron and then tossing them into a gunnysack hanging from an inner tube.

In high school, I became fascinated with the marine world, driven by an occasional day of surfing at nearby beaches. I could easily spend eight hours a day in the water. During this time, two men were particularly influential in guiding me down the path I eventually chose to follow. My mother kept the books for a local rancher who sometimes allowed me to tag along on his hunting and fishing trips. I spent many weekends fishing and free diving from his forty-foot powerboat off Catalina Island. I remember once we were enveloped in thick fog while crossing the channel to Los Angeles. I was told to sit on the bow and blow a little fog horn every ten seconds. The next thing I remember was a loud blast from a big fog horn and a huge ship appearing out of the mist that almost ran over us. I do not think my little horn had much affect. Another time we were tied up to a buoy off Catalina when someone came up at 2:00 a.m. and said it was his buoy and we had to move. I thought I recognized the voice—it was Humphrey Bogart.

The other influential man was a biology teacher who was hired during my junior year in high school. I was mesmerized with all of the animals, dead and alive, he brought to class and I became his enthusiastic assistant during my senior year. I even took taxidermy lessons by mail and our house soon filled with odd-looking lopsided stuffed birds and animals. The only things I wanted for Christmas one year, much to my mother's bewilderment, was a pair of glass wildcat eyes and a brain spoon.

High school placement tests pointed me toward a career in architecture and I enrolled at USC (the University of Southern California) in the fall of 1954. I struggled for one semester when, during Christmas break, I discovered that thirty of my Santa Paula classmates were joining the Army. They all had volunteered for the draft and convinced me to join with them. I was underage but my Mom reluctantly signed my enlistment papers, which eventually resulted in my being one of the youngest Korean War veterans. I was only seventeen when the war officially ended two weeks after I was inducted.

I endured eighteen weeks of infantry training at Fort Ord, California, before traveling to Seattle by train to board a troop ship heading to Korea. My infantry company was standing in formation, in the rain, waiting to march onto the ship when a Captain walked by and asked if anyone could type. I raised my hand. Luckily, I had taken a typing class in high school so, as my unit continued to board the troop ship, I stepped out of line and became a supply clerk assigned to a Fort Lewis, Washington, tank battalion. My official job title was "tank driver" which was interesting as I had never been in a tank. I later received a few driving lessons and became adept at knocking down trees in the forest.

When it was time for me to be discharged, I was sent to the re-enlistment barracks. I declined to re-up so I was given the job of tending a furnace during the Christmas-New Year's break. I brokered a deal with another soldier so I could take Christmas day off. He covered for me and I returned the favor by being on duty twenty-four hours at the end of the year. I was alone New Year's Eve shoveling coal into a furnace when some buddies stopped by and convinced me to take a short break to help celebrate the New Year. Unfortunately, a few hours turned into most the night and when I returned early in the morning the furnaces were out and the water pipes frozen. They threatened me with a court martial but after a few days I received my honorable discharge. The Korean Veterans G.I. Bill was available and I was ready to tackle college again.

MEANWHILE JACQUES COUSEAU, an officer in the French Navy, had been thinking of a way to swim underwater unencumbered with heavy diving equipment. He and several friends worked at perfecting their dive equipment during WWII. In 1943, Cousteau and Emile Gagnan, an engineer with *Air Liquide* in Paris, fabricated the first demand valve, which allowed divers to breathe normally using compressed air underwater. They named their new invention the Aqua-Lung regulator. Cousteau tried to sell these regulators after the war but few people were interested until 1953 when he published a book, *The Silent World,* which featured many color underwater photos taken by Cousteau and his diving buddies. His book was a bestseller and interest in scuba diving started building. A film version of his book then won the 1956 Oscar for the best documentary. After the film won awards, *U.S. Divers*, a USA subsidiary of *Air Liquide*, started selling a few scuba regulators and other dive equipment. About the same time I was eager and ready to return to the ocean.

Chapter One

School & Tar Mounds

A vivid sense of delight takes hold of one, when for the first time one penetrates the surface. A palace untouched by human hands with its gardens of rock and water where living creatures play the part of flowers, is the goal of all our striving.

—Philippe Diole, *The Underwater Adventure* (1953)

I ENROLLED IN A GEOLOGY class during the spring of 1957 while attending Menlo College (near San Francisco). The class was really enjoyable as geology is a science where you can spend a lot of time outdoors so I decided to major in geology. That same spring, a friend introduced me to the new sport of scuba diving* and I quickly purchased my own equipment.

Learning to scuba dive   *Hiking to Big Sur dive site*

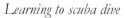

* Scuba is an acronym for self-contained underwater breathing apparatus.

My first ocean dive was off Carmel's Monastery Beach, after a few lessons in a swimming pool, and I soon became addicted. I continued to drive down to the Monterey/Carmel/Big Sur area for diving weekends in 1957 and 1958, and became adept in making multiple dives on just one tank of air—I did not have much choice; there was no local dive shop to refill scuba tanks. We used war surplus cartridge belts, for extra weight, adding or tossing out lead fishing weights, or rocks, for trim.

This was a fascinating time to be underwater; most of the seascape was untouched by divers. Rock scallops were very common on the Carmel Submarine Canyon walls, I still have several of these large beautiful shells I use as soap dishes.

I had dated a girl from Oregon while stationed at Fort Lewis and continued to see her on occasional weekends by driving to Portland from San Francisco. We were married in the summer of 1958. That fall I transferred to the University of Oklahoma, considered one of the top petroleum geology schools in the nation. My plan was to follow family tradition by eventually working for a major oil company.

In 1959 my son David was born in Oklahoma and, in 1961, I graduated with a B.S. in Geology. The oil business was in a down period and there were few job opportunities. I had not planned on attending graduate school but when I could not find work, and still had a couple of years left on my G.I. Bill, I decided to return to USC for a master's degree.

Combining scuba diving with geology and oceanography classes at USC helped me develop into a marine geologist. Scuba divers were uncommon in 1961 and there were even fewer diving scientists. I managed the USC dive locker where I taught scuba to scientists in the indoor pool, filled air bottles, and signed out USC diving equipment to students and faculty. By 1961, anyone using the school diving equipment had to have a dive certification card. The problem was the only card I had was my Freddy Frogman Club card. I quietly signed up at a local dive shop for scuba lessons as I continued managing the USC dive locker.

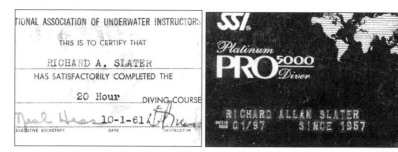

First dive card   Dive card after 5,000 dives

We lived in several places around Los Angeles, including a Watts apartment directly under planes approaching LAX. In 1962, my daughter Melinda was born and we moved uptown to South Pasadena, which was a longer commute for me but a much nicer area for my growing family.

Mapping and collecting rock samples, Santa Barbara Channel (1950s)
(photos from Jim Vernon collection)

Most weekends were spent diving, while I attended USC, to collect specimens and data for non-diving scientists and to work on my own projects. I earned a little extra income by diving with a consulting group owned by oceanographers from Scripps Institute of Oceanography and the San Diego Naval Lab. Oil companies, interested in offshore exploration, were now hiring a few diving geologists. A 1962, *World Oil* magazine article stated:

Diving geologists are starting to study formations, obtain rock samples, and otherwise map ocean-floor outcrops in much the same manner as geologists do onshore.

Suisun Bay, located at the north end of San Francisco Bay, was my USC master's degree thesis study area. It is part of the Sacramento/San Joaquin River delta. I collected hundreds of bottom samples using a small outboard motor boat, and then analyzed them at USC. One of my objectives was to calculate how much gold was washed down to the Bay from the Sierra foothills during the gold rush. If there was any gold, it was too fine for me to measure.

In 1962 and 1963, I sailed on several oceanographic cruises aboard the USC research vessel *R/V Velero IV* (a ship that would reappear in my life forty years later).

USC research vessel Velero IV, *Los Angeles*

One bonus while diving off Southern California during the 1960s was providing an occasional family dinner. Lobster, fish and abalone were common near shore and easily available. Spearing fish was an acceptable way of collecting a meal. Once, I brought a live octopus home in my "goodie" bag. An octopus is not hard to catch; what is difficult is containing them as they can escape from anywhere. I threw my bag into the kitchen sink and planned to return later, after a warm shower, to clean my catch. That's when I noticed the octopus had disappeared and after a long search it was still missing. That evening when my wife turned on the garbage disposal we found the octopus. It took a day to take the disposal apart and clean up the mess.

I volunteered to assist a fellow student who was studying seafloor sand movement in the Southern California surf zone. We would plunge into the surf, collect sand in a bag, stain it with fluorescent dye, and return it to its original location. Then, every few hours over a twenty-four hour period, we collected surf zone sand samples by pressing Vaseline-smeared 3" x 5" index cards onto the seafloor along the beach. Using a fluorescent light we counted the number of dyed sand grains versus non-dyed grains to determine which direction the sand was moving.

Consulting group dive boat Discovery, *San Diego*

We needed sand samples in deeper water off Coronado Island, south of San Diego, so we used the geological consultant group's dive boat *Discovery*. Everything went fine until late one afternoon when I was scuba diving, with a buddy; about a hundred yards off the beach, *Discovery* started drifting into the surf and the student on board could not start the engine. He threw out the anchor, called the Coast Guard, and signaled us to return. *Discovery* was moving closer to the beach as we climbed on board. We dove back into the water in full scuba gear, grabbed the dragging anchor, and started pulling *Discovery* seaward by walking along the seafloor. We kept the boat off the beach until the Coast Guard arrived. They towed us to a Point Loma dock where we jumped off, exhausted. My seasick dive and sand sample partner collapsed on the dock, in full dive gear, and started rolling around while he was vomiting. Tourists scurried out of the way, not knowing what kind of weird creature this was. (My seasick friend was Jim Ingle, now a well-regarded Professor Emeritus at Stanford University.)

A USC doctoral student was studying submarine canyons off Monterey and Carmel for his dissertation. He wasn't a diver but had bought all new diving gear so I taught him how to use it. He then asked me to accompany him on a Monterey diving field trip to take underwater photographs and to collect rock specimens from the canyon walls. We decided to make our first dive off my old dive site, Monastery Beach, south of Carmel. I demonstrated how best to swim beneath the rough surf as we prepared to dive, he with his new shiny equipment and I in my tattered gear. He was to follow me along the seafloor under the waves but when I surfaced beyond the waves he was nowhere in sight. I finally spotted him floating face down in the surf. Swimming back quickly, I grabbed him by his wetsuit collar and the seat of his pants, and propelled him toward shore where a large wave tumbled him onto the beach. After lying there for a few minutes he waved for me to go ahead so I dove alone to take photos and to collect his samples.

When I returned to the beach, about an hour later, he was with some nuns—visitors to the nearby Carmelite Monastery. He was showing how he used his dive equipment, especially his large diving knife. No one paid any attention to me as I hauled myself up the beach with my bag of rocks and camera. On the drive back to Los Angeles he sold me all his new equipment for one hundred dollars and I was set for the next few years with the latest diving gear.

In 1963, I co-authored a paper on some submarine tar seeps discovered off Santa Barbara County—my very first scientific publication. Tar floating on Southern California nearshore waters was commonly found washed up on local beaches and stuck on the feet of annoyed beach-strollers. As a youngster, I was not allowed to enter my home after a visit to the beach without scrubbing my feet with turpentine from a bottle my mother left by the door. Leaky tankers traveling in the Santa Barbara Channel were the suspected culprits until the late 1950s when scuba-diving oil geologists, mapping underwater, discovered unique mounds of tar on the seafloor off Point Conception, thirty miles west of Santa Barbara. Gas bubbles and tar issued from these tar mound vents but little else was known. (Scientists now estimate that about sixty-five percent of all ocean surface oil originates from natural seafloor seeps.)

Fresh tar from mound vent, ≈90', Pt. Conception, CA

A fellow USC graduate student, Jim Vernon, and I decided to investigate these tar mounds. To our knowledge, they had never been photographed. For dive support, we used the local rancher's boat I had gone to sea on in the early 1950s. During two dive trips to Point Conception in the winter of 1961-62, we photographed tar mounds, one-and-a-half miles offshore, in approximately ninety feet of water. My German underwater Rolleimarin camera used disposable flashbulbs that had to be replaced after each shot. I cut up an old bicycle inner tube and added some slits to hold the flashbulbs. Our support boat was to keep close to us by following the line of floating flashbulbs as they popped to the surface. However, spotters on the boat still lost us occasionally. Once, it took over an hour to locate us on the rough choppy surface while we drifted out to sea during a particularly windy day.

Some tar mounds were up to a hundred feet in diameter and eight feet high. They resembled miniature shield volcanoes or cow pies. The tar formed when heavy California crude oil seeped up through seafloor cracks and struck cold water. Thin whip-like strands of fresh tar, some up to twelve feet long, rose up into the water column from a mound's central vent. These long strands, waving in the current, would eventually break off and float to the ocean surface where they would be torn apart by waves and shaped into small balls of tar. Many of these balls eventually washed ashore on nearby beaches. Thus, we helped solve the mystery of tar on Southern California beaches. Today there is much less tar on the local beaches as offshore drilling reduced the pressure that forced the heavy oil to the surface.

These at-sea experiences would prove valuable in the years ahead. The practical knowledge plus the academics at USC, helped me secure my first job, after graduating in 1963, with the Richfield Oil Corporation Research Center in Anaheim, California. I was excited to work for Richfield Oil. My great-grandfather toiled as a carpenter, building wooden drilling rigs for Richfield in the Bakersfield area. My grandfather was a pipeline inspector for Richfield along the Ridge Route between Los Angeles and Bakersfield. My father, as a teenager, worked as a Richfield roughneck on drilling rigs on Signal hill in Long Beach. I would have stayed at Richfield for my entire career but certain events, out of my control, led to a different career path.

Chapter Two

Richfield & Hudson Bay

The Hudson's Bay Company has always been the guardian of the North.

—Ernest Thompson Seton, *The Arctic Prairies* (1923)

RICHFIELD OIL CORPORATION was a Los Angeles based oil company that employed about a hundred geologists. I began my job there by visiting Richfield field offices where I received an education on the diversity of a major oil company. I was given a few research projects including mapping oil-bearing formations outcropping on Ventura and Orange County cliffs.

In the fall of 1964, I was the Richfield representative, aboard a research vessel off San Diego, witnessing a demonstration of Jacques Cousteau's diving saucer *La Soucoupe*, a sluggish two-man submersible that Cousteau was hoping oil companies might lease. Shell Oil used *La Soucoupe* a few weeks later to inspect an underwater drilling complex off Santa Barbara, probably the first manned submersible used by an oil company. I also spent two weeks aboard *M/V Exploit*, a self-propelled drilling ship, to collect rock cores off the Oregon coast.

Richfield leased fifty million acres of Hudson Bay, Canada, in 1965 for potential oil production. Geologic data was needed for exploratory well sites. I was assigned to a summer field party to collect rocks by diving in the Bay, from a small boat, while others would map and collect rocks onshore. Churchill, York Factory, and Winisk would be our ports of call.

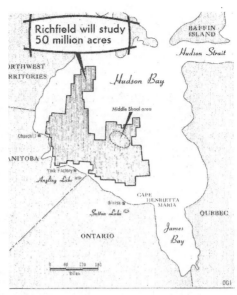

Richfield Oil Canadian Hudson Bay lease area (1965 Oil and Gas Journal)

A second Richfield field party gathered geologic data along Alaska's North Slope the same summer. Their fieldwork led to discovery of the Prudhoe Bay Oilfield. The data gathered by my group around Hudson Bay did not lead to any discoveries but we had a great summer. Our field party consisted of two geologists from Richfield's Calgary office, a cook, a cook's helper, a helicopter pilot, a mechanic, a professional diver, a ship's Captain, two Indian guides, and me.

My adventure started with a visit to Vancouver in the spring of 1965 to see the submersible *Pisces** being built for Richfield. This was to be the first oil company submersible, and we were going to use it in Hudson Bay, but it was not finished in time so it was left to scuba-divers to collect the seafloor data.

---

*International Hydrodynamics built *Pisces*, a two-man submersible capable of diving to 1,200 feet, in 1965. It was the first of nine *Pisces* submersibles used worldwide by the oil industry for work on offshore platforms and pipelines. *Pisces I* was constructed in a backyard garage that was eventually destroyed in order to remove the submersible. International Hydrodynamics went bankrupt in 1978.

First arrival, in 1965, of Richfield personnel, Hudson Bay

Hudson Bay is a large, 850-miles-long and about 650-miles wide, very shallow inland sea, part of the Arctic Ocean. It is the drain for most Canadian rivers and even several from the United States. It was an active area during the 17th and 18th centuries when France and England often fought over its rich supplies of fur.

Churchill*, population between 700 and 800, was the only Bay community of any size in 1965. It was called the "Polar Bear Capital of the World." Most of the area around Hudson Bay was sparsely populated, with Cree Indians living east of Churchill and Eskimos (now called Inuit) to the north. There was bad blood between them so we had to hire Cree guides in the east and Eskimo guides in the north. They would lead our field party down rivers so they could collect rock samples and

---

*In the summer of 2013 I visited Churchill and found it to be almost identical to what I observed in 1965. Same muddy streets, a couple of stores, lots of geese, white beluga whales, polar bear traps, very cold and very windy.

map the local geology. Meanwhile, the forty-foot hull-hardened diver support vessel, *Hudson Explorer,* was shipped by rail from Vancouver to Churchill. It was stuck in Churchill all of June, waiting for the ice to break up, so I joined the field party for several weeklong canoe river trips.

Rock outcrops are rare in the swampy tundra surrounding Hudson Bay, except for a few locations where rivers cut through bedrock. These are big rivers; the Severn is 610 miles long. A Sikorsky helicopter and Beaver seaplane assisted our field party in this vast area. The helicopter carried our field party and canoes up rivers, allowing us to paddle back to our main camp while collecting rocks and fossils along the way. Our main camp moved as we worked our way west. We were on our own while traveling down a river. The seaplane helped move the main camp hundreds of miles between rivers, brought in supplies, and flew out our geologic samples

Helicopter approaching main camp

Main camp on the Severn River

Severn River

Severn River island camp

As with most river trips, there were hours of boredom while drifting through flat lying tundra, a spongy blanket of green and brown vegetation. This was occasionally interspersed with moments of great excitement when we shot through rapids where the rock samples we needed were usually located. Once, on the Severn River, we caught several trout during a typical day's outing. That night, while camped on a river island for safety, a bear put his paw through the bottom of our overturned canoe trying to reach the fishy smell. This caused a one-day delay in our journey while we patched the canoe.

Geologists collecting fossils   *Severn River rapids*

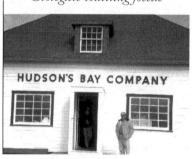

Fort Severn trading post on the bank of the Severn River

The Fort Severn Hudson's Bay trading post, established in 1689, is located near the mouth of the Severn River. When we arrived, the entire local Cree tribe was waiting for the annual visit of the Company supply barge. Sadly, the barge ran into heavy ice and radioed in that they would have to pass but would return next summer—the Cree's celebrated with a big party anyway. There was some excitement when a seal was spotted swimming in the river. Everyone started shooting, including the local priest, but the seal escaped.

Cree's set up camps early each summer near Hudson's Bay trading posts scattered around the Bay. During winter, these same tribes traveled by dogsled across the frozen tundra while checking trap lines for fur-bearing animals. They traded furs for supplies at the nearest Hudson's Bay trading post each spring, and then waited for the first snow to travel across the frozen tundra again. Cree children were sent to Ottawa for schooling in the winter but in the summer entire families camped together. Their camps were noisy affairs with dogs constantly barking and boisterous children. Chained-up sled dogs were kept half-starved because, "they work harder that way." Each dog received one fish to eat every few days.

Sometimes we camped in deserted radar stations, once part of an early warning system (DEW line) to detect Russian bombers flying across the Arctic to bomb the United States. They were abandoned in the early 1960s when intercontinental missiles replaced bombers. The Cree's stripped most stations, but the huts still provided us with shelter and warmth.

Bears were a constant problem, especially polar bears. Once, we encountered a swimming polar bear while paddling a canoe along the south shore of Hudson Bay near Winisk. The water was shallow, three or four feet deep. I could just touch the Bay floor with my paddle. The bear suddenly stood up and I could see daylight between his legs, he was about twelve feet tall. We immediately started paddling in a different direction.

Another time, while waiting for a ride, the helicopter landed nearby and the pilot was waving frantically for us to run. We jumped up, ran to the helicopter, and climbed in. After the helicopter lifted off we could see two polar bears, about a hundred yards away, heading in our direction. We carried M-1 firecrackers to scare bears and high-powered rifles to shoot one in an emergency—we did not shoot a bear that summer.

The helicopter skis were removed and inflatable pontoons installed as the weather warmed up and the tundra began to thaw. We could now land on marshy tundra or small lakes. One day, after spotting a polar bear, we asked the helicopter pilot to move closer. As we hovered over the bear it suddenly reached up and punctured one of the pontoons with his claws. When we landed back at camp the helicopter blades were damaged when we tipped over, causing a major delay and trouble back at our Calgary headquarters.

Polar bear from helicopter

Fishing near insect-repellent oil drums

Our cook and his helper kept moving ahead to set up the next main camp. Black flies and mosquitoes abound in this part of the world so some scientists, back in California, came up with an idea to make a ring around each camp with a mixture of oil, DEET, and who knows what else. We were told to make the width of the swath about fifteen feet since mosquitoes cannot fly more than ten feet without landing so now they would land in the goop and not bother us. Richfield pilots had placed oil drums filled with this magic elixir at our proposed campsites. Most of the drums were never opened after our first attempt at mosquito abatement failed. The scientists did not realize that the wind blows constantly around the Bay and insects were easily blown across our line of defense. Mosquitoes sting while black flies just bite a chunk out of your skin. We had to cover almost all of our exposed skin to avoid these irritating insects.

After a few very long canoe trips, I took the company plane down to the south end of Hudson Bay to join up with the *Hudson Explorer*. It had finally escaped from Churchill when a navigable channel opened between the Bay ice and shore. The return trip was not easy. There were no harbors for shelter and we could not travel within a hundred yards of shore because of the extremely shallow water. This left a very narrow open channel between the ice and the shore that we could travel along. The unusually heavy summer ice pack kept us away from all the areas where we wanted to dive. I did not make a single scuba dive into Hudson Bay all summer and neither did anyone else.

One day, while we were traveling back to Churchill, on the *Hudson Explorer*, the wind suddenly blew hard from the north and we were unexpectedly trapped between onrushing ice and the shore. While trying to escape, we hit some ice, damaging our propeller drive shaft, and needed to make quick repairs. Luckily, we were close to the mouth of the Hayes River and, after several hours of running, we finally entered the river and motored up it a few miles. We anchored off York Factory, which now consisted of only a couple of deserted buildings. Hudson Bay ice that night not only closed our open channel; we had been traveling in, but also piled up on shore while moving several hundred feet inland. We were trapped in the river for several days but had escaped having our boat crushed. Prop repairs were made during low tide after we ran the boat up on a mud flat.

Hudson Explorer, *Hayes River*   *Fixing the propeller drive shaft*

Hudson Bay ice on horizon and close up

York Factory

Cannon found near York Factory   *Richfield float plane at main camp*

The Hudson's Bay Company was founded in 1670. It is the oldest commercial corporation in North America and was once the largest landholder in the world. It was also the de facto government for most of Canada. York Factory, the company's longtime headquarters, is located near the mouth of the Hayes River about sixty miles southeast of Churchill. Here the Hudson's Bay Company controlled fur trade by connecting with their trading posts throughout much of North America. The large wooden structure was constructed in 1831 after some earlier buildings and a nearby fort were destroyed by permafrost. The Hudson's Bay Company used this building until 1957, when it was finally abandoned. It is the oldest and largest wooden structure in the north of Canada. York Factory was deserted when we arrived after escaping from the ice.

Exploring the area around York Factory was interesting. Several of the boat crew found artifacts, including an old Bible written by hand in the Cree language. We all carved our names, as did many others dating back to the 1830s, in the uppermost cupola. I knew the former fort site was nearby and realized that they would have shot cannon balls into the river during a battle with the French. I paced off the distance from a cannon I had found in the bushes and began searching until I discovered a cannon ball exposed on a mud flat during low tide. Excitedly, I brought it back to the boat and proudly showed it around. The ship's captain was concerned that the cannon ball might still contain gunpowder so he placed it into a bucket of water on deck where I could clean it after dinner. When I went to retrieve my cannon ball the bucket was empty. The cook, needing a bucket, had thrown the dirty water—and my twelve-pound cannon ball—overboard. The next day we made several dives into the river but it was gone, probably rolled away by the strong current.

As we approached Churchill, our Cree guides began to get nervous. They did not want to travel into Eskimo territory so we arrived in town on our own and met our Eskimo guides. The field party continued traveling north, but my work was over so I flew back to California. Richfield employees always flew first class and I was the only person in that section. I had a beard, was dressed in scruffy clothes, and was carrying a tube containing my fishing pole. The stewardess must have thought I was a prospector with maps and had hit it big (there had been several recent gold discoveries in northern Canada). She wanted to help me remove my boots but I told her that it was not a good idea.

> [Note: A flood destroyed Winisk in 1986 and it is now a ghost town. York factory is a National Historic Site and still uninhabited. Fort Severn is a center for First Nation (Cree Indians) today with about 400 residents.]

I did not know it at the time but my days at Richfield would end only months after returning from Hudson Bay due to the merger of Richfield Oil and the Atlantic Refining Company. I always thought I would remain at Richfield for the rest of my career and would been happy to do so.

Chapter Three

Australia & South Africa

I can only think of one experience that might exceed in interest
a few hours spent under the water, and that would be a journey
to Mars.

—William Beebe, *Half Mile Down* (1934)

EARLY IN 1966, Richfield Oil announced a merger with the
Atlantic Refining Company to form Arco. Unfortunately for
me, the Richfield Research Center in Anaheim was closing and
I was asked to relocate to Atlantic's Research Laboratory in
Dallas. Working for a large multinational corporation in Dallas
was not the same as working for a small exploration company
in Southern California. There were few job opportunities
available for marine geologists, so I started checking graduate
schools for a Ph.D. program in marine geology. My first
choice was the Scripps Institute of Oceanography near San
Diego. Several of the professors were my friends from the
geological diving company I had worked for while attending
USC. I discovered, much to my surprise, it would take nearly
seven years to obtain a degree there and it would include a lot
of sea time assisting professors with their research. This would
be difficult with a family to support.

Everything was unsettled until a letter arrived from Charles
Phipps, professor of marine geology at Sydney University in
Australia. He was on sabbatical leave at Scripps and had heard
that I was looking for a scholarship. I met him in San Diego
and over a few beers, he convinced me I could obtain a Ph.D.

degree at Sydney University while employed by an Australian mining company that was looking for someone to survey their offshore Tasmania mineral leases. I jumped at the chance, even though I had no experience exploring for tin and gold. I quit my job and shipped a crate with the family possessions to Australia. My wife and children visited relatives in Oregon until I could find a place to live. I flew to Australia with Roger Enright, a former Richfield employee from Australia. There weren't any non-stop flights from Los Angeles to Sydney in 1966; planes needed to refuel twice along this route. One stop was either Hawaii or Tahiti and we decided to disembark and spend a few days in Tahiti. We did not leave for ten days, the time I had planned to locate a house in Sydney.

I wore my thirty-pound lead diving belt under my coat, on the plane, as we were only allowed forty pounds of luggage. After landing in Papeete, I put the heavy belt into my camera bag and strung my camera around my neck. Upon entering Tahitian customs, I was asked if I had anything to declare and just as I said "No" the camera bag strap broke and the bag hit the floor with a big thump. I ended up in an office explaining that I was not smuggling gold while a custom's officer was cutting my lead weights to uncover any evidence

Our money went quickly as we had planned only a brief stay in Papeete. We ate meals at a Chinese restaurant with a menu written in French and Tahitian. Knowing neither language, I would point to a number by one of the twelve one-dollar items. The waiter would go out the back door and immediately return with a plate of hot steaming Chinese food. One evening, I went out the same door and discovered it opened to a back alley where a squatting old Chinese woman was tending fires under large galvanized trash cans numbered one through twelve. We decided to extend our stay by moving to the nearby island of Moorea. The cheapest way to travel was on a boat that was used to transport pigs back and forth from Moorea to Papeete for luaus. Several of the pigs became seasick on our trip.

Riding the "pig-boat" with Roger Enright

The community of Pao Pao, Moorea's capital on Cook's Bay, consisted of a Chinese general store, a pool hall, a gas station, and the "One Chicken Inn"*. We rented a room behind the Inn, which was actually just a popular local bar. Moorea was my first visit to a tropical island. I enjoyed staying there, hiking around the island and snorkeling on the coral reef. I ate ceviche, the standard lunch at the "One Chicken Inn", every day and there was always a party every night at the nearby tourist hotel "Bali Hai" run by a couple of ex-USC students.

I finally arrived in Sydney a few days before my family. There were no household goods waiting on the dock and I still had to find a house. I visited several real estate offices looking for something near a beach, preferably on the north side of Sydney Harbor. Anything half decent was out of my price range and I was running out of time. While waiting for a real estate agent to show me another dumpy place, far from the beach, I happened to see a photo of a new brick house located in Palm Beach renting for $100 a month. This was more than I had planned to pay but I was starting to worry about finding anything. I asked the agent about this house and she said it

---

* When I returned to Moorea in 2006 I was disappointed to find the "One Chicken Inn" gone. Pao Pao is now the site of several large resort hotels.

was too far north for a commute to the city. When I asked how far, she said, "about twenty miles." Having lived in Los Angeles, I had commuted a lot farther than that so I insisted she drive me there. As we drove north, I was happy to see a series of beautiful beaches and small beach communities that reminded me of Southern California. When we arrived in Palm Beach, I immediately signed the rental papers.

Palm Beach is located on the far north end of a peninsula and now has some of the most expensive properties in greater Sydney. However, in the 1960s, it was considered a weekend getaway area with numerous rentals. The only reason I could afford to rent a house there was because the architect and builder did not use standard Australian red bricks. They built the house with used bricks—Australians disliked the look. Used-brick houses were popular in California so I thought it looked fine. A pathway led from near our house down to the beach and we were next to a koala sanctuary.

My family arrived on time and everyone was happy with my choice of house and location. The only problem was that our household goods were still on a Los Angeles dock because, unbeknownst to me, I still owed the shipping company thirty dollars. During our first winter in Australia we lived in an empty new house, sleeping on the kitchen floor, with the oven on to keep warm. Our household goods arrived six months later after I finally paid the bill. We all loved Australia. My children quickly acquired Aussie accents and received excellent educations over the next three years.

It took a while to get used to Aussie accents, slang, and food. I thought the food was very bland and overcooked with few spices. No Mexican food, no BBQ ribs, and no American hamburgers. Australian hamburgers included a fried egg and a slice of beet. Steak was often eaten three meals a day but was tough—they did not age their beef. Everything seemed to be fried in mutton oil and tasted like it. A milkshake was a glass of milk with a tiny scoop of ice cream floating on the top. Chicken was a delicacy and very expensive. However, prawns, fish and chips, and meat pies were delicious. I invited some of my new surfing mates, who had never tasted Mexican food, over for a Mexican dinner after receiving a relief package from California with tortillas, refried beans, and salsa. I needed chili powder, for the chili, so I bought some at the Chinese market in downtown Sydney. There was plenty of beer and when I served the chili, as a starter, the guys were gagging and begging for more beer. Laughing, I told them Mexican food was spicy. I finally tasted the chili and it was awful. I had bought Indian chili powder, which is many times more potent than Mexican chili power.

Soon after arriving, I went to the local Sydney Telephone Company and applied for a phone. I told the lady they could install it any time. She looked at me in amazement and said we would be on a two- to three-year waiting list—we never got a telephone. In 1968, I decided to call home. I had to sign up several weeks in advance and then appeared at the main post office where I was assigned to a waiting booth. The operator finally connected me to California. I could hardly hear my mother, due to static, and we were both yelling. I finally hung up after a few minutes and received a bill of over fifty dollars. Getting news from the States was also a problem. Friends and family would mail me newspapers, but I had to wait several months to find out how USC's football team did.

I bought a used VW bug for transportation. One weekend we decided to drive to the Blue Mountains, located just west of Sydney. After traveling for several hours, I stopped and asked how much farther to the Blue Mountains. I was told we had passed them some time ago; those foothills we crossed were the Blue Mountains. Since we were in the outback, we started looking for kangaroos. A passing truck threw up gravel (the road was dirt) and our windshield exploded—there was no safety glass. Then, for the first time in ten years, it started to rain and we could not keep the water out of the car. It was not a very pleasant trip back to Sydney. I totaled the VW several months later by not yielding to the right.

In 1968, my daughter Kylie was born. Kylie is an aboriginal word for a one-way or runaway boomerang. When the time came, I drove my wife to the nearby hospital and sat in the waiting room. Nurses kept running by me to assist at least six other women in various stages of labor. I seemed to be the only husband waiting. One nurse stopped and asked why I was there. I told her I was waiting for my wife to have a baby. She told me to go home and they would contact me after the baby was born. It was late at night and I had two children at home, so I agreed and left. I was not sure how they were going to contact me since we had no telephone. The next morning, my neighbor ran over and said my wife called and I better get down to the hospital right away. When I arrived, my wife was standing in the hospital doorway. The nurses quickly wheeled her back to her room. Women in Australia enjoyed having babies; they could stay two weeks while being waited on in the hospital. My wife came home the next day.

The University of Sydney is considered by most to be one of the best universities in the world and it is the oldest one in Australia. The campus mimics Oxford University in England, with ivy covered walls and classroom buildings located around grassy quads. It was a great place to study, conduct research, and to get a degree. For the one hour commute, I would take the bus, drive, or hitchhike to school. No one would pick me up the first day I tried to hitchhike. Drivers honked or shook their fists at me. I later learned that putting out my thumb meant "up yours" in Australia, I needed to point to the ground to obtain a ride.

The Utah Mining Company and Broken Hill Proprietary, Ltd., in Melbourne, employed me to map their mineral leases in Banks Strait (SE section of Bass Strait) with an emphasis on possible tin and gold mining prospects. These companies also paid for a new University Sedimentology Laboratory I helped set up and used for my research. The new laboratory was very familiar to me, similar to those where I had worked at USC and Richfield.

My first task was to collect and study heavy mineral deposits from the seafloor off the northeast corner of Tasmania and around the Furneaux Islands. This is a remote, fairly wild, little known area of Australia. I needed a field assistant and luckily found a good one, Tom Landis, a fellow Southern Californian who was working part time at the University. Tom was a champion swimmer and introduced me to the Surf Lifesaving Club environment prevalent in Australia. Sadly, he was kicked off the New South Wales water polo team when he went on a field trip to Tasmania with me instead of participating in the Australian Championships.

Tom suggested I join the Whale Beach Surf Club, located just south of Palm Beach. After going through six weeks of training I became a full member, eligible to enter competitions and obliged to be a weekend lifeguard about once a month during the summer. I started a routine of swimming and body surfing in the warm water for a few hours most mornings, followed by a trip into the University where I usually worked well into the evening. I missed the heavy traffic hours. Family life revolved around the beach and, looking back now, I realize we were living in a paradise. We had little money but the beach was free. Our Australian friends were some of the kindest, most generous, fun-loving people I have ever known.

Slater family, Palm Beach, Australia

Whale Beach Surf Club members (I am far left, front row)

Tom and I, and later other assistants, flew down to Melbourne about once a month for a meeting with my Utah Mining and Broken Hill bosses to update them on our progress. Then we would fly over to Flinders Island, the largest of the Furneaux Islands, or to Launceston, Tasmania, where we would work along the beaches or nearshore for a few weeks.

There were several places to stay in Tasmania but only one rundown pub* on Flinders Island. One night, Chris Kendall, a University friend, stayed there with me and locked our rental pick-up truck. The next morning we couldn't open it. I called the local farmer who had rented us the truck and asked for a key. He was not happy. He said, "You are on a small island with only a couple of dirt roads. Why would you lock my truck?" I had to pay for the window we broke to retrieve the keys. Another time, a Tasmania pub was fully booked but the bartender finally let us have a single bed late that night. When we awoke in the morning, the other beds in the room were still empty and Chris and I were squeezed into a single bed next to a wall splattered with blood from the mosquitoes we killed during the night.

---

*An Australian pub usually has a couple of bars and a few rooms you can rent for the night.

Furneaux Islands and northeast Tasmania

Bass Strait separates the mainland of Australia from Tasmania and contains some of the world's roughest waters. Antarctic westerly swells, prominent westerly winds, and tidal currents move water easterly through this shallow Strait, dotted with numerous islands, straight into a southerly current flowing down the east coast of Australia. Many ships have disappeared or been wrecked here due to the treacherous combination of wind, sea conditions, numerous shallow submerged rocks, and islands. Currents between the Furneaux Islands average two to three knots, with speeds up to six knots not uncommon. The water becomes exceedingly rough when the wind blows against the current, sometimes forming six- to ten-foot standing waves in restricted areas. In the 1998 Sydney to Hobart yacht race, only 44 of the 150 yachts made it past Bass Strait, and six men died when winds reached near hurricane force. This occurred during the usually mild summer weather.

Tasmania from Flinders Island   *Flinders Island pub*

Charlie Phipps   *John McCarthy*

My professor, Charlie Phipps, introduced me to a fisherman from the tiny community of Lady Barron, located at the south end of Flinders Island. His name was John McCarthy and he was the owner of a small lobster fishing boat. He was a good guy, a hard worker, a chain-smoker, and one of the greatest characters I have ever known. He could not say a full sentence without at least five "f-bombs" in it. John and I made an agreement: I would help him set his traps in the mornings and pull them in the evenings, and he would let me use his boat during the day to collect my seafloor samples. The center of his thirty-foot boat was a lobster holding pen open to the sea, which left little room for us. We rarely ate lobster; since they were valuable, but occasionally a broken leg ended up on my plate.

John's boat had a winch for hauling up lobster traps. I used it to recover my small dredge or grab (a simple instrument that recovers a hand-full of sediment when it hits the seafloor). I collected over 500 samples with this arrangement. John's winch was an ingenious piece of equipment, it was an old truck rear-end axle, and gearbox, sitting on end with the wheel at the top. This wheel turned when the gears engaged. You looped the line around the rotating wheel and it pulled up the lobster trap, or the grab, and neatly curled the line into a pile on the boat deck. It worked well; even the day Charlie's hand went around the wheel pinched by the line. Charlie was a very brilliant scholar but a bull in a china closet.

Flinders Island lobster boat with traps on deck and Bass Strait lobster

Recovering the dredge   *McCarthy's boat with winch*

I spent many months at sea during the three years I worked on McCarthy's lobster boat around northeast Tasmania and the Furneaux Islands. I used a sextant for navigation; scientific samples are worthless if you do not know exactly where they came from. Using the sextant horizontally, I measured angles between various known shore locations and triangulated our position at sea. This was easy during rare calm seas as there were many charted islands and rocks in the area. There was no GPS (global positioning service) in those days and rough seas were a constant problem. They caused the little boat to rock back and forth, and sometimes shook us quite hard. There were no toilet facilities on board. I had to hang my rear over the railing and several times my bare butt was hit by a wave, much to John's amusement. John's boat sank years later, I would guess on purpose, and the insurance company replaced it with a new one. He wrote me a letter saying I was welcome to return as his new boat had an inside toilet so he would not have to listen to me complain so much.

John's boat had no refrigeration or stove so we used a hot plate to cook on. Food became a bit ripe after a week at sea. In Australia, bright red sausages are called snags and one of my chores was to cut the green mold off the snags every day. By the end of a trip, the sausages were about the size of a pencil. There were four berths below deck. There were two upper and two lower bunks that were so close together I had to get up in order to turn over.

Bad smells on the boat were a serious problem. The boat was a stinkpot with diesel fumes and cigarette smoke blowing in my face most of the time. Another bad smell came from the dead wallabies lashed to the boat's railing until they were good and ripe. Then John chopped them up for lobster bait—lobsters prefer rotten bait to fresh bait. Some evenings we went ashore on Flinders Island and used John's truck to hunt wallabies. I stood in the back of the truck, my gun on top of the cab, blasting away as John, using his truck spotlight, chased wallabies at breakneck speed over the rough terrain.

There were many shipwrecks in this area. One, just south of Cape Barren that we could scramble on board in good weather was the *Farsund*, a freighter that sank in 1912 while trying to take a shortcut through the islands. John took shortcuts when returning to Flinders Island and this meant passing through narrow passages that separate the Furneaux Islands. There were many shoal areas with large standing waves in these straits and it was often difficult to find safe passage. John would tie me to the forward mast, on the bow, so I could point out any fast approaching shallow areas. I sometimes wondered if I could untie myself in time if we hit something and sank.

Dead wallabies being loaded onto boat   Wallabies lashed to railing

Tom Landis and me with the Farsund *shipwreck*

Farsund *south of Clarke &Cape Barren   Rough seas between islands*

John took shortcuts when returning to Flinders Island and this meant passing through the narrow passages that separate the Furneaux Islands. There were many shoal areas with large standing waves in these straits and it was often difficult to find safe passage. John would tie me to the forward mast, on the bow, so I could point out any fast approaching shallow areas. I sometimes wondered if I could untie myself in time if we hit something and sank.

There are many Furneaux Islands, including two populated ones, Flinders and Cape Barren. There were not any tourist facilities and very few visitors to these islands while I worked there. About four hundred inhabitants, mainly farmers, lived on Flinders, the largest island. The much smaller Cape Barren was home to about a hundred aborigines and one white couple who ran the local store, the only commercial building on the island. All welfare checks went directly to his store where the aborigines could obtain food and other goods against their credit. The aborigines did not like the manager and once, while I was there, started a fire to burn down his store. The wind direction changed at the last moment and the store was saved but their church was destroyed. The store manager and his wife ended up in the ocean waiting for the fire to burn itself out.

Cape Barren store and Post Office   Our Cape Barren shack, church in back

Sometimes one or two of my Whale Beach surfing mates would travel to Tasmania with me. The most helpful, and fun to be with, were Kim Davidson and Tom Landis. Tom, Kim, and I would often stay in a small one-room shack on Cape Barren with a beat up Land Rover for transportation. At night, we would play cards to see who would clean up after dinner; Kim always lost.

The Queen Victoria Museum in Tasmania discovered we were working around Bass Strait and asked me to collect some biological samples for them. They gave me a collecting box full of labeled bottles and some large rat traps. Scientists were interested in discovering how rats, escaped from early whaling vessels, evolved on the different Islands. We kept hearing rats moving around at night inside our Cape Barren shack, so one evening I set a rat trap and turned off the lights. Within minutes, there was a loud bang, I switched on the light and we saw a huge rat running out the door with our trap snapped onto his nose. We never recovered the rat or the trap.

Aborigines control Cape Barren Island today with less than a hundred inhabitants. These natives are all descendants of Tasmanian and Australian aborigines that were abducted by white whalers and sealers in the early 1800s. The women, used as short-term wives, were forced to stay on the Islands where they clubbed seals and boiled down whale blubber. Tasmanian aborigines were exterminated on Tasmania in 1876 and their only descendants today live on Cape Barren. There was a lot of inbreeding on the Island. There were only a few family names and nearly everyone was descended from the same ten ancestors.

Soon after the seals and whales were nearly exterminated, the islanders started earning a living off birds (short-tailed shearwaters), that appeared every spring. These birds make the long flight to Alaska and back every year, the longest known bird migration. They return to the Furneaux Islands each year to lay eggs, feed their young, and prepare for the journey back to Alaska. To fuel up for this monumental flight, they eat and feed their young a tremendous amount of krill and small fish. The sky turns dark from the thousands of birds flying out to sea every morning and returning each evening. When these birds were eaten, it was said they tasted like mutton, hence the nickname "mutton-birds". The young birds, fatter than their parents, are very tasty and an industry was developed on Cape Barren to catch and preserve them. The Islanders became known as the mutton-bird people.

Mutton-birds dig deep burrows all over the islands, where they deposit eggs and keep their hatchlings safe. Islanders lie on the ground and reach into these nesting holes to capture the young birds. Black tiger snakes also live on the islands. There are only three types of snakes in Tasmania and they are all deadly poisonous. The Furneaux Island tiger snakes, up to six feet in length, are considered one of the deadliest snakes in the world and they feed on young mutton-birds. It is very dangerous to reach into a mutton-bird hole as you could grab a snake instead of a bird. I asked a young islander how he knew when a snake was in the hole. He told me, "When you grab something warm, it's a mutton-bird. If it's cold, you drop it immediately because it's a snake." Young mutton-birds were cooked, salted, and sealed in oaken barrels. These barrels were sold to a Flinders Island man who shipped them over to New Zealand and around Australia.

Cape Barren Islanders collecting and cooking mutton-birds (Smith, 1965)

The Cape Barren Goose is another well-known bird from this area. About the size of a Canadian Goose it is considered one of the rarest birds in the world. It is also one of the tastiest.

McCarthy said we should shoot a goose, as "They are great tucker."* During a trip from Flinders to Cape Barren in our little aluminum boat, a goose flew over and I shot it. Down it came to our great joy—no peanut butter sandwich for lunch. We grabbed it, traveled to the nearest beach, plucked the bird, and lit a fire. Having no utensils we heated up our large metal gold pan, used for heavy mineral panning, to cook the bird. It tasted awful. Later, when I saw McCarthy, I told him it was the worse bird I had ever eaten. He asked me to identify it and when I told him, he laughed and said, "You ate a Black Swan, one of the national symbols of Australia." Then he added, "However, a young swan is good tucker." A Black Swan does not look much like a Cape Barren Goose.

Tom and Kim cooking the "goose"   *Resting on Cape Barren*

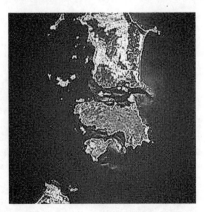

Cape Barren Island, Flinders to the north, Clarke & Tasmania to the South

---

*Tucker is Australian slang for food.

Once, while we were working off northeast Tasmania, John noticed Kim constantly picking at his groin with tweezers. He asked me to investigate and I discovered that Kim had "crabs." McCarthy banned Kim from most of the boat and we headed straight to the nearby small town of Bridport. We dropped Kim off to find a cure and returned to our lobster traps. Kim saw a doctor who gave him some powder to solve his problem. He then checked into a room above the local pub to clean up and rest for the remainder of the day. He washed the clothes he'd worn for the past week and hung them up to dry. Borrowing an iron from the bartender, he set it on the ironing board to heat up when a breeze blew a curtain against the iron and it caught fire. Kim tried to douse the fire but it spread quickly. We'd just arrived back at the dock when Kim, nearly naked, came running toward us with smoke pouring from a nearby building and sirens blasting. Kim yelled, "Go!" and we sped away. To further complicate things, I put several of Kim's "crabs" into the museum collecting bottle labeled crustaceans and returned it with the other bottles. Several years later I received a letter, while I was working in Colorado, from the British Museum asking for more data on those interesting specimens from the Bass Strait seafloor. I didn't answer the letter and never heard from them again.

Sydney newspaper article

Aussie diver

I WAS INVOLVED IN several other interesting projects in Australia. One involved searching for abalone along the east coast and another was diving off the New South Wales for a local mining company, searching for gold. I introduced many of my surfing mates to abalone and I'm not sure if we found any gold. I never saw the assay results and I did not notice any new gold mining operations starting up.

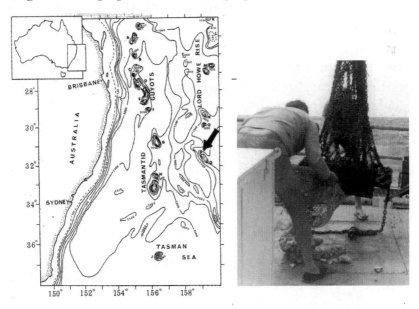

Location of Tasman Sea guyots   Dredge with rock samples
(arrow points to Lord Howe Island, from Slater and Goodwin, 1973)

Another of my "down under" projects involved a 1968 search for Tasman Sea seafloor phosphorite and manganese between Australia and New Zealand. These minerals are found as crusts on the sides of guyots, flat-topped extinct volcanoes, which form two north-south trending Tasman Sea submerged ridges. Some of these guyots rise up over 14,000 feet above the seafloor. Their flat tops, resulting from wave action when the volcanoes were once at sea level, have now sunk to depths of 300 to 3,000 feet. We searched for manganese crusts by dragging a large dredge up the guyot sides.

Several elaborate twenty-foot long spar buoys were built with radar reflectors on top to help us navigate while dredging (again still no GPS). These surface buoys were attached to the guyot flat tops by lines and chains tied to large railroad wheel anchors. Before setting our first buoy, we asked the captain to run over the guyot and, watching his echo sounder, yell when we should shove the railroad wheel and chain overboard. He yelled, we pushed, and the anchor headed to the seafloor. The line tightened when the anchor hit the guyot and the large spar buoy rose up to vertical and the radar reflector unfolded. This was very dramatic and everyone cheered. Suddenly, the spar buoy went straight down and disappeared. We had missed the guyot top and the railroad wheel was dragging our spar buoy thousands of feet down the side of the guyot. The other buoys were placed correctly and we recovered over a hundred large dredge samples.

The weather was poor most of the time. The one hundred and fifty foot ship, *Imlay*, rocked and rolled making work and mealtimes difficult. The cook had a bad habit of throwing knives when upset. Once, we ran in to Brisbane to replace the large shack that once sat on the stern filled with sampling gear. It simply disappeared one night, washed overboard by a large wave. The project was successful, though it was determined the deposits were not economic to mine at that time.

Imlay, *Lord Howe I., with shack that disappeared and with Kim (far right)*

One Tasman Sea Island, rising 3,000 feet above sea level, is the crescent-shaped Lord Howe Island. It is the eroded remnant of a seven-million-year-old volcano. This was my first trip to Lord Howe and this beautiful World Heritage Island would play an important role later in my life. About 200 people lived on Lord Howe and there were very few tourist facilities. We anchored the *Imlay* off Lord Howe one night and the local's panicked thinking that the Russians were invading. Our bright work lights made us appear to be a huge ship at night. I have no idea why they thought we were Russians.

ONE OF MY Australian adventures was with a professor on a three-year project to map the Great Barrier Reef, the largest coral reef in the world. In early 1967, I eagerly volunteered to accompany him on a one-month cruise to the northern section of the Reef. This area off the northeast tip of Australia and south of Papua New Guinea was both largely unexplored and unpopulated. Another graduate student and I drove over 1,500 miles from Sydney to Cooktown in far northern Queensland to meet the professor and the dive boat, *C-Gem*.

Dive boat C-Gem, *Cooktown*   *Shelter on the Great Barrier Reef*

Cooktown consisted of a couple of buildings, a general store, and a few unemployed Aussies on the dole in 1967. When we arrived, the forty-foot dive boat *C-Gem* was waiting. As we climbed on board, the skipper asked, "Where is the food?" and the professor said, "The food was part of the charter." We were leaving for a four week trip on a boat with no food and nowhere to buy any. We walked up to the Cooktown general store and bought a bag of flour, a case of melon jam, and a few other items. We were going to live off the sea. We made damper (an unleavened Australian bread) in a skillet and we had plenty of melon jam. At dusk, I would go ashore onto one of the small reef islands to shoot pigeons and collect coconuts. We caught lots of fish with spears and line. Turtle eggs were great for breakfast—they were easy to find. Many mornings we followed a fresh turtle tracks leading up the beach to a newly buried nest. You peel, not crack, turtle eggs.

Preparing coconut lunch   *Turtle tracks, Great Barrier Reef*

C-Gem *shower*   *Great Barrier Reef fish for dinner*

We collected seafloor sediment samples and I photographed sea life and reefs. I still have a giant clamshell from this expedition, the largest I could bring to the surface. This trip was a great success and, in 1968, our fieldwork was published as part of the *Atlas of the Great Barrier Reef*.

We finished the trip at Thursday Island (TI), an old pearl diving center located in the Torres Straits between Papua New Guinea and Australia. We stayed on *C-Gem* because a typhoon had recently ripped through the island and wrecked the only pub. The locals cooked a turtle to celebrate our arrival. They dug a pit and lined it with rocks heated with a fire. They put the recently deceased turtle upside down on the hot rocks and filled the hole with sand. After a few hours of drinking beer in the hot sun anything would probably taste good but the turtle was every tasty. We flew back to Sydney with great memories.

I WAS FORTUNATE to be the Australian representative on two legs of the 1966 Scripps Institute "Nova" South Pacific oceanographic expedition. I flew to New Caledonia and met several graduate students waiting for the ships to arrive from New Zealand. One student talked me into accompanying him on a native open bus, carrying more chickens than people, for 200 miles to the tiny village of Poum located at the northern tip of New Caledonia. We passed by several World War II airstrips while bouncing along the unpaved beach road. At Poum, we met a diver who collected seashells and he offered me a fresh green turtle shell. He explained how to polish it by scraping the shell with a broken Coke bottle. I scraped and polished my turtle shell daily for the next four weeks while cruising back and forth on the Tasman Sea.

The "Nova" expedition crisscrossed the Tasman Sea from New Caledonia to Brisbane, Australia, and then from Brisbane to Auckland, New Zealand. This was the first geological and geophysical survey* to study the history of the South Pacific

---

*Geophysical surveys at sea help determine the types of rock that underlie the seafloor. We used instruments similar to an echo sounder but much more powerful. First a loud noise is made underwater by dynamite, compressed air or electrical sparks. The resulting sound waves travel through the water, seafloor sediments, and the underlying rocks at different speeds. The returning echoes are picked up by another ship or from a hydrophone towed behind the shooting ship and recorded. This recorder then produces a seismic profile (x-ray) of the ocean seafloor over which the ship is traveling. Knowing the speed of sound through different types of rocks and sediments helps identify the different types.

seafloor and there were several new oceanographic research tools on board that I was excited to see in action. I was a member of the scientific team from six different countries. Everyone enjoyed working at sea. It was a two-ship expedition and I was on the older ship R/V *Horizon*, the first research ship acquired by Scripps. The *Horizon*, fondly called the *"Hor,"* was a 140-foot rough riding vessel. The other, much smoother riding, ship was the 213 foot R/V *Argo*, with a much larger crew and group of scientists.

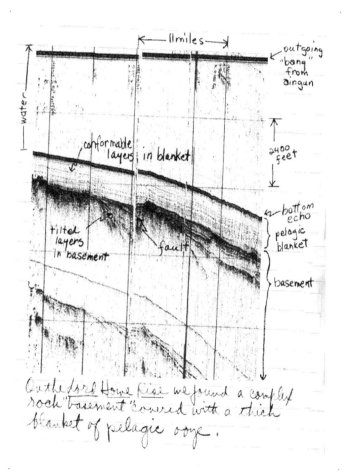

Geophysical record from the Tasman Sea Expedition (Menard, 1969)

R/V Horizon, *New Caledonia*   *Two ship operation at sea*

TNT ready to launch   *Waiting for a sample*

Sleeping presented a problem as our ship constantly swayed back and forth in the deteriorating weather. Meals were exciting, with lots of food ending up on the floor. The *"Hor"* was the shooting vessel so we launched dynamite overboard on a set schedule while the *Argo*, miles away, received the return signals. With a rocking boat, I was hoping the dynamite, with a set time to explode, did not end up on our deck.

We had an unscheduled stop in Brisbane because of damage by a large storm we had battled against for many days. Local officials did not let us to dock in downtown Brisbane because of the dynamite on board, so we anchored near the mouth of the Brisbane River. While at anchor, I observed thousands of huge jellyfish and hundreds of hammerhead sharks swimming around us. We decided not to swim in this area. The trip back to Auckland was uneventful; we sailed by Lord Howe Island, where I was destined to return one day.

ONE BENEFIT FOR a scientist in Australia was being able to visit the Heron Island Research Laboratory on the Great Barrier Reef. Heron Island is a small sand cay with a lab and dormitory. I made several trips there and once took along my family. The diving was great but my best memory involved Kim Davidson, who was following me underwater one day when he happened to look away and ran his spear into my leg. Bleeding in shark-infested waters is not a good idea. I quickly swam to shore with no problems except a really sore leg.

Kim and his spear   *My family and friends on Heron Island*

With Kim ready to dive on Heron Island

THE CITY OF SYDNEY wanted to construct a tunnel under the harbor as traffic on the Sydney Bridge was becoming very congested. Charlie Phipps received a contract, through the University, to survey the harbor floor. He decided it was too dangerous for us to scuba dive across the harbor, due to the heavy boat traffic, so he built an underwater diver sled to be towed behind the new 35-foot University of Sydney research vessel *R/V Matthew Flinders* he had designed and helped to construct. Charlie wanted to be the first to dive when the big day arrived. We played out the line and started to tow him north across the harbor from a southern beach. He descended with his sled to start running along the harbor floor. While dodging ferryboats and other traffic, we continued to tow him across the harbor. When we reached the north shore, the sled floated to the surface—without Charlie. We began a search for him immediately. This was difficult as there were many ferries, motor boats and hundreds of sailboats in a race being held in the harbor that day. There was no sign of Charlie until we reached the south shore and there he was standing on the beach. He had driven his sled into the mud and was thrown off near the beginning of his transect. That was the last time, to my knowledge, that Charlie's sled was used. The tunnel was built many years later, too late to assist me with my daily commute to the University.

I worked for three years on my Bass Strait research, and the mining companies seemed satisfied with my results. My Ph.D. dissertation was 340 pages thick with many maps and charts. The doctoral committee passed it, and I was left to wonder how many had actually read the entire three-inch thick tome. The University of Sydney now owned a new Sedimentology Laboratory and I received my Ph.D. degree. I was offered a full-time teaching position at the University and was going to accept, but my wife wanted to return to the States. The only problem was how to get there. My original plan was to buy a boat, live on it during our stay in Sydney, and sail it back to California. That never happened.

WHILE PERUSING JOB opportunities, I found an opening for a research position at the University of Cape Town in South Africa. I applied and was accepted for a two-year post-doctorate fellowship, which included transportation for my family. I would be working for the South African CSIR (Council for Scientific and Industrial Research) with my office on the University campus. It was a good opportunity, even though it delayed our return to the States. With deep sadness, we sailed on the *Chusan* from Sydney in April 1969. A festive crowd gathered to see us off at Circular Quay. A friend handed me a bag of nylon stockings, all tied together, while continuing to hold on to one end. I tied the other end to the ship's railing. As the *Chusan* sailed we stretched the nylons, with a large brassiere in the middle, clear across the Quay until it snapped to the crowd's enjoyment. After crossing the Indian Ocean, we arrived at one of the most beautiful cities in the world, Cape Town.

Chusan, *Sydney Harbor*

The beautiful University of Cape Town campus, at the base of Table Mountain, overlooks the city. I rented a small house near the University, not near the beach, with only a ten-minute commute. This was the time of racial segregation, apartheid, even though I witnessed little evidence of it as the Cape was very liberal compared to the rest of South Africa. Most white South Africans had full-time help. We hired Edith who was a member of the Xhosa tribe whose language contains many different clicking sounds. Most homes had a small house in back where the hired help lived but I did not think Edith needed to live with us. I also thought the normal salary of twelve dollars a month was not enough so I paid her eighteen, which brought down the wrath of our neighbors. Edith took the bus home every night. I was not allowed to drive her home; it was against the law for a white man and a black woman to be in a car together. My only problem with Edith was she kept calling me "master." When I asked her not to call me that, she would say, "Yes, Master," so I finally gave up. Edith spoke four languages and took home our old magazines and newspapers to read.

Edith, Kylie, and Melinda   *Table Mountain from our house*

I was pleasantly surprised to find the cold waters around Cape Town similar to those off Southern California including large kelp beds. Lobster and abalone were abundant locally and South Africans had yet to discover how tasty both were. On one dive, I entered a cave that contained hundreds of lobsters. I had to fight my way through the small ones which kept bouncing off my mask to catch several very large ones clinging to the ceiling. It was only a few months later when someone discovered they could sell lobster tails to Europe and North America, and the lobster population was quickly depleted.

I needed a South African oceanographic project and hoped for something off Cape St. Francis, near Port Elizabeth. I had recently seen the famous surfing movie *The Endless Summer*, a story about two surfers traveling the world looking for the perfect wave. They found it at Cape St. Francis. I got my wish but worked offshore where minerals might exist that could be mined from the seafloor. I only saw the backside of Cape St. Francis surf. I sailed on the University of Cape Town research vessel, *R/V Thomas B. Davie*, for several cruises to the Cape St. Francis area. This was an interesting ship with the officers, crew, and scientists divided into separate groups. We had to clean up and put on a white shirt for a very proper lunch, no matter how dirty we became while working on deck with muddy sediments. The food was not very good, everything was overcooked and had little flavor. Meanwhile, the crew ate their meals down in the hold and the most wonderful aromas drifted up to the deck. When I asked if I could go down and have some curry for lunch, both officers and crew informed me that it was not possible. I continued eating boring tasteless food in the galley.

I did find several interesting objects while dredging the seafloor off South Africa, including several tektites (meteorites that freeze when they hit the ocean) and a fossil shark tooth. While at sea, we often listened to four- and five-day cricket matches over a loudspeaker. It made time pass quickly.

The ship's officers were white Afrikaners and the crew were Cape Coloreds, the descendants from intermarriages of white settlers, African natives, and Asians who were brought to South Africa from Dutch colonies in Southeast Asia. Cape Coloreds make up a large percentage of people living in Cape Town today and are known for their spicy food. Sadly for them, whites considered them black during apartheid and blacks now consider them white. On several occasions, we hired a Cape Colored lady, Mrs. Robinson, to stay with our children while my wife and I traveled around southern Africa. Mrs. Robinson was very worried about staying in our house because we did not have bars on the windows and she was afraid blacks were going to break in. On one trip to Rhodesia (now Zimbabwe), which I thought was the most beautiful country in Africa at that time, I met a local farmer who invited me to return with my son for a hunting safari. I was excited about this opportunity and could not wait to get back there.

On returning to Cape Town, there was a telegram waiting for me from Jim Vernon. Jim was the USC graduate student who had co-authored the California tar mound article. He was now the president of General Oceanographics, a California offshore geological consulting company created from the old diving consultant group I had previously worked with. Jim asked if I would return home to pilot a manned submersible off Alaska for three months. It was a tough decision. I was enjoying South Africa and still had nearly a year left on my fellowship. I also was looking forward to a project where I would be searching for diamonds off Southwest Africa (now Namibia). However, I would probably never have another chance to dive a submersible off Alaska. It was just too good an opportunity to pass up, and a way to return home.

We gave Edith all our household furniture and everything else we could not pack into a few suitcases. I decided to break the law and drove her home while pulling a fully loaded trailer. I watched Edith for the last time when she was leading and directing a conga line of singing Xhosas, carrying my family goods on their heads down a path to her village.

It was good to be going home after more than four years of living overseas and I was going to make $12,000 a year plus dive pay. I could earn $15,000! I was going to be paid a large amount of money for doing something I would have been happy to do for free just for the opportunity.

Chapter Four

Submersibles & Alaska

Click! The hatch cover locks. Ballast air hisses out, ballast water gurgles in. Waves splash against the view ports of our yellow U-boat. Then silence, sinking, and sinking, and sinking. In a tranquil dream of fading light, 100, 200, 400, 800 feet, into the edge of night.

—James Vernon, *The Sea, Over, On, and Under* (2006)

AFTER SEVERAL FAILED opportunities to make a dive in a manned submersible, I finally got my chance during the summer of 1970. I would log nearly 2,300 submersible dives over the next thirty years, and submersibles would be involved in most of my future adventures. The term "submersible" is used for a small self-propelled submarine that needs a surface support ship while at sea. The main objective for a manned submersible is to carry people down to great depths in order to observe, take photographs, and collect samples. Divers are limited to shallow depths without exotic mixed gasses or using manned submersibles. There are many types of submersibles but all have much in common. Most manned submersibles are untethered and have enough space for a pilot and one or two observers. A dive will usually last from one to eight hours then the submersible is brought back aboard its "mother" support ship where maintenance and battery charging takes place.

The heart of the submersible is the steel (sometimes titanium or aluminum) passenger cabin, or "pressure hull." These hulls must withstand incredible hydrostatic pressure from the ocean depths to enable a submersible to dive deep. At 1,000 feet, there are 430 pounds of pressure per square inch on a sub, and at 20,000 feet, there are nearly 9,000 pounds per square inch. Most pressure hulls are either cylindrical or spherical. A sphere can withstand more pressure than a cylinder but a cylinder is more maneuverable and is easier to tow on the ocean surface. Most shallow diving submersibles are cylindrical and most deep diving ones are spherical.

Because steel is heavy, steel submersibles need supplemental buoyancy compensation. Some submersibles have floatation devices, but most use compressed air and seawater to fill buoyancy containers (ballast tanks) that enable the submersible to rise and sink and to be neutrally balanced at any depth. Clear acrylic Plexiglas ports, or windows, fit into portholes cut into the pressure hull. These ports let the pilot and observers see outside the hull.* Several submersibles used clear acrylic spheres for their pressure hulls allowing occupants to see in all directions. Acrylic spheres and curved ports, however, distort views whereas flat ports give observers a truer, although somewhat magnified picture.

Occupants inside a submersible pressure hull breathe air at surface pressure, so it does not matter how deep they are or how long they stay down. During a dive, oxygen is added or "bled" into the submersible from an oxygen bottle. Carbon dioxide build-up from occupants exhaling is removed, or "scrubbed," by a chemical scrubber. This leaves the inside pressure and air content during a dive similar to those at sea level. Compressed air, used in buoyancy control, is usually available for emergency life support.

Rechargeable batteries supply power for most submersibles but restrict the amount of time a vehicle can stay underwater. Limiting factors include the distance a sub travels, how many

---

*General Motors, in Santa Barbara, built the *DOWB* submersible (Deep Ocean Work Boat) with no ports in 1968. The occupants used a TV monitor to see outside. This 20,000 pound two million dollar vehicle was not very successful and ended up in a local schoolyard play ground.

lights are used, and how much auxiliary equipment is deployed during a dive. Batteries are usually charged overnight while the submersible sits on its support ship. A propeller driven by an electric motor, is used for propulsion. Some subs have lateral thrusters.

Radio waves do not penetrate very far through seawater so communications from a submersible to and from its support vessel are by an underwater wireless telephone (UQC) that can send and receive acoustic signals through the water using transducers. Sound travels very well in water so a submersible communication transducer, while underwater, can pick up all types of noises in addition to voice communications. Most submersibles have a mechanical or an articulated hydraulic arm to pick up objects and place them in storage containers.

The first successful modern submersible was built for Jacques Yves Cousteau in 1959. It was a two-person diving saucer, *La Soucoupe* that I witnessed diving off San Diego in 1964. It was a flattened sphere capable of diving to a thousand feet but very sluggish and slow. Several large corporations and a few individuals in the late 1950s and 1960s designed and built manned submersibles hoping that the future Ocean Age would be like the Space Age. Most of these submersibles were economic failures and now reside in museums and garages, or ended up in junk yards.

Douglas Privitt, a machine shop operator from Torrance, California, built submersibles that were the exception. His submersibles were very practical, safe, and easy to use. He built his first submersible in the 1950s, followed by several more in the early 1960s. In the late 1960s, my geological diving consultant friends from USC and San Diego wanted to dive deeper. They asked Doug to design and build a rugged sub they could use to break off rock samples, have good visibility for seafloor mapping, be able to dive off different kinds of support vessels, and be economical to use. With their input, Doug designed and built *Nekton* (later called *Nekton Alpha*). The name "Nekton" comes from the Greek word for things that swim or move in the ocean independent of water motion. *Nekton Alpha*, a two-person submersible, was fifteen feet long, weighed 4,800 pounds, and could dive down to 1,000 feet. Its cylindrical pressure hull was forty-two inches in diameter with a conning tower on top. It was powered by lead-acid batteries, similar to those used in golf carts, and was rugged enough to withstand the rigors of deep-sea diving. Two ballast tanks, one located in front and the other behind the pressure hull, were filled with seawater to make it descend and filled with air, from compressed air bottles, for it to rise. No electrical power was needed to bring one of Doug's submersibles to the surface, one of many safety factors built into all his submersibles.

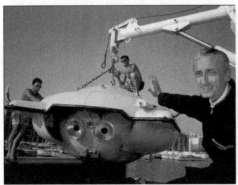 

Cousteau with La Souscoupe   *Doug Privitt*

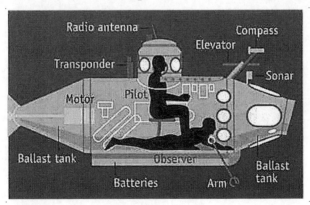

Cutaway of Nekton *type submersible (McCosh, 1996)*

Doug built four *Nekton* type submersibles: *Nekton Alpha, Nekton Beta, Nekton Gamma,* and *Delta.* All had cylindrical pressure hulls with many flat acrylic ports. They were simple, extremely reliable, easy to transport, and could dive off almost any support vessel anywhere in the world. They were also an immediate success. I logged over 2,000 dives off six continents piloting Doug's submersibles. Once, while traveling to dive in Lake Tahoe, *Beta* rolled off its trailer and tumbled about a hundred feet down a steep slope. It was undamaged, even when a tow truck dragged it back up to the road. That's how rugged Doug's submersibles were.

Nekton Beta

OBTAINING GULF OF ALASKA seafloor geologic data was important for oil companies because a Gulf lease schedule had been recently announced. Everyone thought somewhere in the Gulf of Alaska would be the next large offshore oil field discovery. General Oceanographics had contracts with several oil companies to collect geologic data from the Gulf during the summer of 1970. The General Oceanographics two-man office was in Newport Beach, California, and Larry Headlee, a USC classmate of mine, was the only employee. Jim Vernon, who asked me to return from South Africa, was the president. I was invited to help collect data because their Gulf of Alaska project needed another diving geologist.

After arriving from South Africa, I immediately went to work in Long Beach, helping to mobilize General Oceanographics' 105-ft. *M/V Oil City*. My first chore was to construct a mat of automobile tires that would hang over the side to protect the sub from touching the support ship during launch and retrieval. I went around town collecting old tires, drilled one-inch holes through them and connected the tires with chain.

A few weeks later I flew to Alaska while studying *Nekton's* instruction manual during the flight. I was the pilot on my first submersible dive, June 4, 1970, to 363 feet with Jim Vernon, my observer and instructor. After four dives I was on my own and piloted all my submersible dives that summer. Most of my three months' work in Alaska was spent dredging and coring for seafloor samples. Tom Crawford was the *Oil City* Captain, a great guy who I had sailed with off Oregon when I was with Richfield. He made our jobs much easier and was the best Captain for recovering a submersible after a dive that I ever sailed with. Larry and I kept the ship busy around the clock— diving, dredging and coring during the day and then collecting geophysical data at night. Unfortunately for us, there were only a few hours of darkness in mid-summer and the clients wanted us to dive fifteen hours a day. Fortunately for us, a full charge on *Nekton's* batteries was only good for about eight hours of diving.

Captain Tom Crawford

Enjoying the weather

M/V Oil City, *Gulf of Alaska*

Guppy *submersible*

Alaska diving

With Larry Headlee

Working on deck

Halibut fishing in Alaska

The Gulf of Alaska has some of the roughest ocean water in the world. Much of the time we worked in foul, windy, cold weather and occasionally had to run for cover. Once, we measured the wind speed at 100 mph while hiding behind an island. When I went outside to check on *Nekton*, I could feel salt crystals piercing my skin like needles as the salt water evaporated in the fierce wind.

There were geologists on several ships collecting data for oil companies that summer. One ship had a different type of manned submersible on board. While anchored behind an island during a storm, Larry and I went aboard the Sun Oil ship and inspected their submersible *Guppy*.* It did not dive more than a few times that summer as the sea had to be flat calm, a rare occurrence, before the crew would even attempt a launch. *Guppy* did not perform well when it was in the water either. This submersible was tethered to its support ship and soon after it was launched, the strong currents would spin the submersible like a fishing lure on the end of a line. *Guppy*'s pilot told us, "It was like being tumbled in a clothes dryer." The support ship had to be anchored, unlike our ship, throughout a dive and *Guppy* once wrapped its tether around the anchor line—it took most of a day to free it. We did not volunteer for a dive in *Guppy*.

We needed to know our exact location at all times while gathering data. There was no GPS available in the 1970s so we relied on signal generating shore stations for the most accurate navigation. These signals enabled us to plot our exact position each time we collected a sample, made a dive, or were running a geophysical transect. It took three line-of-site signal-generating stations to obtain an accurate navigation reading. We usually worked many miles offshore so navigation stations

---

*Guppy was a tethered two-man spherical submersible built in 1969-70 by the Sun Dry Dock and Ship Building Company. It depended totally upon the 1,200-foot umbilical cord to deliver electrical energy to the vehicle for propulsion and maneuvering. All the difficulties *Guppy* experienced in the Gulf of Alaska led to the abandonment of this submersible and it was never used again.

had to be positioned high on hilltops. One unpleasant task was rowing a small wooden boat ashore, sometimes through high surf, landing on a beach, usually soaking wet, and then, while carrying heavy car batteries and other equipment, trudging up a very steep hill overgrown with thick dripping-wet brush where we finally installed a battery-powered black box that transmitted signals to the *Oil City*. Every time we moved to a new area, which was often, someone had to climb three hills several miles apart to set up these transmitters.

One day, when working far offshore, one of the stations went dead. We rowed back to the beach, got roughed up in the surf and then hiked up the wet hill with a spare battery where we discovered a bear had destroyed the original battery. One of our oil company clients on board *Oil City* suggested something he found to work well for inquisitive bears. He wired raw bacon to a large spray can of OFF, the mosquito repellent, and we placed it next to the new battery. Later, when the bear bit into the spray can, it must have exploded in his mouth, as he did not bother us again. We used this successful technique several times during the summer.

One time, we rowed to an island beach with several oil company executives. A large wave flipped our wooden boat over and we all tumbled into the surf, ruining several cameras. I recall the water being very cold and yelling at the executives to move. I knew, from rowing Australian surfboats, what was coming. The next wave rolled our boat toward the beach, knocking the men over like bowling pins. We built a fire to warm up and dry our clothes when a large unfriendly Kodiak bear appeared. He was unhappy with us because we had been catching some large salmon in a nearby creek. This was his hunting ground. We hurriedly dressed, jumped into our bailed-out boat, and returned to the *Oil City* without further incident. Later, I found a huge whale skeleton while beach combing and dragged a large vertebra back to our rowboat. The whalebone now resides in my backyard along with several glass balls I also collected while beachcombing in Alaska.

Salmon from bear's creek   *End of a dive*

One day, we were asked to collect samples from a little, smooth, rocky island, about twelve feet across, in the middle of the Gulf of Alaska. One of the crew rowed Larry and me, wearing our wetsuits, over to the rock that was covered with sea lions. Sea lions are big, very nasty, and can bite like a dog. We scared them away, leapt onto the rock, and landed on sea lion droppings. Our feet went out from under us and we both slid up and over the little island, landing in the water on the other side, amidst angry sea lions. Luckily, neither of us were bitten. We quickly climbed back onto the rock and collected our samples.

During a visit to nearby Lituya Bay, when we had to run for shelter during a storm, we came across a grumpy old seal hunter, with two Indian wives skinning seals. He had shot the seals and dragged them to a shack where his wives worked. The large 8.3 earthquake in 1958 caused a lot of damage around Lituya Bay, when it triggered a massive landslide of over forty million cubic yards of rock and ice. When this big landslide hit the Bay water, it generated a 1,720-foot surge of water, the highest wave known in modern times. The wave rocked back and forth in the narrow inlet, knocking down trees up to 1,700 feet above the Bay. They looked like lots of matchsticks all lying on the ground pointing uphill. It was very difficult to get into Lituya Bay, but sometimes we did not have much choice as the weather in the Gulf of Alaska can become nasty in a very short time.

Seal skinners and hunter, Lituya Bay (our wooden row boat in background)

Visiting a port for a day ashore was a pleasure everyone looked forward to. Someone once said, "Working at sea is similar to being in jail with the added chance of drowning". It is not that bad, but a day on land was always welcomed. The *Oil City* needed to visit a port every few weeks for fuel, supplies, and to exchange several oil company personnel who monitored our project for their respective companies. There were only a few Gulf of Alaska ports large enough to handle *Oil City*. In 1970, we used Seward, south of Anchorage, and the tiny town of Yakutat located about 200 miles east of Seward.

M/V Oil City *and fishing boat at Yakutat and Yakutat Liquor Store*

Yakutat was once the largest city, by area, in the United States but with a population of only a few hundred, mainly Native Americans. There was one motel, which was weird as there were no roads in or out of Yakutat. A railroad was built to Yakutat in the early 1900s, but the tracks were now covered with weeds and trees—a lone locomotive stood rusted at the terminus. We met a friendly priest early in the summer but, during our last visit in August we were told a drunk native had recently clubbed him to death. We tried to time our visits to Yakutat to coincide with their weekly outdoor movie that started at 11:00 p.m. We had to bring our chairs from the ship or sit on the grass.

Bob Parks, the *Oil City's* engineer, was a great shipmate who would later save my life. He enjoyed pulling practical jokes. Anytime a client was feeling a little seasick, Bob bet a few of us that he could make him throw up and then walked by the poor guy while gagging on a partially swallowed piece of raw bacon attached to a string hanging out of his mouth. When Bob pulled up the bacon by the string, the seasick client would run for the door. Bob's best prank that summer involved an unpopular client. The *Oil City* had one-inch pipe bunk frames so Bob drilled a hole in the client's frame, inserted a marble, and covered the hole. Then every time the ship rolled, and it rolled a lot, the marble traveled back and forth through the pipe driving the client crazy. I discovered the best way to sleep on the *Oil City* was to lay spread eagle with my elbows, knees, and feet jammed into the bunk frame. One night, when the ship's bow slammed down, I found myself up in the air over my bunk. The ship rolled and I landed on the floor, luckily I was in the lower bunk.

Near the end of summer, we made a fuel run to Seward which has very large tides, as does most of the Gulf of Alaska. The *Oil City's* deck was level with the dock when we arrived but at low tide, the deck was about twenty feet below the dock. A deckhand repeatedly had to retie our mooring lines. One of the crew, who was a good seaman but a disaster on land, could not wait to visit the nearest bar. When he left the ship, he just stepped off onto the dock. When he returned, very drunk, that night, he stepped off the dock thinking the ship's deck was still there. He fell twenty feet, landed on the ship's railing, and then flipped onto a log floating in the water between the ship and the dock. He would have drowned if he had not landed on the log. We found him later after one of the crew on watch heard his moans. He broke several ribs and was not much use to us for the remainder of the trip.

We tied up alongside a large modern scallop fishing boat from Seattle during an earlier port visit to Seward. I mentioned to the owner/captain that I had observed frightened scallops propelling themselves up to six feet off the seafloor as *Nekton* passed by. His scallop dredge was only about three feet high so I thought he might be missing a lot of scallops. He then modified his dredge and subsequently made a big haul. Later, when I was flying home from Seward, at the summers end, he gave me some frozen scallops wrapped in brown paper and tied with string. After a few hours delay in Sitka, my airplane finally left for Seattle, then flew on to Los Angeles. I placed the frozen scallops under the seat in front of me. When the pilot hit the brakes hard while landing in Los Angeles, my package broke open and a flood of water and scallops shot forward under the seats in front. I ignored the commotion and left the plane minus my scallops. Sadly, the scallop boat, with the owner and his family, disappeared during a storm in the Gulf of Alaska a week after I left Seward.

I was excited to return to Southern California after four years living overseas and three months working on the *Oil City* off Alaska. Unfortunately, a tragedy was about to happen that would alter the lives of many people.

Chapter Five

Accident & Catalina Island

The greatest depth of an actual escape without any equipment has been from 225 ft. by Richard A. Slater from the rammed submersible *Nekton Beta* off Catalina Island, California on Sept. 28, 1970.

—*Guinness Book of World Records* (2010)

I RENTED A BEACH apartment in Newport Beach, after returning from Alaska, and needed to make a decision for my future. Larry was General Oceanographics' senior employee and I knew they were not going to need two full-time marine geologists on their payroll. I was thinking about applying for a University teaching position but everything changed a few weeks later during a dive off Catalina Island.

Doug Privitt had finished construction of two more Nekton class submersibles, *Nekton Beta* and *Nekton Gamma*. The first *Nekton* was now called *Nekton Alpha*. During the summer, while we were in Alaska, Jim Vernon had found a sunken pleasure boat off Catalina Island, using the new *Nekton Beta*, in 225 feet of water. The twenty-seven-foot speedboat with two Corvette engines had flipped at high speed. An insurance company paid for the search, thinking there might be drugs on the boat, and General Oceanographics had acquired the rights to the wreck itself. Jim was anxious to recover this boat but waited until we had returned from Alaska as he needed *Nekton Alpha*, the *Oil City*, and Larry and me for the recovery. A local LA underwater photographer was going to film the episode for a TV show.

Nekton's Alpha, Beta, *and* Gamma

Beta *and* Alpha *underway to Catalina Island*

Beta *and* Alpha, *Catalina Island, September 21, 1970*

On Monday September 21, 1970, both *Nekton's Alpha* and *Beta* were onboard the *Oil City* when we arrived around 10:00 a.m. at the Catalina dive site, a few miles east of Avalon, off the rock quarry. There were several guests on board including a good friend who brought his teenage son along to observe the recovery operation. The *Oil City* captain Tom Crawford and Larry made the first dive, in *Alpha*, to decide the best approach for the recovery. We then held a one-hour discussion where everyone agreed that Larry and I would dive in *Beta* to carry down a recovery line with a snap-hook to the wreck. Doug and Dick Anderson, the local underwater photographer, would be in *Alpha*. My job was to use *Beta's* arm to snap hook the heavy nylon line, connected to the *Oil City* winch, to the sunken vessel. Larry would be the pilot. It would be the first time the two submersibles were diving together, the first time Larry and I had dove together, and the first dive in *Beta* for both Larry and me. After rough cold water dives in Alaska, this was going to be enjoyable.

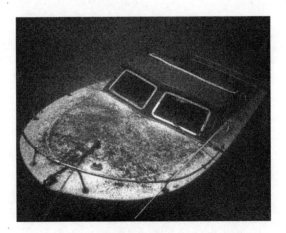

Sunken speedboat, 225'

It only took a few minutes to locate the sunken speedboat that was sitting on the seafloor near some rocks. I snapped the hook to the speedboat's bow and then decided to rearrange a line to help distribute the boat's weight while it was lifted up.

After I tied a few knots with *Beta's* mechanical arm, Larry was eager to have a turn so we switched places. This was difficult in the limited space. After Larry tied some knots, he continued playing with the arm and I remained the pilot. I moved *Beta* about 200 feet away from the wreck as we did not want to be under the *Oil City* during the recovery. The winch on the *Oil City* then hauled the speedboat quickly to the surface and it was secured to the tire mat.

Meanwhile, the speedboat's owner arrived in his water-ski boat to retrieve personal items from his wrecked speedboat. The *Oil City's* crane, holding the speedboat, was not available to lift us on board so we had to wait on the seafloor for the okay to surface. We started up very slowly, after receiving a message from Jim Vernon, on the *Oil City*, that everything was ready for us.

Someone decided to retie a line securing the speedboat to the *Oil City*. Suddenly, the speedboat broke loose from the tire mat and sank quickly, stern first, toward the seafloor. It did not travel straight down but sliced through the water column at a sharp angle. Both submersibles were in mid-water, around 150 feet, and slowly rising to the surface. Larry and I were talking when suddenly there was a crash—a tremendous crash! The three-ton speedboat had smashed into us. The quarter-inch stainless-steel trim tab, connected to the speedboat's stern, struck *Beta's* starboard conning tower port only inches from the right side of my head. In an instant the port cracked in several places and a triangular piece of Plexiglas from the center of the port imploded into the submersible, shattering my right cheekbone. It also sliced through my upper lip, cheek, and along the right side of my head, opening up wounds that bled profusely. The implosion, caused by the five-fold difference in pressure between the ocean at 150 feet and the inside of the submersible, destroyed our eardrums and instantly knocked us both out. It also buckled *Beta's* quarter-inch steel plate floor that sealed off the batteries located in the keel. We sank rapidly as *Beta* quickly filled with water.

When I came to about a minute later, *Beta*, nearly full of cold water, was lying on the seafloor in the dark. It had crashed onto the steeply sloping seafloor between 225 and 240 feet, and was leaning over about forty-five degrees. I stuck my nose into the air pocket forced up into the conning tower, above the broken port, by the incoming water. My first thought was to escape quickly but I had to wait a few more seconds until *Beta* completely filled with water. I could not open the hatch until the pressure was equal on the inside and outside of the submersible. I wrenched open the hatch, stood on the pilot's seat with my torso outside the submersible, and tried to jump free but I could not move. I was facing the stern and my Levi's rear pocket had snagged on the protruding rudder control knob. I could feel Larry's hands on my legs but there was no panic as I gave a mighty effort which resulted in ripping off my pocket by popping out the rivets. The pocket was found later in *Beta* after it was recovered.

There were two sets of emergency scuba gear in *Beta* but neither Larry nor I, the two most experienced *Nekton* pilots, grabbed them. Some people later wondered why we did not use the scuba gear. I have no idea but it just never occurred to me. I was wearing a dark T-shirt, Levi's, and running shoes as I swam toward the surface. It was very peaceful, quiet and dreamlike—everything seemed to be in slow motion. I had to exhale all the way to the surface. If I had held my breath, even for a moment, it might have resulted in a fatal air embolism. The urge to take a breath is caused by carbon dioxide build-up in your lungs. Halfway up is the toughest time in a free ascent; once you pass it the urge to take another breath lessens.

My last breath of air, while in *Beta*, was from the trapped air pocket where the pressure equaled the outside sea pressure. My lungs, holding six or seven times the usual amount of air, were still normal size as this air was compressed by the pressure. The pressure decreased as I headed to the surface so the air in my lungs increased in volume and I had to expel this air at roughly the same rate as my lungs were expanding.

Even though I was semi-conscious, I remember saying over and over to keep blowing out. My free ascent probably took about two minutes and I blacked out somewhere along the way, probably near the ocean surface. I have read that ninety-five percent of free diver blackouts occur in the last fifteen feet. The blackout can last for nearly two minutes, after that your body will take a breath and if you are still underwater it will cause instant death. Later, I mentioned seeing a bright green light during my ascent. This caused a stir as some people in near-death experiences have reported seeing a bright light. In my case, I was probably on or near the ocean surface. Clear shallow ocean water, on a sunny day, usually looks bright blue or green.

My friend and his son, on board the *Oil City*, had borrowed the small wooden rowboat to go fishing in the nearby kelp beds during our dive. When rowing to a new location they noticed a fountain of rising air bubbles in the water. They moved over to investigate and found me floating face down in the water. I was cut so badly they did not recognize me but held my head out of the water and started shouting for help. I was not breathing. Hearing their yells, the *Oil City* engineer Bob Parks jumped into the water-ski boat, still tied to the *Oil City*, and directed the owner over to the dinghy. Bob and the owner lifted me into the ski boat and we sped off for nearby Avalon. Bob told me later, "Although we were good friends, I did not give you artificial respiration because I could not locate your mouth with all the blood and gore." I was lying face down, unconscious, and not breathing on the boat floor when we hit a large swell. I went up into the air a few inches, came down hard on my stomach, vomited, and started to breathe.

Several timely events probably saved my life. What if Larry and I had not changed places in the submersible? What if the speedboat owner had not arrived in his water-ski boat to claim his gear? What if my friend and his son had not rowed over to a kelp bed near where I eventually surfaced? What if the water-ski boat had not hit the swell that caused me to start breathing again? What if the ships engineer had not reacted quickly when he saw that there was a problem? What if I had not been close to the Avalon hospital that was well known for treating diving accident victims?

I was offloaded at the end of the Avalon pier where large game fish are usually weighed. A crowd gathered as I was placed into an ambulance and transported to the hospital. I awoke, nearly one hour after the accident, on the operating table where a doctor was sewing up my wounds. Jim Vernon and some of the *Oil City* crew were standing around me. I asked about Larry and someone said he did not survive. I was shocked and could not comprehend what had happened. I thought maybe we had come up under the *Oil City*, which would have been my error as pilot.

Doug, piloting *Alpha*, saw us sinking rapidly and realized something was wrong. He immediately descended and landed near us with *Beta* enveloped in a cloud of dirty water stirred up when we crashed. When the water finally cleared, a minute or so later, *Beta's* hatch was open and Larry and I were gone. Doug was searching for us when he heard on *Alpha's* UQC that I was on the surface but Larry was still missing. He kept searching until he found Larry nearby on the seafloor. After grabbing him with *Alpha's* arm they surfaced immediately, less than ten minutes after the accident. For nearly an hour the Captain and Mate applied artificial respiration but could not revive Larry. Later, his knee-high rubber boots were found together on the seafloor. They probably filled with water when he tried to swim to the surface. It was assumed that he landed back on the seafloor, took his rubber boots off, and tried to swim up again but this delay proved fatal.

I was in the hospital a few days with a tablespoon of water in one lung, and I was almost deaf due to my ruptured eardrums. They eventually grew back from tiny nubs so I did not have the planned operation to put in new ones from my neck skin. My hearing is fine except for occasional tinnitus, a ringing in my ears. Doctors told me the cheekbone is the strongest bone in your face. If the Plexiglas chunk had hit me an inch higher, in my temple, I probably would have died instantly. If it had hit me an inch lower, it could have ripped my jaw off. I was very fortunate not to lose my eye.

Beta *on the seafloor, 240' (starfish on hatch)*

Beta and the speedboat were recovered a few weeks later. Doug completely restored *Beta* and it was soon ready to dive. He also repaired the damaged speedboat and sold it. Everyone said I was lucky, but I always thought my son Stephen, born ten months after the accident, was really the luckiest one. I decided to stay with General Oceanographics and bought a home in Mission Viejo, just a short commute to the office in Newport Beach.

My ascent is listed in the *Guinness Book of World Records*. They have the date wrong and the depth was just an estimate.

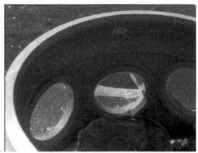

Submersibles after Beta *recovery*   *Broken conning tower port*

Wooden rowboat at time of accident   *Recovered speedboat*

According To Guinness

The greatest depth of an actual underwater escape without any equipment has been from 225 ft. by Richard A. Slater from the rammed submersible *Nekton Beta* off Catalina Island, Calif. on Sept. 28, 1970.

From The Guinness Book of World Records
© 1984 Sterling Pub. Co., Inc.
© Guinness Sup Ltd
Dist. by Universal Press Sync.

J-L

Chapter Six

California, Colombia, & Belize

> The excitement of the search, even the months of waiting and despair have provided moments that could not be bought. Every find comes as a gift from the sea, and our best reward will always be the unforgettable thrill of discovery.
>
> —Kip Wagner, *Pieces of Eight* (1966)

SIX WEEKS AFTER the accident, Doug and I dove *Nekton Beta* off Point Conception, near Santa Barbara, on oil company projects. Some people wondered if I would climb back into a submersible, but I knew what had happened was an accident and I was fortunate Doug had designed *Nekton* so I could open the hatch during an emergency. My escape would have been impossible from most other submersibles, where you need someone outside to open the hatch. I was now the only person who could manage a General Oceanographics at-sea project. For the next several years, I would be busy working and diving around the world.

Diving off Southern California is typically a real pleasure. The water is normally very clear and the seafloor scenery can be stunning. In 1971, I made over a hundred submersible dives off Southern California for commercial seafloor projects along the coastline, around the offshore islands and on several outer banks. Visibility on the outer banks was usually over a hundred feet and small pink anemones, like wild flowers, blanketed acres of the seafloor. It was very spectacular and unforgettable diving.

We often entertained prospective clients near the Isthmus at Catalina Island by diving on a shipwreck we had discovered in 180 feet of water. It was the remains of a large old sailing ship, anchored fore and aft with two magnificent anchors, which had burned before sinking. Later we discovered this was the ship used in the *Mutiny on the Bounty* movie filmed at Catalina in 1935. The wreck provided shelter for many lobster and schools of fish. Nearly everyone we took down to view this wreck kept asking us if we had found any treasure, so Doug decided to put a treasure chest on it. He purchased an old wooden chest at a swap meet, scorched it with a welding torch, and added cheap jewelry so when the lid was left slightly open you could see the riches. We then carefully placed the chest on the shipwreck. Doug and I relished taking observers down, cruising by the treasure chest and, when they were screaming to stop, just kept going while saying we did not see anything. Some macho scuba divers removed the chest a few years later; they probably wondered about its origin.

Large anchor and "treasure chest" on shipwreck, Catalina Island Isthmus

In 1969, Doug used *Nekton Alpha* at the Isthmus for a Jacques-Yves Cousteau TV special on submersibles. Most of the other submersibles just sat on the seafloor while *Alpha* sprinted around. Cousteau called *Alpha* "the roadrunner." Doug showed the shipwreck to Cousteau's divers and they removed one of the six-foot anchors, which they later threw overboard into the harbor. The USC Marine facility at the Isthmus eventually used this anchor to secure their sea lion cage. During filming of the submersible show, thousands of squid appeared one night, had a mating frenzy, deposited their eggs, and then swam away or died. Their bodies covered the seafloor. Cousteau put together a TV special on squid called *The Night of the Squid*, which implied that they followed them to this area. We had trouble collecting our fee from Cousteau for participating in the submersible show—he finally settled after we hired a lawyer.

My son David, Nekton Alpha, *and shipwreck items, Catalina Island*

We enjoyed the Catalina Isthmus diving so much that we spent many weekends there, with friends and family, using scuba and submersibles off General Oceanographics' sixty-five-foot *M/V Dawn Star*. My son David's first submersible dive, in 1971, was at the Isthmus. Rising insurance costs put a stop to those wonderful weekends.

The oil spill off Santa Barbara in 1969 generated so much bad publicity we needed to rename the *M/V Oil City* (M/V - motor vessel). This was not easy. We spent weeks going over lists of names before deciding on the *R/V Seamark* (R/V - research vessel). A seamark is any object used as a navigation guide at sea. This title seemed appropriate as we planned to use it as a navigation station during scientific operations.

OUR FIRST MAJOR *SEAMARK* voyage took us down to Cartagena, Colombia, in 1971. We worked for Exxon, taking deep-sea cores and gathering geophysical data from an area offshore the Magdalena River Delta. I was the project manager and Tom Crawford the ship's captain. Tom had been on more seafloor sampling expeditions than anyone and together we made a good team. We installed a large winch with 12,000 feet of cable, built an A-frame on *Seamark's* stern and secured *Beta* onboard, just in case we might have an opportunity for a dive. Friends and family came down to the Long Beach Harbor to see the ship off. I planned to meet *Seamark* later in Panama. During the first night at sea, one of the main engines failed off San Diego and *Seamark* limped back to Long Beach. It took several weeks to replace the blown engine (and the other main engine so they would be compatible). This was not a good start for *Seamark's* first foreign adventure. Fortunately, the break down did not occur in a third world country, many miles from home.

Before leaving for South America, we had a visitor from the CIA. This was my first of many CIA contacts over the next 30 years. The Agency often used businessmen traveling abroad as an extra set of eyes and ears. Our contact always warned us of dangerous areas and asked that we let him know of anything that seemed suspicious. He was more help to us than we were to him so we kept in contact over the years.

Jim Vernon and I flew to Panama City to transit the Panama Canal onboard *Seamark*. During a brief layover in Mexico City, I ate a ham sandwich that immediately made me ill. As the plane lifted off I rushed to the bathroom and stayed there all the way to Panama City. We rented a room at the Canal Zone military base where I was bedridden for several days. I finally ventured out by walking into town on a Sunday afternoon, where a large rally was being held in the central square. The local Indians, many dressed in colorful native attire were listening to a man giving a frenzied speech from a balcony. When I returned to the Canal Zone the gate guard asked where I had been. When

I told him, he said Americans were banned from downtown that day because of the anti-American rally held by the future dictator Manuel Noriega. We easily transited the Canal with no further problems, Jim flew home, and we sailed for Cartagena.

Bandits controlled much of the Colombia countryside in 1971 so we had to hire an armed guard while at the dock in Cartagena. We also had to keep all our portholes closed, as kids on the pier were using fishing poles to snag things out of our cabins. One day, during an afternoon tropical downpour, several bandits with knives clenched between their teeth climbed aboard *Seamark*. They jumped up from dugout canoes they had paddled from under the pier and ran through the ship grabbing anything that might be valuable. When I returned from shopping in town, our armed guard was holding a man he had captured while Captain Tom was calling the police. I felt something was wrong, as our armed guard was very pale and sweating profusely. Suddenly, when our backs were turned the bandit leaped overboard and swam under the pier. It was good riddance because we did not want to get involved. We later discovered our lone captured bandit was the "Robin Hood" of Colombia featured on Most Wanted posters all over town. The guard would have been in deep trouble if he had turned him in.

One of the world's most famous shipwrecks, the *San Jose*, lies on the seafloor just a few miles off Cartagena. It sank in 1708 and is thought to be the richest shipwreck in the world. It contains billions of dollars' worth of gold and jewels, plus possibly a six-foot solid gold Madonna statue. We did not search for the *San Jose* on this trip, but several years later we finally received permission from the Colombian government. Unfortunately, that government was overthrown before we got started and the new government cancelled our permit. Over the years, several potential clients inquired about diving on this wreck—I always thought it was too dangerous. One treasure hunter asked us to submerge off Panama and travel 300 miles to Cartagena underwater!

Armed guard and gravity coring from Seamark, *Colombia*

The sampling and geophysical work went very well. I ran the day shift where we recovered sixty cores, some from water depths down to 10,000 feet, while a technician ran the night shift collecting 1,200 miles of geophysical data. This technician was quite a character who had spent years on Scripps research vessels. I learned a lot about electronics from him. One day, I asked how he could tell 110-volt from 220-volt lines; we had both on the ship and I noticed he never used a voltmeter. "It is easy," he said, "I can hold on to 110 but 220 knocks my hand away." I never tried his technique.

Seamark sailed north to British Honduras after the Colombia project and I left for home. I hired a driver to take the recently fired, macho first mate and me about seventy miles over the mountains to the Barranquilla international airport. About halfway on our journey, as we turned a corner on the narrow winding jungle road, there was a tree blocking our path. We stopped and bandits, wearing dark glasses, jumped out of the bushes with guns and crossed bandoliers. I thought we had entered a movie set but this was the real thing. Our driver got out, told us to be quiet, and went over to talk to the bandits. Finally, he returned and said if we paid twenty dollars they would let us pass—I wondered if it was a set-up. We paid, they pulled the tree out of the way, and we proceeded on.

AN OPPORTUNITY AROSE to dive the new *Nekton Gamma* submersible after I arrived back in California. *Gamma* was nearly identical to *Beta* and we now had three operable subs. General Oceanographics was hired to examine oil pipelines running from shore out to several Santa Barbara Channel oil platforms. My job was to video every pipeline, each about three miles long, and to inspect for any leaks or damage. Video recorders and cameras were very large in 1971, and we had to find a unit that would fit through the eighteen-inch *Nekton* hatch opening. It was boring work. I am sure I startled many drivers on the Pacific Coast Highway when I followed one pipeline into the surf zone with the sub conning tower sticking out of the water. Before the first dive, I asked our clients if there were any problems, as one pipeline was new and had never been surveyed before. The answer was, "No, they are all clear." When an ocean pipeline is laid down they usually float it to the final location and then cut off the large, roughly six-foot diameter, metal buoys that kept it afloat. We were at full speed along a pipeline in very dirty water and poor visibility, when we ran right into a large buoy they had neglected to cut off. It stopped us in our tracks and gave me a nasty bump on my head, but, luckily nothing broke and we continued on while I suffered a headache. These pipelines provided shelter for lobsters and abalone. I noted several good locations where I could later return to collect a future meal.

WHILE WE WERE IN South America, Dr. Robert Ginsburg from the University of Miami inquired about using *Beta* for his biological and geological studies of the second largest barrier reef in the world. This reef is located along the east coast of British Honduras (now Belize) in Central America. This was exciting news; my only dives on the Great Barrier Reef were in shallow water with scuba. Now I would be diving down to 1,000 feet along the front of a barrier reef with one of the top coral reef experts in the world. Funding would be through NSF (National Science Foundation) and NOAA (National

Oceanographic and Atmospheric Administration). This was the first of many NOAA and NSF funded reef diving projects I would be involved in over the next thirty years off Florida and in the Caribbean.

I rejoined the *Seamark* crew at Belize City in early December. British Honduras was the only Latin American country with English as the official language. Working with local officials was much easier here than in most other foreign countries. During the day we explored the deep fore-reef zone of the barrier reef and one atoll with scientists in *Beta* taking many photographs, making direct observations, and also collecting samples. At night another crew ran geophysical profiles and recovered deep-sea cores.

Studying modern coral reefs is important as many ancient fossilized reefs are of economic interest for petroleum and other mineral deposits. There had been a great deal of research done on shallow modern living reefs but this was the first *in situ* study of a deep barrier reef below scuba depth. It was also a test to see how well *Beta* and its crew would perform. During the five working days, we made thirty-two dives and produced the first precise documentation of depth limits for many reef-animals.

Placing and exploding small packages of dynamite stuck into crevices in water depths down to 350 feet enabled us to collect reef rock samples. We wrapped explosives around one end of a ten-foot long PVC plastic pipe and then attached primacord* that was connected to the ship. *Beta* carried the pipe down to the seafloor, looking like a yellow horse in a medieval jousting tournament, while primacord was played out from the ship. Once the explosives were in place, I would bring *Beta* to the surface and crack open the hatch, then the primacord would be ignited from *Seamark*. The loud underwater explosion could have damaged our ears if we were not on the surface with the

---

*Primacord is a high-speed flexible tube used as a fuse. It explodes rather than burns and is used to detonate high explosives.

hatch open. Even on the surface, an underwater explosion sounded like someone hitting the submersible with a large hammer. After each explosion, the *Seamark* cook and a fish biologist collected dead fish floating on the surface for dinner and identification while we dove to collect the blast samples.

> [Note: Explosives are no longer allowed on coral reefs so obtaining deep reef rock samples is very difficult now]

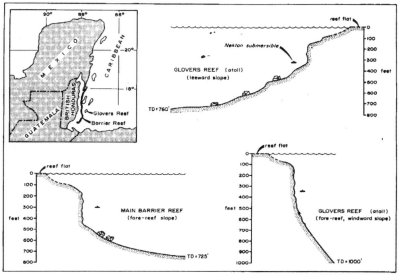

BATHYMETRIC PROFILES OF DEEP REEF in three areas investigated by NEKTON submersible, British Honduras barrier reef and atoll.

Submarine Reef Exploration
In British Honduras

By Dr. John L. Wray*

British Honduras dive locations and profiles, 1971-72 (Wray, 1972)

British Honduras (Belize) Barrier Reef   *Doug with TNT package*

R/V Seamark *and* Nekton Beta   *Scientists off British Honduras*

British Honduras Deep Reef Slope, ≈500'
(James and Ginsburg, 1979)

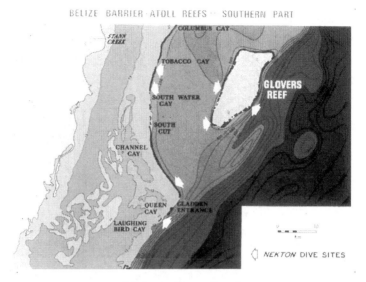

Nekton Beta *dive sites*

British Honduras reef escarpment 200-300' and collecting blast samples
(James and Ginsburg, 1979)

Local fishermen often came out in their handmade dugout fishing boats to trade fish, coconuts, and lobster for motor oil and steaks. We ate well on this trip. Diving was spectacular; we witnessed things no one had ever seen before. During one dive, a three-foot fish swam between *Beta* and the nearby reef wall. It became excited and while trying to escape rammed into *Beta*, shattering a light. Bob Ginsburg, my observer, was taping his observations. As slivers of glass from the broken light floated and shimmered around *Beta*, Bob became excited and whispered into his tape recorder, "We have just been attacked by a huge fish that smashed into our submersible and shattered a light." At that moment, a very large sea bass swam out of a nearby cave and swallowed the stunned fish in one gulp. That was the end of the giant fish that had attacked our submersible. On another dive, a huge sea bass swam right up to us. It seemed nearly as big as the submersible and when it looked into a ten-inch *Beta* port, his eye seemed to block the entire window. *Beta* proved to be an ideal platform to assist scientists study the deep reef.

Belize City had recently been hit by a hurricane and the city was a mess with many ruined buildings. Raw sewerage ran down open ditches along the city streets. I took one of the ship's crew into the Belize City hospital after an accident with his knife. The hospital was extremely unhealthy looking and I was concerned as they sewed up his wound that he would get an infection, but he survived. Our alcoholic deckhand, the same crewmember that fell off the dock in Alaska, was onboard because Captain Tom had a kind heart and did not want to leave him in Santa Barbara. He was about fifty years old but looked closer to seventy. For his upcoming birthday he announced he would dive off the top of *Seamark's* A-frame. This framework was about twenty-five feet high and only a few young athletic crewmembers ever jumped from the top. We did not pay much attention; as we did not think he could even climb that high. However, on the appointed day, while we were eating lunch, he climbed to the top. We ran out onto the deck and tried to talk him out of jumping when he made a beautiful swan dive and neatly cut into the water. We were all amazed. Sadly, we had to leave him behind the next year. While we were gone, he committed suicide by jumping off a Santa Barbara hotel where Captain Tom had arranged a room for him.

SEAMARK SAILED TO Miami, from British Honduras, for the winter. Doug and I flew to Los Angeles where I hoped to stay home for a while but less than a month later I was diving off Miami. It was still just a two-man office in Newport Beach, Jim Vernon and me, although we finally hired a secretary that helped me as I had been doing all the typing.

A dock was found in Miami where *Seamark* was secured for the winter. We hoped to sail to the Mediterranean for pipeline route surveys in the spring. Meanwhile we invited some local scientists to join us for demonstration dives off Miami Beach. *Nekton Beta* was used on thirty dives and we generated some interest for future work.

We checked out the Miami Beach sewer outfall, called the "Rose Bowl", which was a magnet for local Cuban fishermen. It was easy to locate, I would just go out into the middle of the fishing fleet and then dive straight down, landing on top of the diffuser pipe in one hundred feet of water. I'm not sure if I would have eaten any fish they were catching but it did not seem to bother them and the fishing was excellent.

We often inspected sewer outfalls in Southern California and I found the work easy as the pipes are large and water visibility was usually good. Once, with scuba, I helped inspect an outfall off Palos Verdes near the Los Angeles Harbor. I remember swimming several hundred feet up inside the pipe (after the flow had been shut off). The diffuser openings were too small to swim through with diving gear on. It was easier to take off my tank, push it through the small vent, wiggle through the hole, and put the tank back on than it was to swim backwards inside the pipe.

While diving in Miami, I was invited to visit the Bahamas aboard John Perry's private yacht for a chance to observe the filming of a television show. John, owner of several Florida newspapers and TV cable companies, was very interested in underwater habitats and manned submersibles. Marlin Perkins, host of the TV show *Wild Kingdom*, and his assistant joined us for a trip out to Lee Stocking, John's private Bahamian Island, to film a shark show. We dragged a bloody dead cow carcass around for several days trying to convince sharks to approach us so that a small two-man submersible could be launched with Marlin inside. The sharks decided not to partake in our little adventure.

Marlin Perkins and assistant in the Bahamas

Chapter Seven

Canada, Mediterranean, Jamaica, & Belize

One of the problems with oceanography today is that if you get your PhD and write to get grant money through peer review, you might go on five expeditions in your entire life. Science is like baseball or ballet; it's better if you practice it. The problem with most oceanographers is that they don't get to play the game very often.

—Emory Kristoff (2010)

THE COMPANY THAT BUILT *Pisces* for my Hudson Bay adventure, International Hydrodynamics, Ltd., contacted us in March 1971. They requested that we bring a submersible up to Vancouver, Canada, to search for a tugboat that had recently disappeared. I was puzzled why they did not use one of their submersibles but Doug and I loaded *Gamma* on a trailer and towed it up to Canada. The sixty-one-foot long tugboat had disappeared during high winds and sank in approximately four hundred feet of water. The lost crew's families and the local union were demanding an investigation because another of these new, very fast tugs had disappeared the year before. The tug we would be looking for was pulling several large log rafts, and the union wanted to know if the crew had been ordered to open the louvered engine hatch cover to cool the engine, thus enabling the tug to go faster.

We sailed into nearby Hecata Straits aboard the *Pisces* support barge and started searching. The log rafts, still connected to the sunken tug, were floating on the ocean surface the day after the accident but someone mysteriously unfastened the connecting shackle and the steel tow line had fallen to the ocean floor making our search more difficult. Our hosts kept delaying our dives and, when we finally dove; our sonar* did not detect any large targets. After a futile day of searching and meetings, Doug and I wondered if we might be looking in the wrong area. It seemed like someone did not want us to find the tug. Our hosts kept plying us with food and booze; apparently to keep our minds off what we were there for. We were working for some shady operators. Our main contact disappeared a few years later; sailed his boat into the Pacific and was never seen again.

Nekton Gamma on *Pisces* barge, Vancouver
(next to tug boat similar to the one that sunk)

A heated discussion between owners, union reps, and others broke out on the barge while we were waiting to dive on the second day. While the argument raged, Doug and I slipped off and dove to search in a different direction. Within a half hour we picked up a loud audible sonar target that led us to a large

---

*Sonar – Acronym for sound navigation and ranging. It is similar in concept to radar but uses sound waves in water by active transmission or by passive sensing. We used sound to map the seafloor, to find objects on the seafloor, to locate a submersible from the mother ship and to communicate with the mother ship.

shackle connected to a heavy steel cable. We followed this cable in very low visibility for about twenty minutes until we could hear a much larger and louder sonar target just ahead. We slowly inched our way forward, the sonar booming in the submersible, until suddenly the cable rose up into the water column and disappeared. As the observer, I stared straight ahead into the murky water. Visibility was only a few feet. Doug kept asking if I could see anything and I kept answering, "No, only dirty water."

We continued slowly forward until we bumped into a hard object. When the water started to clear I could see something big and shiny, and suddenly realized we were under the tug and up against the propeller. We had found the tugboat sitting upright on the seafloor after searching for about six hours over two days. Doug backed *Gamma* out from under the tug and started up slowly until I grabbed the tugboat's railing with *Gamma's* arm to steady us. The water was clearer above the seafloor and we could now see across the deck. I observed a louvered door in the open position and said, "Let's get out of this spooky place." We had completed our mission and I was ready to head home.

Upon returning to the support barge, we were questioned about diving without permission but not much could be said as we found the wreck. I was describing the open louvered door when someone moaned, "That's the wooden vegetable bin door."

We had to dive again the next day. It was easier this time. We ran along the seafloor until we found the cable, followed it to the wreck, rose up to deck level and observed the correct louvered hatch cover. It was shut, case closed, job finished. We handed over our photos and videos of the wreck, plus a written report, to the Canadian Department of Transportation. They later came to the conclusion that a strong wind had blown one of the log rafts up on its side and the raft, acting like a sail, had pulled the tug over backwards.

IN APRIL 1971, we were hired to search for a missing scuba diver off the San Pedro breakwater outside the Los Angeles Harbor. He was a commercial diving class student and had disappeared during an underwater lesson. We did not find the diver but discovered a couple of interesting objects. One was the skeleton of an old single engine airplane that, regrettably, I didn't photograph. Later, when I described this plane to a World War II expert he said it sounded like the remains of a Japanese Zero. During the war there were rumors of a Zero flying around Palos Verde and possibly this was that plane. Unfortunately, we never found the plane again.

We also ran into a large three-bladed propeller still coupled to a twenty-three-foot long broken drive shaft. We raised the propeller and shaft with air bags and sold it for scrap. The manganese bronze propeller weighed 14,400 pounds and the shaft 12,500 pounds. We named our project "Get the shaft and screw up." It had apparently spun off an old WWI Navy ship entering the L.A. Harbor over forty years ago.

Recovered propeller and shaft, Los Angeles Harbor

THERE WERE SEVERAL interesting non-diving projects I was involved with in 1971. One concerned a hang glider Doug designed and built. There was great interest in the late 1960s and early 1970s in hang gliders and many different designs were being built and tested. In May 1971, the first ever hang glider meet was held on a Newport Beach hill. Doug wanted to be there. We tested the plane several times near Doug's shop before taking it down to Newport Beach. Doug and I were too heavy to pilot the hang glider so my son David, age twelve, was selected. I watched several spectacular crashes, and then it was our turn. Doug and I, each holding one wing tip, ran along the hilltop and launched the plane. It flew a short distance, took a nosedive, and crashed. David was uninjured but the plane was totaled. An interesting highlight to me was the introduction of the triangular flexible wing Rogallo* hang glider that eventually became the standard. It was the clearly the best performer of the day. Doug's design never became popular and the wrecked plane was relegated to the back of his shop. Doug later built a self-propelled bi-wing plane with a hand carved propeller that also did not fly very well.

> [Note: In May 2011, the city of Newport Beach erected a monument at the site commemorating the first hang glider meet on its 40th anniversary. The area is now covered with expensive homes and a city park.]

Doug's bi-wing hang glider, Newport Beach

---

*The Rogallo hang glider was originally designed in the 1950s to bring space capsules back to earth and was not adapted for the sport of hang gliding until after the Newport Beach event.

DOUG AND I, plus two other friends, drove my Volkswagen bus over 2,000 miles, on mainly unpaved roads, from Newport Beach to Cabo San Lucas, Mexico, and back in 1971. We had discovered that the road was going to be paved in the near future and wanted to drive the old road before it disappeared. We carried our own food and gasoline, as there were few stops along the way. Fortunately, Doug brought tools to repair the road, which was impassable in many places. Friends said to carry candy and cigarettes for the locals. The candy worked fine but we ended up with a lot of leftover cigarettes—none of us smoked. We camped for a few days at Bahia de Los Angeles and enjoyed the company of local fishermen who invited us to sit around an open fire in their beach hut where we boiled and ate shrimp while drinking Mexican beer. A ferry ride across the Gulf of California from La Paz to Mazatlán made the return trip easier on a paved road all the way home.

Camping and fixing the main highway, Baja California

A MEDITERANEAN CONTRACT was finally received after a Spring of Catalina Island Isthmus diving, surveying pipelines, and inspecting sewer outfalls. *Seamark* crossed the Atlantic Ocean in May 1972 with few problems except the engineer somehow lost 3,000 gallons of diesel overboard, resulting in an emergency Azores fuel stop. I flew to Spain and met the ship and our clients in Algeciras, across the bay from Gibraltar. A pipeline company from Tulsa, Oklahoma; hired us to survey potential Mediterranean tunnel and gas pipeline crossing routes from Spain to Algeria and Morocco. Our job was to gather subsurface geophysical data, collect rock samples, and to use *Beta* to video and survey the seafloor along each route.

The work was easy but having government representatives from three countries always on board made for a very difficult situation. Between Catholic Spain and Muslim Algeria, and Morocco, there was a religious holiday almost every day.

R/V Seamark *off Gibraltar*

Obtaining cores off Gibraltar   *Mediterranean crew*
(I am in the middle, top row, Bob, the engineer who saved my life off Catalina, is far right, second row)

We were in port more often than at sea. The diving was okay, but the Mediterranean has been over-fished for centuries and there was little marine life left. One of the more exciting events occurred when we snagged and dredged up a three-inch cable still attached to the seafloor. It put so much strain on our winch that *Seamark's* stern was being pulled under, until we finally cut the cable with a welding torch. We watched with some concern to see if the lights in Tangiers went out as the cable was severed—they did not. Later we decided it was a World War II cable to detect submarines passing through the Strait of Gibraltar. Subsurface geophysical data revealed a very complex contorted geology. It would be difficult material to tunnel through.

My field assistant and I rode a Strait of Gibraltar ferry to Morocco during one four-day work break. I wanted to find an Australian friend who was mapping up in the Atlas Mountains on a project funded by Exxon through the University of South Carolina. He had rented a beach house in Casablanca and I thought he would be easy to find. Arriving in Casablanca in the late afternoon, I was shocked to find a large city of several million. My search suddenly became a lot more difficult. We headed down to an upscale beach area and starting asking if anyone knew an Australian living nearby. A young man who spoke English helped me by talking to locals.

I thought we might have found the right person, during one lively conversation. When I asked our guide, "What did he say?" the answer was, "How do I know? All white people look alike." We continued our search. Finally, a man pointed to a back alley door and said an Englishman lived there. Our situation was becoming hopeless and the sun was setting, so I knocked on the door. A voice in English said, "Come in." A man sitting on the floor, puffing on a hookah, looked up. As I peered through the smoke, I recognized Chris Kendall, my friend from England and Australia. The last time I saw Chris was when he locked the rental truck on Flinders Island and I had to break the window. I said, "Dr. Kendall, I presume," which resulted in a startled look. He was also working on the University of South Carolina project and took us on a wonderful three-day trip, in a tiny car, into the Atlas Mountains where we observed some spectacular geology and visited several Berber villages. It was market day at one village and tribes from miles away gathered to trade and shop. One group on horseback came galloping through the open market, firing guns into the air. The jugglers, snake charmers and other entertainers fascinated me. I finally located my Australian friend's house in Casablanca but did not see him; he was still mapping high up in the mountains.

Casablanca alley   *Filling up our car in Morocco*

Snake charmer at Berber market

I invited my wife to fly to Europe so we could have a holiday together after the Gibraltar project was completed. I met her in Paris, where I also received a telegram the same day saying I was needed immediately in Jamaica for a deep-reef project. There went our vacation. I promised my wife a trip to Jamaica instead—she went home, not happy, after two days in Jamaica.

SEVERAL SCIENTISTS who dove with us in Belize wanted a *Nekton* submersible for the deep-reef off the Discovery Bay Marine Laboratory located on the north shore of Jamaica. The problem was how to transport a submersible there and back. We finally requested and received permission from the Kaiser Company to place *Gamma* in the hold of a bauxite ore carrier that ran between New Orleans and Discovery Bay every week. *Gamma* was then shipped from California to New Orleans for the ride to Jamaica. It rode on a large pile of red bauxite ore during the return trip. Tiny pieces of red ore were still stuck to the submersible months later.

Another problem was finding a support ship for *Gamma* in Jamaica. We finally decided to tow it back and forth to the nearby reef from the Discovery Bay Laboratory pier with a twenty-two foot *Aquasport*. No one wanted to ride in *Gamma* for twenty minutes while it was being towed—it was a very bouncy and extremely hot ride. We took a chance, except in very rough weather, and transferred submersible personnel from the *Aquasport* while outside the reef. At night, we tied *Gamma* to the Lab's small sheltered pier to charge its batteries. One problem was the algal beard that *Gamma* grew from being in the water twenty-four hours a day. Every few days, I jumped into the water and gave *Gamma* a good scrubbing. We used a Kaiser Bauxite facility crane to pull *Gamma* out of the water when we needed to make repairs, such as fixing the drive shaft leak. Most observers did not like diving in a leaking submersible but it was not a serious problem and easily fixed. Between these repairs, we pumped *Gamma's* bilges every night of the water from sweat and condensation from our breathing.

The diving was very successful with thirty-one scientists making 128 dives, many to 1,000 feet, in twenty-eight days. It was a wonderful month of diving and being around scientists who were excited about deep coral reefs. I stayed with several scientists at a nearby house where long evening discussions over a few Red Stripe beers were a magnet for all. We drove an old beat-up Land Rover, when it would start, back and forth to the Discovery Bay Lab every day from our home away from home.

Gamma *being loaded on bauxite ore*   Aquasport *and* Gamma
(notice how beat up the sub is from diving)   *(bauxite carrier in background)*

Discovery Bay Marine Lab and reef   *Pulling out for repairs*

Repairing Gamma's *drive shaft leak*   *At Discovery Bay Marine Lab dock*

Towing Gamma *out to dive*   *Diving with sample rack*

Discovery Bay Marine Laboratory, Jamaica

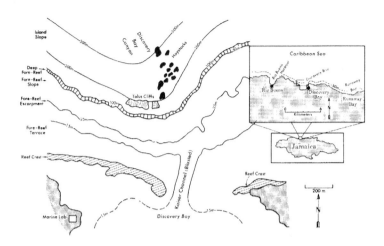

Discovery Bay dive area (Land and Moore, 1977)

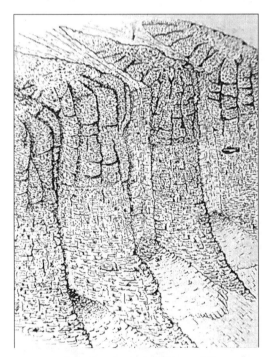

Jamaica deep-reef, "the wall"
Gamma *and scuba diver (near top) for scale (Land and Moore, 1977)*

Tom Goreau, a Yale biology professor, founded the Discovery Bay Laboratory in 1965. Tom had passed away a few years earlier and one of my first tasks was to take his widow on a dive down to an area designated as his memorial site near where his ashes had been placed outside the reef.

After several weeks of diving I taught a University of Texas geology professor, Lynton Land, to pilot *Gamma*. I needed some relief; the diving was strenuous because of the intense heat and humidity inside *Gamma* during shallow dives. Lynton and I were down about 400 feet during a training dive on the steep slope below the reef "wall*" when I spotted a pair of diving fins on the seafloor. I asked Lynton to move *Gamma* over to see if he could maneuver the submersible close enough to enable me to pick up the fins with the mechanical arm. I got a grip on the flippers when I saw that there was a diving mask attached. Lynton asked if there was a cigar box and when I said "Yes" he quickly replied, "Drop it—you found Tom Goreau." If Lynton had not been diving with me, I would have brought everything back to the dock where Tom's widow was waiting. Lynton saved me from an embarrassing moment.

Jamaica reef collecting techniques, similar to those we used successfully in British Honduras, were aided with dynamite and primacord. During one dive, a student in a small boat played out the explosive primacord to us as we descended down the "wall" with the dynamite lashed to a plastic pipe. Unknowingly, he was drifting toward shore over the shallow pristine reef. This resulted in laying down the primacord across the living reef and the explosion made a destructive track right across a study area. The doctoral student, who was measuring growth rates of coral in this area, was very upset.

---

*Below the living reef there is the deep fore reef or more commonly known to divers as the "wall". At Discovery Bay the "wall" is a rugged near vertical cliff found between the depths of about 90 and 400 feet. Below this cliff is a steep talus slope, dipping thirty to forty-five degrees, consisting of loose and cemented sediment and large chunks of debris, which had broken off and fallen down from the living reef up above.

Most sponges are usually soft and attached to rock; however, calcareous sponges (sclerosponges) are hard and form part of the reef framework along with coral and algae. Sclerosponges are difficult to collect without explosives. A few months after I left Jamaica, several Discovery Bay scientists went over to nearby Montego Bay to collect a few sclerosponges off the an underwater cave ceiling. They chose the Widowmaker Cave, a famous dive site just outside Montego Bay. Using too much of our leftover dynamite, they collapsed part of the cave. Divers from Discovery Bay Marine Laboratory were not welcome in Montego Bay for many years.

Jamaica living reef ≈100' and upper reef groove (photos by Phil Dustan)

There are many large blocks, called "haystacks", sitting on the island slope at depths below 600 feet. These are large chunks of the shallow reef that broke off, tumbled over the "wall," and rolled or slid down the upper slope. Some of these blocks are as big as a house. I made one dive to examine a haystack with Pat Colin, a tropical fish expert from the University of Miami. He was interested in finding tiny tropical fish that use haystacks for shelter. While we were examining a large block in about 1,000 feet of water, I noticed a cave on the downslope side. I stuck *Gamma's* nose into the cave and Pat became extremely excited (this was his first submersible dive). I realized the cave was actually a tunnel about twenty feet long and I decided to go through the tunnel instead of backing up. Maneuvering a submersible in reverse is difficult. As *Gamma* approached the exit, it came to an abrupt halt. We were stuck; the exit was not as large as the entrance. I tried to unwedge the submersible by using both forward and reverse gears, to no avail. Meanwhile, Pat was having a wonderful time discovering fish never observed before. I broke into a cold sweat. I could not radio the surface with the antennae jammed into the cave roof and the submersible wouldn't move.

I finally noticed a large air bubble in the forward ballast tank. This meant that *Gamma* was left heavy when it was prepared on the surface for this dive. Depending on the weight of the occupants, we add or remove five- and ten-pound lead weights before diving so the submersible weight is approximately the same for every dive. Not enough lead was removed for our dive so I had to inject a lot of air in both ballast tanks early in the dive to neutrally balance *Gamma*. We still were carrying this extra ballast tank air when we were trapped in the cave. I dumped all this air, which allowed seawater to completely fill both ballast tanks, resulting in a heavier submersible. I then shifted to the lowest gear and pushed the accelerator to the max. After a few seconds, *Gamma* plowed ahead and popped out of the cave while shearing off the conning tower antennas. We were very lucky. *Gamma* could still be hidden there with two skeletons; no one would have ever found us. I never again drove a submersible anywhere where I could not go straight up to the surface after that dive.

Some beautiful animals live at great depths below the living reef. One that is very interesting is the stalked crinoid, a close relative to starfish that can be up to three feet high. Stalked crinoids can move slowly along the seafloor but usually grab hold of a rocky surface and spread their arms into the water column to catch plankton that are floating by. One of the most valuable coral reef animals is the slit shell. These are very attractive primitive gastropods (snails) three to five inches wide that live on the "wall", usually hidden under ledges. They are rare and can best be collected using a submersible. Nearly everyone who dove with us anywhere in the Caribbean wanted a slit shell.

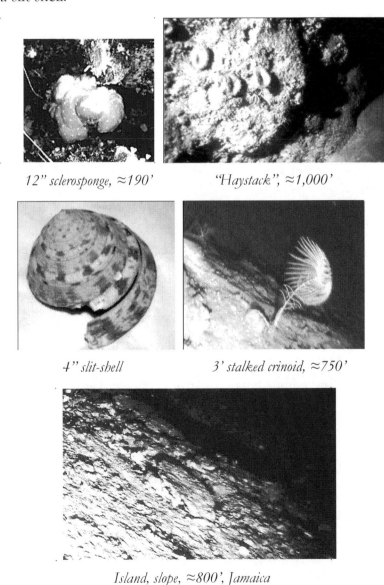

12" sclerosponge, ≈190'   *"Haystack", ≈1,000'*

4" slit-shell   *3' stalked crinoid, ≈750'*

Island, slope, ≈800', Jamaica

I wore a brief Speedo swimsuit while diving in tropical waters where high temperatures inside a submersible can be brutal. The surface ocean water temperature around Jamaica is nearly ninety degrees. It was very hot, probably near 100 degrees, and extremely humid inside *Gamma*, especially during any dives shallower than 400 feet. I lost up to seven pounds per day from sweating, but put the weight back by drinking lots of water and having a few Red Stripe beers after work.

A very attractive young female scientist from the Scripps Institute of Oceanography was visiting Discovery Bay while I was there and I offered her, as I did others, a short demo submersible dive. She wore a very brief red bikini around the lab and everyone was wondering what a dive with her would be like. By the luck of the draw it was my turn to pilot on her dive. Down the wall we went and everything was going well. She was lying on the submersible floor in her tiny red bikini and I was sitting over and straddling her in the very hot sweaty atmosphere. It was a little difficult to concentrate during the dive as she kept wiggling around and occasionally placed her posterior between my knees. We were starting back up the island slope when she spotted a slit-shell that had fallen down the "wall" and wanted to collect it. I showed her how to use the mechanical arm * but she had trouble due to the outside pressure trying to push the arm back into the submersible. Finally, I crawled down on top of her, and, using the arm, picked up her slit-shell and dropped it into the sample bag. There was a great deal of squirming and slipping around in the tight space to accomplish this mission. While on the floor of the submersible I could not reach the UQC microphone and

---

*This arm was one of Doug's innovative ideas. It consisted of two metal tubes, one inside the other, with handles at one end and claws at the other. These tubes ran through a cue ball that rotated inside a metal frame. By opening and closing the handles you could grasp objects on the seafloor Doug measured hundreds of cue balls before he found one with a perfect shape. The only problem was using this arm at depths over 200', not only did it become more difficult to push out against the sea pressure but sometimes a needle like squirt of water, from around the cue ball, would hit the observer in the face.

the support boat kept calling, wondering why we were not surfacing as we had passed our allotted dive time. Returning to the pilot's seat, I finally grabbed the microphone, and asked for permission to come up. After reaching the surface I drove the submersible over to the small support boat and opened the hatch. We climbed out sweaty and exhausted with our hair and bathing suits in some disarray. My support crew and many others still think we were doing more than retrieving a slit-shell during this dive. I hope she still has that shell.

There was an unfortunate scuba diving accident when I was in Jamaica. One of the visiting English scientists was checking his shallow reef experiment while we were making a deep submersible dive. Waiting for another diver to finish with his observations, he casually turned a few cartwheels in the water, which probably resulted in his subsequent air embolism. We surfaced immediately when told what happened and hurried in to help. There was no dive chamber in Jamaica so the injured diver was rushed to Montego Bay and put aboard a plane sent by the U.S. government. They flew him to the nearest dive chamber, which was at Guantanamo Bay, Cuba. Later he transferred to Walter Reed Hospital in Washington, D.C. but the damage had been done. He survived but is still crippled today. He undoubtedly held his breath during his underwater acrobatics. This episode reminded me how fortunate it was that I kept exhaling during my free ascent off Catalina Island just a few years before.

Sir Maurice Yonge, a famous marine biologist from England, flew over to dive with us in Jamaica. He had led the famous Great Barrier Reef Expedition in 1928 where he dove down to thirty feet with two aborigine's hand pumping air to him from a dugout canoe. This was his first dive since that time. In the evenings, we swapped Great Barrier Reef stories—he envied our deep diving. Before he left, he bought a round-trip ticket for someone to fly a slit-shell to him; if we could find one. Later, a live slit-shell flew first class to London in a plastic bag filled with seawater on the lap of a Jamaican.

I would return to Jamaica many times over the next twenty years—it was one of my favorite dive destinations. Several hurricanes have recently destroyed much of the coral reef. Like forest fires, this is nature's way of generating new growth and in the future the reef should be beautiful again.

Gamma made the *Nekton* submersible's 1,000th dive while in Jamaica. Special envelopes were mailed out to commemorate this historic event. Stamp collectors around the world sent us self-addressed stamped envelopes that we put our logo on and then filled out the details from a dive. These envelopes were supposed to make the dive with us but we rarely had time for that. Occasionally, we would drip water on them to make them look authentic. I often received complaints from certain stamp collectors if I did not send them an envelope for some special dive. Sometimes I took over 100 collector envelopes to a local post office before leaving a dive area. Some of these collectors published a monthly newsletter listing covers they had recently received, which enabled us to keep up with other submersible activities. There were only a couple of manned submersibles working in the 1970s. Several companies tried to compete with us but we had made our own special niche for marine scientists.

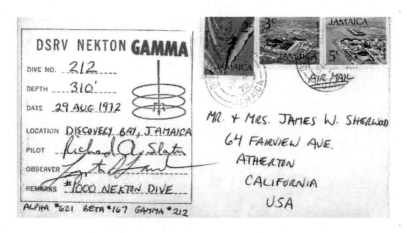

Envelope for Nekton *Dive #1,000*

ONE WEEK AFTER flying home from Jamaica, I returned to British Honduras. *Seamark,* with *Nekton Beta* on board, stopped there on the way to California from Spain so we could dive on the Barrier Reef for the second consecutive year. Bob Ginsburg headed the project again with another outstanding group of marine scientists. We accomplished eighty-four dives in fourteen days with half between 500 and 1,000 feet deep. With the help of explosives, we hauled in 1,500 pounds of reef rock, including a valuable sample later called the "Genesis Rock." This sample contained evidence, that porous reef rock could be filled with cement while underwater. A professional underwater photographer from Pennsylvania accompanied us to produce a documentary film. We dove during daylight hours while other scientists gathered geophysical data at night.

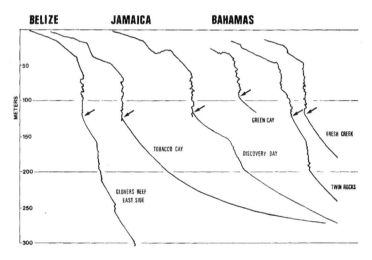

Caribbean reef profiles from Nekton *dives (Special Publication No. 3)*
(arrows point to notches cut during the last low-level sea stand)

Several scientific papers were published from the two years of Belize research, including the 190-page Special Publication 3, *The Seaward Margin of Belize Barrier and Atoll Reefs* by Noel James and Bob Ginsburg. (British Honduras was renamed Belize in 1973.)

A dive on a deep reef can be humbling, exciting and one of the most beautiful of life's experiences. Sometimes it felt like I was in a helicopter hovering along a skyscraper looking into windows. The water visibility was usually hundreds of feet and using very fast film, we were able to take natural light photos along the fore reef wall and on the deep slope. The inside submersible temperature during deep tropical water dives is very pleasant—it was always difficult to leave tropical deep-diving projects.

The Seaward Margin of Belize Barrier and Atoll Reefs

Special Publication Number 3 of the International Association of Sedimentologists by Noel P. James and Robert N. Ginsburg published by Blackwell Scientific Publications Oxford London Edinburgh Boston Melbourne

Special Publication No. 3, Miami, Florida
(Ginsburg and James, 1979)

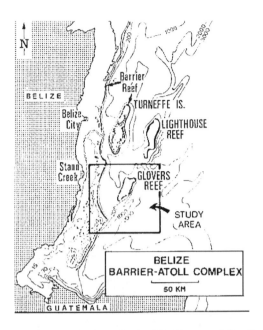

Study area, Belize (Special Publication No. 3)

Upper slope below "wall", coral debris on surface, 430'
(photos from Nekton Beta, *Special Publication No. 3)*

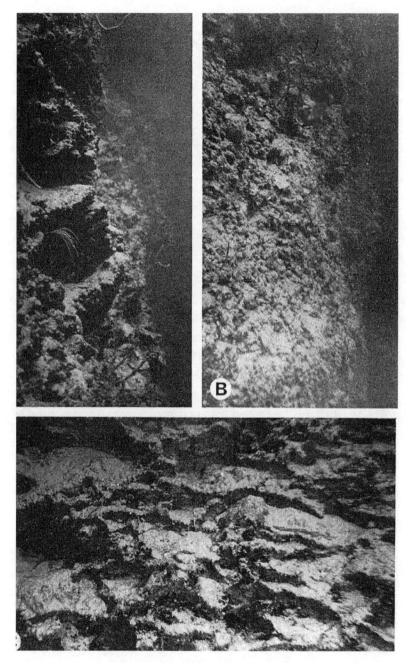

Fore reef "wall" between 300-350'
(photos from Nekton Beta, *Special Publication No. 3)*

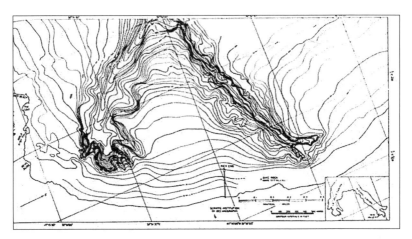

La Jolla and Scripps submarine canyons, California (Shepard, 1973)

I HAULED *GAMMA* down to the Scripps Institute of Oceanography, near San Diego, in December to discover and recover a lost $11,000 current meter. It had been placed in one of the nearby submarine canyons several months earlier. We used the fifty-five-foot *Dawn Star* for support, as we did for most diving off Southern California. Offshore of Scripps are two of the most studied submarine canyons in the world. The heads of both La Jolla and Scripps Canyons are close to shore and scientists have been scuba diving in them for years. The two canyons merge in about 900 feet of water and I became the first, and probably the only, person to pilot a submersible down one canyon and return up the other. It was like diving in a miniature Grand Canyon with near vertical walls sometimes only inches away.

We found the missing current meter on the Scripps Canyon floor in 300 feet of water. It was completely entangled in a mass of kelp, which gave it the appearance of a fifteen-foot-tall green ghost. The heavy kelp blanket kept it from rising when release signals were beeped down from the surface. The meter, with its ghostly covering, had been slowly moving down the canyon into deeper water. We removed some of the kelp and released the meter. It slowly rose to the surface where *Dawn Star's* crew retrieved it.

Nekton Gamma *on support vessel* R/V Dawn Star

A Scripps student once dumped an old car body containing a radio transmitter into the Scripps Submarine Canyon during the late 1950s. Every few days he checked for the car location until one day he discovered the car had disappeared. I kept looking for this car during my dives but it had obviously been flushed out of the canyon into deep water during one of the periodic cleaning out episodes known to occur in submarine canyons. Luckily, we recovered the current meter before it ended up in deep water. Scripps oceanographers, including the dean of marine geologists, Dr. Francis Shepard, dove with us for their first look at the canyons they had been studying for many years. Unfortunately, Dr. Shepard fell through an open hatch on the *Dawn Star* and was unable to continue diving.

It was great to be diving close to home. In just three years, we had made 1,100 dives in *Nekton* submersibles and had been underwater, off four continents, for over 1,200 hours.

AT THE START OF 1973 Doug and I made a twenty-foot dive in the Long Beach Harbor with *Gamma's* stern tied to a piling. We ran the submersible, in place, for three hours to test the batteries in order to obtain the needed certification from ABS (American Bureau of Ships). This was important. The U.S. Government and many oil companies were now requiring certification before they would hire any submersible. I drew up detailed blueprints for the *Nektons* as Doug only had rough sketches from their construction. We then traveled to New York to appear before the ABS Board to present our case and to answer any questions. With their certification, we could now dive on future projects funded by the MUST (Manned Undersea Science and Technology) division of NOAA and NSF. We still needed an annual inspection by ABS and a dive down to 1,000 feet every three years with an ABS inspector.

One time, several years later, the ABS inspector did not want to dive, so Doug made the certification dive with a boat crew member. This upset Doug so he only went to 200 feet while he continued to call up the depths as 300, 400, 500, 600, 700, 800, 900, and finally 1,000 feet. I was the onsite navigator and could see he was suspended at 200 feet but the inspector never figured it out. We had made many dives to 1,000 feet and knew the submersible was safe at that depth. All of the *Nekton* submersibles had been tested to 1,500 feet in the U.S. Navy Port Hueneme, California, pressure chamber.

Doug and I went up to the top of a Trade Center building during our New York trip and he mentioned we were 1,000 feet off the ground, the same distance as the depth the *Nekton* submersibles could officially dive to. Looking at a yellow taxi from 1,000 feet, I realized how small we would have looked from the ocean surface when diving to those depths.

Chapter Eight

East Coast & Colorado

What is a scientist after all? It is a curious man looking through a keyhole, the keyhole of nature, trying to know what's going on.

—Jacques Cousteau, *Christian Science Monitor* (1971)

I HAD BEEN DISCUSSING a *Nekton* based research project for several years with Dick Cooper, manager of the National Marine Fisheries (NMF) laboratory in Booth Bay Harbor, Maine. Dick finally received funding and we entered into a contract to help his group study lobsters living near the New England continental shelf break. Lobsters have been caught in shallow-water for centuries but deep-water lobster fishing was new. Our first objective was to research the effectiveness of present-day trapping techniques in the deep environment around the heads of fourteen submarine canyons located along the southern edge of Georges Bank.

My assistant and I drove a rental truck across country, in June 1973, to Newport News, Virginia, where we mobilized *Nekton Gamma* aboard the 154-foot oil field supply ship *M/V Pierce*. Working off this large vessel in bad weather with a crew that had never supported a diving operation was not easy. However, our dives were successful and led to many years of diving with Dick's group. I ultimately made more dives off New England than anywhere else. Our many dives produced a better understanding of lobsters and also helped set limits and future fishing seasons.

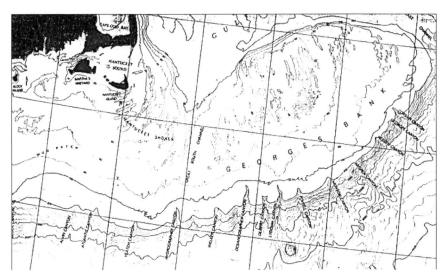

Georges Bank submarine canyons off Cape Cod (Backus, 1987)

A Rhode Island based deep-water lobster fisherman made a dive in *Nekton Beta,* with me, near a Georges Bank Canyon in 1973 to witness his traps in action. He became very excited when he observed a large lobster walking across the seafloor and then entering one of his traps; but quickly became upset after the lobster tore off a chunk of bait, backed out of the trap, and continued walking across the seafloor dragging the bait. He decided to redesign his traps. We captured several lobsters, with *Beta's* mechanical arm, for the scientists to tag and release. I grabbed a very large lobster and was looking forward to eating it for dinner. After trying to smash the large claw with a hammer, I finally pulled the meat out with a wire hanger and saved the claw. The lobster was delicious and the claw still sits on a shelf in my office.

Dick Cooper and I made our first dive into the Veatch Submarine Canyon, south of Nantucket Island. Over the next decade, we gathered more scientific data from this small Georges Bank submarine canyon than from anywhere else. We were amazed to find the canyon walls teaming with fish, crab, and lobster living under ledges and in caves of all sizes.

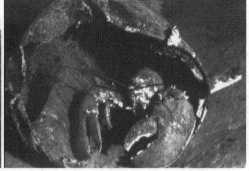

My big lobster   *A really big lobster in an oil drum*

Beta *and scientific crews on the* M/V Pierce *off Georges Bank*

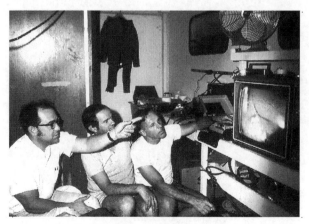

With Dick Cooper and Joe Uzman reviewing dive tapes on support vessel

Gamma *transit stick and chain*   *Brittle stars off New England≈800'*

One objective of Dick's fishery research was to compare three sampling techniques to determine lobster and crab abundance and distribution on the New England continental shelf. In addition to sub transects, a camera sled was dragged behind the *Pierce* and a fishing trawl was towed behind a chartered fishing boat—all over the same areas. We mounted a stick on the submersible bow plane, which stuck out about six feet with a chain hanging down to the seafloor, to mimic the width of the sled and trawl. We counted every crab and lobster that came between *Beta* and the chain during every sub transect. The overall advantage of a submersible was in the direct visual assessments not equaled by the other methods. It was also better in rugged environments such as submarine canyons. Starting with Dick's project, *Nekton* submersibles were kept busy on East Coast lobster, crab and fish research for many years. These projects led to many other contracts including environmental and geological studies.

I observed lots of new things off New England, including many fish and seafloor animals I had never seen before. Hake and codfish occasionally swam by, and, on deeper dives I saw thousands of brittle stars—probably the most common large invertebrate living on the seafloor. I enjoyed watching them scoot around using different pairs of arms to pull their bodies in various directions without climbing over each other. At times, the entire seafloor seemed to be moving while we sat still in the submersible.

Dick Cooper and his team of scuba diving biologists were great to work with. One day, while diving for lobster, they took a break for lunch. A biologist offered Dick part of his chocolate bar that Dick quickly consumed. About an hour later, while preparing to dive, Dick suddenly ran around the deck tearing off his dive gear. The other divers were rolling on the deck in laughter; the chocolate bar was an Ex-Lax. Lucky for him, and for me, we were not diving in the submersible that day. Dick held the distinction of being the only person to vomit in a *Nekton* submersible. At the end of a dive off New Jersey, as *Gamma* was coming alongside the support vessel, a line became tangled in the submersible propeller and we had to drag *Gamma* backwards for a short time until we could free it. Being inside a submersible on the ocean surface is not very enjoyable; waves make it roll and bounce. After ten minutes or so Dick finally lost it. The pilot handed him a plastic bag but, sadly, it was full of holes and he spewed all over inside *Gamma* —he cleaned it up later. Thankfully, I was not the pilot on that dive.

There can be hurricanes topside but it will always be calm thirty feet underwater. No one ever felt seasick in a *Nekton* submersible while underwater. The less time I spent bouncing on the ocean surface, the better I liked it. I always tried to dive a submersible as fast as possible after launch and to surface close to the support ship for a quick retrieval. Captain Tom Crawford was the best at retrieving us quickly. He would spin the support ship around a surfaced submersible, laying the water down flat between the submersible and the ship. This slick would last for nearly a minute, no matter how rough the surrounding sea. I would quickly motor across this smooth patch while aiming at the tire-mat hanging from the support vessel railing. Two crew members would then reach over the railing and snap the bridle to the submersible as I rammed into the tire-mat at full speed. The crane would lift us out of the water quickly and hold the submersible tight against the tire mat so we could disembark safely.

While working our way south I made a dive in a submarine canyon located under the Navy shipping channel off Norfolk, Virginia. We were careful diving here because of the numerous surface ships. A submersible is a small target bouncing on the ocean surface; a large ship could easily and unknowingly run over us. On one dive, near the canyon head, I kept hearing weird sonar signals when suddenly it sounded like we were being hit with a chain. I quickly maneuvered *Gamma* behind a large rock. The sonar signal frequency and direction kept changing—someone was searching for us. I called the *Pierce*, our support ship, on the UQC and asked if there was a Navy vessel nearby. "Yes," came the answer, "a destroyer." I played games with them for a while by running along the seafloor a short distance and then hiding again. Frustrated, they finally radioed our support ship, and when told that the *Pierce* was tracking a small manned submersible they turned and left.

MY CONSTANT TRAVELING and being away from home was difficult for my family, and for me. So, during the spring of 1973, I started searching for a teaching position, hopefully a professorship at a small university where I could continue my research. I answered an ad in a geological magazine for an opening in Colorado. In June, while trucking *Gamma* to the east coast again, I stopped at UNC (University of Northern Colorado) in Greeley. The interview went well and I liked the school. They offered me the position of Assistant Professor of Oceanography and I accepted. I then tendered my resignation to General Oceanographics. Late in August, I set off for a new chapter in my life. I thought I left submersible diving behind, but the future was to prove me wrong. I had completed 344 submersible dives in three years and needed a break. A Ph.D. is a teaching/research degree and I was excited to see how I would do, even though I was taking a big pay cut.

Soon after I resigned, General Oceanographics underwent a major overhaul, Jim Vernon and Doug Privitt both left. The owners asked me to return to be company president. They offered me a great salary and said I could move the office to Santa Barbara. It was a tough decision, but I had not given my academic career much of a chance so I turned it down. I did manage General Oceanographics office during the summer of 1974 and volunteered to pilot *Nektons* in the future on a job-by-job basis.

Slater family 1975 Christmas card from Colorado (notice my swim fins)

I discovered how much I enjoyed teaching both beginning and advanced geology, and oceanography courses, even though some of the beginning classes were so big I had to lecture in a large auditorium. It did not take long to settle in and to start planning my own research projects. One advantage of not working for a company is being able to participate on many different scientific projects and I wanted to take full advantage of any opportunities. Being an oceanography professor in the Rocky Mountains and working on deep-sea diving projects during school breaks generated a lot of local publicity. The move to Colorado did not help my marriage though, my wife and I separated after a few years in Colorado. Our marriage ended amicably in 1976.

I CONTINUED DIVING *Gamma* for lobster research off New England during summer school breaks. In 1974, a 110-foot catamaran, the *Atlantic Twin* from New Jersey, was used to support *Gamma*. It had a great crew and was very stable, making launching and recovery much safer and easier than from our previously larger support vessels. Most dives were in submarine canyon heads just south of Georges Bank studying cusk, goosefish (now called monkfish in restaurants), and wolf fish—although the emphasis was still on lobster. We became intrigued with bioerosion (erosion by animals) that was very common on the canyon walls. It was not a familiar geological process in submarine canyons until our discovery, we named them "Pueblo Villages." I first noticed bioerosion during dives in Scripps and La Jolla Canyons but nothing on the scale we found in Veatch Canyon. I co-authored several papers and two book chapters on bioerosion in submarine canyons.

M/V Atlantic Twin

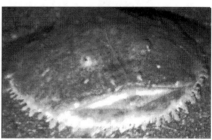
Goosefish (monkfish) ≈250'

Cusk in bioeroded cave ≈300'

Wolf fish ≈150'

(fish photos from Cooper's research around Veatch Canyon)

Sketch of "Pueblo Village" (Warme, Slater and Cooper, 1978)

In 1974, while diving in the large Oceanographer Canyon, south of Georges Bank, we positioned a well-known Harvard professor's experimental two-meter package, composed of various compressed waste remains, under a ledge. She wanted to learn how organisms interacted with waste products on the seafloor over time. We planned to return in 1975 to recover it. The idea was to hide the block so fishermen would not scoop it up while trawling. This study was very important as there was concern in New York City, and other places, on where to dump treated sewerage and garbage in the future. We sailed back to New Jersey and, as we pulled into *Atlantic Twin's* slip, I noticed our waste material package sitting on a nearby fishing boat. The fisherman, a friend of our Captain, knew we were studying lobster so he had been following us for the past few weeks. He moved in when we were finished diving and trawled our study areas, including where we had hidden the waste block. So much for that expensive study. I was not through with the New York garbage dump problem. It would appear again in a few years.

During the summer of 1974, *Gamma* dove in six different Georges Bank submarine canyons and made two dives flying across shallow Georges Bank while being pushed by very fast tidal currents. There were two unique incidents during dives in Oceanographer Canyon. First, a large shark attacked us. It was hard to tell how big it was, all I saw was a lot of white skin pressed against several ports. You could hear our shouts on the video, "What in the hell was that?" Then, "Whatever it was, it was huge." I think *Gamma's* lights attracted him. That's what happened to the *Alvin* submersible when a swordfish attacked one of their lights, got his bill jammed, and was still stuck to the submersible when they surfaced.

The other incident was more important for science. It was the first time a turbidity current* was witnessed *in situ*. We were moving up the Oceanographer Canyon floor in about 700 feet of water, thirty to forty-foot visibility with lights, when I noticed the surrounding water temperature started to rise rapidly. This was puzzling. Suddenly, a turbid cloud of sediment arrived, visibility dropped to one foot, and we were pushed sideways down the canyon while being pelted with gravel and shells. I added air to the ballast tanks and *Gamma* slowly rose to the 650-foot level where we suddenly popped out of the muddy roiling current. I could see the turbid water below me. It was a strange and exciting experience for about five minutes. Several scientists later asked me why we did not go back into the cloud to take pictures, measurements of water temperature and current speed. "It did not seem like a good idea at the time," was my usual answer. We had been caught in a turbidity current, known in the geological past for moving organisms and sediment from shallow to deep water. This one probably started with a tidal current direction change, causing the heavier, more saline and warmer water on top of Georges Bank to be funneled down the canyon. I discovered that the highest and lowest Georges Bank tides of the year occurred on the day we dove. My observer and I were the first to be caught in a turbidity current and we had no pictorial evidence; the cameras were turned off as we were preparing to surface. This phenomenon caught me again years later in the Bahamas

---

*A turbidity current is a fast moving current full of suspended sediments. It flows along the seafloor under the influence of gravity.

"Tongue of the Ocean" and on the Great Barrier Reef near New Guinea. Turbidity currents undoubtedly had moved the missing car down Scripps Canyon into deep water.

It was not easy to track a *Nekton* submersible in any kind of rugged terrain or during rough sea conditions. The navigator, on the support vessel, had to lower a hand-held hydrophone into the water, while leaning over the support ship railing, to receive signals from a pinger strapped to the submersible. This system was not very accurate and did not work well under any adverse conditions. It gave the navigator the rough direction but not distance the submersible was from the support vessel. Occasionally, the navigator would count to ten into his UQC microphone and the pilot would continue counting from ten in the submersible. By knowing the time delay it took for the pilot's voice to return to the surface, and knowing the speed of sound in seawater, the navigator could fairly accurately judge the distance from the support ship to the submersible. It was primitive navigation but it usually worked. The navigator still lost us occasionally so we would surface and be directed back to the support ship by CB radio. Radio transmissions only work in the air; radio waves do not travel underwater. On the surface I could see the support ship more easily than they could see me. Occasionally, when we were back on the surface and it was foggy, I had to open the conning tower hatch and listen for the ship's whistle to help me locate the direction to the support ship.

Sometimes we towed a surface buoy, usually a red tetherball, during a dive. The constant tugging of the ball made piloting the submersible difficult but at least the support ship knew where we were and I could release the buoy line if it became entangled. While working off New England, our buoy line occasionally tangled with deep lobster trap lines. Once, the buoy line caught on a lobster line and the red buoy broke free. It floated away with our support ship dutifully following it. We slowly lost voice contact through the UQC as the distance grew until suddenly we found ourselves with no support ship.

They were at least five miles away following the buoy thinking it was still attached to us. We always surfaced after ten minutes if we could not make voice contact with the support ship, so I slowly brought *Gamma* up to the surface and discovered a thick fog had moved in with visibility not more than twenty feet. I could converse with the ship on the CB radio but they could not see us on their radar, we were too low in the water. They recovered our red buoy and started searching. One good thing about thick fog is the ocean surface is usually very calm. Finally, after about one hour, I opened the hatch, stood on the pilot's seat and held a scuba bottle up high. The Captain saw this target on the ship's radar and came over to pick us up.

Scuba diving biologists often accompanied us on our dashes across shallow Georges Bank. They were also tethered, from the seat of their pants, to surface buoys—we did not want to lose a diver. Without GPS, we had to rely on Loran stations, sending out signals from shore, to locate ourselves on the ocean surface. Working with Loran was not easy so we had to hire a consultant to navigate for us. Twelve years later, we added a more sophisticated computerized system for tracking submersibles. By the end of my diving career, we had our own computerized navigation system with GPS and a computer to achieve pinpoint location accuracy and complete data storage. We no longer needed a consulting navigator or a red buoy.

When we arrived at a dive site, a crane would lift the sub off the support ship deck and swing it over the ship's railing, so we could secure it against the tire mat. This was a difficult and dangerous maneuver, especially on a rolling deck, for the four people holding lines attached to the submersible. Trying to keep your footing on a rocking, wet deck while holding a three-ton submersible steady when it is swinging from a crane is not easy. No one would be inside the submersible during this maneuver. Once the submersible was secured against the tire mat, the observer and then the pilot climbed in. After the pilot completed his checklist, he would give the okay and lock the hatch. The navigator on the bridge would work with the

Captain to make sure we would launch in the proper place and would then give the word to go. Using the crane wire, the submersible would be lowered a few feet into the water and quickly released from its bridle. We reversed this procedure while retrieving the submersible. Two crewmembers would reach over the railing, or lie on the deck, to hook the bridle snap hooks to the submersible after it came alongside the tire mat and then the crane would then lift it out of the water. We determined this method of launching and retrieving superior to working off a support ship stern because we could dive in rougher weather, and we felt that it was safer. When launching or retrieving a submersible over the stern, as with most other submersibles, occupants have to climb into a submersible while it is sitting on the support ship deck and are in the sub during the entire launch and retrieval procedure. This is more dangerous for the occupants, as well as for the divers that are needed in the water to release and then, later, to reattach the submersible bridle before the sub can be brought back aboard its support vessel. This technique is very limited by weather conditions as most submersibles are not secure until sitting on the support ship deck.

Gamma *being held by crane against tire-mat*

Pilot in Gamma *on* Atlantic Twin *(notice red buoy line hanging down)*

Towing Gamma *to Atlantic City*   *Close up of accident*

The only time our launch system failed, in over thirty years of diving, was in 1975, while diving from the *Atlantic Twin* off New Jersey. I was leaning over the ship's railing directly above the submersible, holding the two release lines, as *Gamma* was being lowered into the water by the crane. I would pull these lines free to release *Gamma* after it landed in the water. As the crane behind me started to lower the submersible, the ship took a slight roll and I heard a scream from a nearby fainting female biologist who saw the crane falling. I turned to see what happened. As I turned, the crane, which had broken loose from the deck, slid by my shoulder leaving a grease stain on my T-shirt sleeve. If the biologist had not screamed, and if I had not turned, the crane would have landed on top of me instead of smashing into the railing. The men in *Gamma* were lucky the crane did not flip over the railing and drag them down to the seafloor—they did complain about the rough launch. The welding that attached the crane to the deck had rusted under the deck paint. This was not noticed when we tested the crane at the dock or during the ship's inspection before we sailed.

We tied a tow line to *Gamma*, after the two men climbed out and up the tire-mat, and then towed the submersible back about fifty miles to Atlantic City. All *Nekton* submersibles were designed to be easily towed at ten knots. Most other sub can only be towed slowly if at all. Before entering the harbor, just at dusk, I pulled *Gamma* up close, leaped onto its deck, opened the hatch, jumped in, closed the hatch, and drove it, with all lights on, straight through the entrance and across the harbor to our berth. People lined up to watch a submersible cruising across, and lighting up, the harbor after arriving from the ocean. This accident caused a tightening of government rules, and in the future any crane used to launch or retrieve a manned submersible had to be ABS (American Bureau of Ships) certified and any welds attaching the crane to a deck had to be x-rayed. Hopefully, our accident helped prevent any future incidents.

THIRTEEN OF MY UNC students accompanied me to Southern California during the 1975 spring break to dive in *Gamma* off Santa Barbara Island. General Oceanographics kindly donated the *Dawn Star* for support but it was left to me to pilot and navigate the boat, as well as the submersible. I grabbed a former *Seamark* crewmember to assist me. We camped on the island, as the ship was too small for everyone to have a berth. It was the first, and maybe the only time a group of students were able to use a sub for an undergraduate scientific project. I had a little trouble getting the students on and off the Island for three of the five days because of rough sea conditions and thick fog. However, they mapped the island during bad weather days and everyone had a great time. Diving highlights included the discovery of a small octopus living in a Coors beer can and salvaging an old anchor that now resides in my garden. Each student made a dive down to 1,000 feet. Another professor, from my department, came along to assist me as he wanted to dive to 1,000 feet. He was a mountain climber and wanted a personal depth record also. He waited until the last dive with the weather worsening. We had to rush the dive and, incorrectly, did not put enough weight in so the sub slowly came to a stop at about 700'. He did not get to set his hoped for 1,000' record.

GENERAL OCEANOGRAPHICS hired me in August 1975 for a project with the USGS (United States Geological Survey) office in Woods Hole. The project leader was David Folger, then a professor at Middlebury College in Vermont. His group was studying the continental shelf submarine canyon, off nearby Delaware and Maryland, located near potential oil lease areas. This work led to several other projects and a 1976 USGS summer job for me. Dave and I were related. My seven times great-grandfather, Tristram Coffin hired Dave's seven times great-grandfather, Peter Folger, to be his interpreter of Indian languages when they first visited Nantucket Island in 1654. Dave told me that Tristram later threw Peter into jail for some minor offense. The families eventually intermarried so Dave and I are distant cousins.

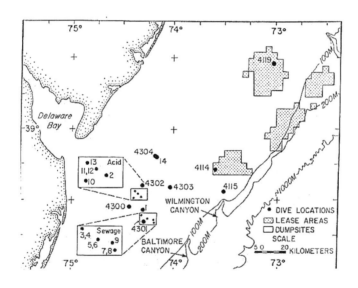

Dumpsite dive locations, Delaware (Folger, et. al., 1978)

In 1974 and 1975, *Beta* was used on two continental shelf waste disposal sites, Philadelphia sewage and DuPont acid, off New Jersey and Delaware for the USGS at Woods Hole. In 1974, I dove the day after they dumped two million gallons of treated sewage and could find no evidence of any sewage in the water column or on the seafloor. I was in *Beta,* just above the seafloor in 1975 when they dumped one million gallons of acid waste on me. I was concerned with any affects from the acid on *Beta's* ports—there was no damage. The acid dump reduced visibility close to zero for a few minutes, as suspended matter flocked together forming clots that sank toward the seafloor as currents swept them away. The results from our dives provided evidence that dumped sewage sludge was being oxidized, eaten, and/or transported away from the dumpsite. The acid waste just disappeared while being swept away by ocean currents.

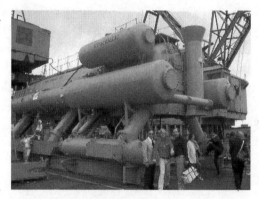

Helgoland *habitat, Boston*

IN SEPTEMBER, 1975, MUST (NOAA) supported a dive program, with the German government, in which aquanauts (underwater astronauts) would live under the Gulf of Maine. *Helgoland,* a German undersea habitat, was shipped across the Atlantic to Boston. The U.S. Navy had sponsored several manned habitats in the past, specifically *Sealab,* a controversial program that ended with mixed results. Scientists hoped the *Helgoland* project would regenerate interest in man living under the sea. We scouted the seafloor off Rockport, Massachusetts, for a suitable spot for this huge structure. A flat, gravelly area in 110 feet of water was finally chosen.

A storm swept through during one of the first missions, the tethered surface support buoy, which provided power to the habitat, broke off leaving the aquanauts in the dark. They had the sensation the habitat was rolling around on the seafloor and at one point thought they were sliding into deeper water. Later we could see that the large surface waves had caused the habitat to roll back and forth a little on the gravel seafloor.

An all-German crew was in the habitat a few weeks later when a hurricane headed their way. For safety reasons, it was decided to bring the men to the surface. They went through decompression in the habitat and prepared to evacuate by swimming to the surface using scuba gear while following the tethered buoy line. One of the men, a diver with seventeen years' experience, stopped for a moment during his ascent when his camera swung up and dislodged his mask. He held onto the taut line while he adjusted his mask and suffered an air embolism.* He died almost immediately, even though he was quickly brought to shore and placed into a decompression chamber. The Board of Inquiry later stated:

> The high seas passing (over them) could have caused a momentary change of pressure to cause air embolism if a diver was holding fast to the mooring line of the buoy and had just taken a full breath of compressed air.

The seas were running ten to twelve feet and you can suffer an air embolism in a difference of only four feet of water if you hold your breath. This would have happened to me if I had held my breath during my free ascent off Catalina. We continued diving although the diver's death put a gloom over the project.

We spent several more weeks in the Gulf of Maine before I headed back to Colorado for fall semester. We searched a few days for a missing fishing boat and crew but could not find it.

---

*An air embolism is one of the dangers in scuba diving. Gas bubbles appear in the bloodstream during a rapid ascent if a diver holds his breath, which causes his lungs to expand past their capacity. Air bubbles are then forced through his lung walls and into his bloodstream. It is best treated by recompression in a chamber. An embolism is the leading cause of death among divers using scuba.

The exact location was unknown and the water visibility was very poor making our search futile.

After these dives, we sailed out into the middle of the Gulf of Maine to retrieve current meters and other scientific arrays deposited the year before by scientists using a Harbor Branch Oceanographic Institute *Johnston Sea-Link* submersible from Florida. Harbor Branch scientists were with us and it created a sticky situation, as everyone was comparing *Nekton Beta* to the *Johnson Sea-Link*. We completed several dives to 1,000 feet and recovered all their equipment, much to my relief and to the scientist's joy.

I RETURNED TO COLORADO in mid-September and did not get back into the water until the next spring when I piloted *Beta* for one week in the Bahamas, for Bob Ginsburg. It was on this deep-reef project that I dove with an old friend, Gene Shinn, who was now managing the USGS office in Miami. Gene was an experienced diver who had put himself through the University of Miami by selling fish he had speared to local Miami restaurants. Gene, in the early 1950s, won the national spearfishing championship when spearfishing was considered a sport. We would dive together on many projects over the next thirty years. I made thirty-three dives in one week and was delighted to return to the now familiar deep coral reef environment.

I worked as a consultant for General Oceanographics (now called Nekton, Inc.) at the end of the 1976 spring semester, when I spent a month off the east coast piloting *Gamma* on continuing projects for Dick Cooper and Dave Folger. The support vessel *Advance II* was leased by Nekton, Inc. in 1976. It was a large ship that proved to be adequate but much more awkward to work off than the *Atlantic Twin*. My only problem concerned the captain from North Carolina who insisted on boiled okra with every meal.

We dove off the New York Harbor during the bi-centennial celebration on the Fourth of July, and it was quite a sight, with hundreds of sail boats around us and firework displays at night. I was there to train new pilots and these would be my last dives in a *Nekton* submersible.

Over the next few years, many of the marine scientists I had worked with went on to other projects or used different manned submersibles. Diving was not a priority for Nekton, Inc.—*Nekton's Beta* and *Gamma* were left in disrepair outside in a San Diego storage yard. They rusted and *Beta* disappeared. *Alpha* was sold to an individual for diving in his private lake and *Gamma* ended up in Florida. I was sure my submersible career was over, but later events proved me wrong once again.

> [Note: A refurbished Alpha is again active, with dives off the east coast in 2014. I was told that Beta is in Southern California and might end up in a Canadian museum. All three Nekton's are still in existence and able to dive even though they are nearly 50 years old].

I TAUGHT A CLASS on coral reefs every fall at UNC. The students that passed had the opportunity to travel with me to the Discovery Bay Marine Laboratory in Jamaica. For the first field trip, during Christmas break in 1975, I took ten seniors and graduate students, all certified divers. Each following year, my coral reef class and the associated spring break field trip became more popular. We usually stayed in the lab dormitories but eventually, I rented a house. Our cook's name was Mrs. Byles, a strange name for a cook. She made a wonderful goat curry, which I requested each year. One night, I was carefully driving her home when I noticed she was horrified with my driving. I finally asked her what the problem was. She said that everyone cuts corners on this road and I should continually honk the horn. She envisioned us hitting a sugarcane truck head-on. There was marijuana and other drugs available in Jamaica in the 1970's and I had to be careful that none of my students were caught buying drugs as it could have meant jail time. Luckily, no student ever got in trouble.

Coral Reef class going diving   *Teaching*

UNC class on the "wall", 100', Discovery Bay

Jamaica Coral Reef class from UNC

The highlight each year was the final deep dive, down to 100 feet, where the students could hang on the near vertical wall below the living reef. Most students followed my instructions but I had my hands full with a few students who wanted to go deeper. This was dangerous because they could be susceptible to nitrogen narcosis at those depths or as divers say, "getting narked". There is a theory formulated by divers called the "martini effect" that best describes nitrogen narcosis. Diving to thirty-three feet is the equivalent to drinking one martini. Each additional thirty-three feet of depth is equivalent to drinking another martini. At around 100 feet, the depth at which nitrogen narcosis becomes noticeable for most divers, the feeling is the equivalent of drinking three martinis. Almost everyone feels woozy if they go deeper. One year, I chased a student down to 150 feet and hauled him back—he was lucky to have passed the course. These trips were worthwhile; many of my students later became teachers or scientists, and almost all claimed the Jamaica trip was one of the highlights of their academic career. I asked a biology professor to accompany me on one trip to Jamaica. He was having personal problems so I thought the trip would be good for him. Unfortunately, he decided to swim out to sea one night after an evening of drinking. We formed a search party and eventually found him, much to my relief. That was the last time I took a professor with me.

On each field trip, I charged students just enough to cover all expenses, including mine. One of my students was killed in an auto accident over the 1976 Christmas holidays so I needed a substitute for the 1977 Jamaica spring trip. It was difficult finding someone qualified because all participants had to have taken my coral reef course and be certified divers. One biology student, Heidi, had approached me the previous fall and asked if her recently divorced mother, whom she was concerned about, could go on the trip and I answered, "No, I do not take parents on my field trips." So in early January, when I ran into Heidi, I asked if she still wanted her mother to go. Her mother begrudgingly agreed because, as I found out later, Heidi had told her the trip would be cancelled if I could not find a girls' chaperon. This was not true but I did need one more person to help pay for the trip, even if it was a student's mother.

During spring break, my geology students and I left first for a field trip to explore mangrove swamps in the Florida Keys. We planned to meet the biology students a few days later at the Miami airport and then fly to Jamaica together. I was stunned when I walked into the airport and first saw Heidi's mother, Lois. She looked like a fashion model, which she had been for many years. I do not think her first impression of the hippy professor was very good. I had been camping out in a mangrove swamp for three days and had some of yesterday's spaghetti dinner on the front of my T-shirt. I saw very little of Lois that week in Jamaica as I was busy with my class and she was enjoying swimming and sunbathing away from the crowd. I asked a graduate student to show her how to snorkel and to take her out to the reef. However on the last night; before leaving for home, I asked her out to dinner and we had a wonderful evening. Lois and I started dating after we returned to Colorado.

With Lois

IN 1978, DICK COOPER invited me to help determine the feasibility of using a different submersible for his research. A dive company from New York had chartered the submersible *Diaphus** and was very anxious to obtain Cooper's and Folger's projects. It was a ten-foot high, twenty-foot long Perry sub that could dive to 1,200 feet. This submersible carried three observers and a pilot. Unfortunately, the support ship was not ready for sea when the demonstration day arrived so we sailed while they were still mobilizing. They continued to mobilize during the cruise and were still hammering and sawing when we returned to port. I was well aware that this submersible had problems in the past.

Diaphus *going to sea and launched over the stern off George's Bank*

When we finally made a dive, a steady leak was coming in around the large, front, dome-shaped port when *Diaphus* was in shallow water. Upon nearing the surface after a dive, the water would pour in around the port edges because the rubber shims that fit between the large Plexiglas port gasket and the

---

*Diaphus was built by John Perry's company in Florida and was originally called PC-1401 before being bought by Texas A&M University. On one dive, off Southern California, its batteries fell out of their pod, which is located under the submersible. This caused the sub to head for the surface rapidly, upside down in the dark, until finally leaping out of the water.

submersible hull kept floating away. The gasket needed to be compressed so we could wedge in larger shims. We decided to hang *Diaphus* by a line from the ship in about 100 feet of water and a scuba diver came down with a sledgehammer to pound the shims into place. While the diver whacked away on the shims, I was in the submersible holding a block of wood against the edge of the port wondering what would happen if he missed and hit the large Plexiglas port. These large, dome-like front viewing ports, found on many submersibles, seemed a good idea, but observations through them were distorted. A beer can lying on the seafloor kept changing size when we passed by. It was like being in a funhouse with a crazy mirror. Cooper's group was not impressed with the operation and they did not use *Diaphus* again. I dove in *Diaphus* later that summer around several Georges Bank canyons for my USGS research project.

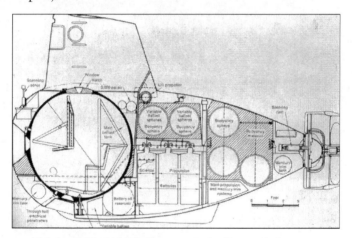

Alvin *(Woods Hole Oceanographic Institute diagram)*

I HAD AN OPPORTUNITY to dive in the deep diving sub *Alvin* in 1980. I was an observer on four dives, including one to 5,500 feet to map the distal end of Hydrographer Canyon, just south of Georges Bank. *Alvin* is America's most famous manned submersible. It was used on the *Titanic* discovery dive by Bob Ballard. A dive in *Alvin* takes time, it usually makes only one dive a day and the crew normally took another day to prepare the submersible between dives. The six-foot titanium sphere held three participants; one pilot and two observers. The observers sat on either side of the pilot and were stuck in one position for the entire dive. It was difficult to sit up straight or stretch your legs so everyone became somewhat cramped by the end of a dive. We listened to old Lone Ranger and Green Hornet radio show tapes during deep dives, as it took several hours to descend to the seafloor and several hours to return to the surface. However, *Alvin* dove deep and the new *Alvin*, rebuilt in 2008-09, is more comfortable. When I dove in *Alvin,* there was very little space and I was crouched over in the front of the sphere for each six to eight hour dive into Hydrographer Canyon.

Diving scientists with Alvin *(I am on the left)*

I WAS APPOINTED Chairman of the UNC Earth Sciences Department in 1975, a position I held until I left the UNC in 1980. After this appointment, I spent less time teaching and working on research projects, and more time playing the part of a politician. Budgets were tight and I was always fighting for a bigger slice of the pie.

Chapter Nine

Aquanaut & Bahamas

Nothing that the ingenuity of man has permitted him to do is
more unnatural than working as a diver in deep water.

—Commander Edward Ellsberg, *Men Under the Sea* (1939)

IN 1975, I WAS CHOSEN by NOAA to be a U.S. aquanaut
and to participate in the International Expedition SCORE
(Scientific Cooperative Operational Research Experiment). I
would be spending a week living inside an underwater habitat,
in sixty-five feet of water, on the edge of the reef drop-off
near Freeport, Grand Bahama Island. Most of the time, I
would be studying the surrounding reef using scuba gear. A
lockout submersible*, Harbor Branch's *Johnson Sea-Link,* would
be available to help me collect sclerosponges from the deep
reef wall. This project included a study of bone deterioration
while weightless underwater. There was concern for future
astronauts, weightless in space, having similar bone problems.
I flew to Miami for training and a physical that included x-rays
of the long bones in my legs and arms. There were three male,
and one female, teams on for this project. I was part of the last
one with two other scientists and a technician.

---

*A lockout submersible has a separate pressure sphere that holds a diver and a
technician. When ready to dive the sphere is pressurized to equal the outside
water pressure. This enables the occupants to open the bottom hatch where the
diver exits while his technician handles the hose that connects the diver to his air
supply on the submersible. After the dive they close the hatch and both undergo
decompression in the sphere.

Training for lock-out dive, Miami

Artist's conception of SCORE project (NOAA drawing)

I was going to live in *Hydro-Lab*, a small habitat built by John Perry's company in Florida. It was a steel tube, eight feet in diameter and sixteen feet long, sitting on legs, with a four-foot acrylic dome window at one end. The pressure in the habitat equaled the outside water pressure so when the bottom hatch was left open, water could not enter. I would be able to easily step off into the water through this "moon pool" hatch, grab a scuba tank and then spend an unlimited amount of time diving every day without worrying about any decompression time. I would reenter the habitat by the same hatch when my work was completed. Each breath at sixty feet would contain nearly three times the amount of air squeezed into my lungs than on the surface. My blood would quickly become saturated with these pressurized gases (from breathing under pressure) so I would not be able to return to the surface without suffering "the bends" or undergoing long decompression.* I could, however, spend all day scuba diving in sixty to one hundred feet of water while a scuba diver diving from the surface can only stay at sixty feet for about an hour without going through decompression stops. At the end of the week, I would have to undergo twenty-four hours of decompression in the habitat before returning to the surface.

One of the scientists on my team was a University of Paris-Sorbonne biologist who spoke very little English. On the first day, he smuggled down a bottle of orange juice and some cheese when we dove to the habitat. After entering *Hydro-Lab* the bottle imploded showering everyone with glass and juice. Not a good start. Our voices were strange, a bit like Donald Duck, and you could not whistle. We were on the last mission and the project nearly ran out of food. The earlier teams had a choice of four astronaut entrees. We ended up eating turkey tetrazzini for the entire week and I have not eaten it since. It took a few days to settle in, but we kept busy diving all day and exhaustion brought about deep sleep at night.

---

*Decompression sickness is better known as "the bends". Any diver breathing compressed air under pressure has dissolved gases (mainly nitrogen) enter his blood from his lungs. The deeper or longer the dive the more gas is absorbed until his blood becomes saturated. When a diver goes back to the surface he must stop at pre-selected depths for predetermined lengths of time to rid himself of these gases. Dissolved gasses turn into bubbles as the diver rises and his lungs slowly absorb these bubbles during decompression stops. If he decompresses too quickly by ascending too fast, the bubbles become larger and can cause joint pain, paralysis, and even death. A diver can also decompress in a habitat or a pressure chamber that will slowly bring him back to surface pressure. Mixed gases are often used for breathing instead of air on extended or very deep dives. Usually mixed gas diving involves replacing nitrogen with helium. This mixture lessens the chance of getting the bends and stops the intoxicating effect of nitrogen narcosis but results in the diver becoming extremely cold.

Divers with Hydro-Lab, *Bahamas (U.S. Navy photo)*

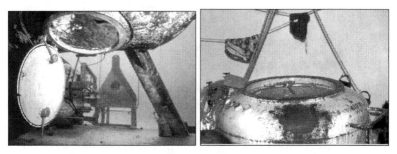

Hydro-Lab's *entrance/exit hatch (exterior and interior)*

Inside Hydro-Lab

My sixteen-year-old son, David, was my support diver. He had to deliver my food, in a pressure cooker, and a steady supply of full twin scuba tanks to me daily. We wore wet suits when diving as water temperatures, even in the high eighties, can chill the body over time. Fish did not bother us when we wore our wet suits. However, if someone swam out of the habitat without a wet suit, he was quickly surrounded by a large school of fish. This happened whenever anyone left to attend to bodily needs; there were no toilet facilities in the habitat. You would grab a scuba tank lying nearby on the seafloor and swim over to the nearest coral patch reef for some needed privacy. The fish knew what was happening, and immediately attacked while you were carrying out your business, much to the hilarity of the guys in the habitat who could see the dive bombing fish as you hid behind a coral patch (one diver got bit on his penis). A well-known scientist wrote an article on this phenomenon that he titled "Tapered Underwater Residue Deposits." It was published in an obscure scientific journal that did not grasp the acronym.

Four underwater "wayside talking stations" were positioned at different depths to provide rest areas during our scuba dives. We used these stations for short decompression stops after venturing into deep water or just to have a conversation with a companion. Most stations resembled large upside down plastic salad bowls on stilts and each held a big air bubble so we could remove our masks. One was even large enough to climb into so we could sit down and chat. One aquanaut on an earlier mission was a heavy smoker. Smoking was not allowed in the habitat so he swam out to a wayside station, stuck his head into the air bubble, unwrapped his cigarette, and lit a match. Because the air was under high pressure at that depth, its oxygen content was also very high. Instantly, the match flared up, burning his eyebrows and the front of his hair. He finally lit the cigarette but it disappeared in one puff.

The SCORE project, with thirteen scientists making lockout dives, had run out of mixed gas, making my lockout dive more dangerous as I now had to use compressed air to breathe. When I was ready for my deep dive, I hitched a ride in the aft diver lockout compartment of a *Johnson Sea-Link* submersible, I quickly swam over from *Hydro-Lab*, without any diving equipment, and climbed into the submersible waiting nearby. A BBC cameraman sat in the front sphere, with the pilot, to film my dive, while I sat in the small, hot, humid and cramped aft sphere with my technician on a large pile of hoses. These hoses would be my life support to the submersible providing my helmet with air and communications during my lock out dive. I was well aware of an accident, just two years before, involving one of the *Sea-Link* submersibles.* It had become entangled in a scuttled destroyer, in 360 feet of water, near Key West, Florida. Unable to free itself, or with the Navy's help, the occupants were doomed until a local wreck salver pulled the sub free hours after everyone else had given up. The two men in the aft sphere died but the two in front survived. Doug and I looked at this sub several years before the accident and Doug mentioned "that is an accident waiting to happen." I asked why and he pointed to the *Sea-Link* snap hooks, used during recovery, unlike our operations where we snapped hooks to the submersible. *Sea-Link* was trapped when a cable on the wreck was caught in a snap hook on the submersible.

Once *Sea-Link* was secured, we pressurized our chamber to 250 feet, opened the bottom hatch, and I swam out and over to the nearby vertical wall. I had locked out at 250 feet, on air, with the seafloor over 500 feet below—the effect on me was like drinking eight martinis and it was difficult to concentrate. I started hammering on a basketball size sclerosponge when,

---

*The two *Johnson Sea-Link*s are lockout submersibles built in 1971 by Edwin Link for the Harbor Branch Oceanographic Institute and funded by the Johnson & Johnson Company. The forward two-man Plexiglas sphere with unlimited visibility holds the pilot and one observer. The aluminum aft two-man diver lockout sphere is forty-eight inches in diameter and has one small view port. The *Sea-Link*s can dive to 2,000 feet, are twenty-four feet long and nine feet high. Each weighs 19,000 pounds. Harbor Branch went out of business in 2011. One *Sea-Link* is now in Brazil and the other sits in a Florida garage, both are inactive.

Locking out of Sea-Link *in the Bahamas (NOAA drawing)*

Sea-Link *waiting outside* Hydro-Lab

Sea-Link *hanging on the wall during lock-out dive*
(Harbor Branch photos)

from the corner of my helmet, I saw something swim by. I thought it was a large shark but it was my technician who was supposed to be in the rear chamber tending to my air hose. He had become bored, so he removed his bathing suit and with no diving equipment, swam out and around the submersible stark naked, on one breath of air. He posed and waved in front of the camera, which ruined the tape for my dive. This was a very dangerous stunt. If he couldn't have returned to the rear sphere, he would have died instantly. We got into trouble over this incident, and my dive was not included in the TV documentary. I did collect a large sclerosponge and gave it to the Yale University Museum.

At the end of our mission we closed the *Hydro-Lab* hatch, slowly re-pressurized the habitat back to surface pressure, and gradually brought our bodies back in sync to the surface. Then we quickly pressurized the habitat to match outside pressure, opened the bottom hatch, and swam up to the surface support boat. I had to wait on Grand Bahama Island for a few days, until most of the dissolved gasses in my blood stream were definitely gone. As far as I know, I was the last, or one of the last scientists, to ever lockout from a submersible as it was considered too dangerous and expensive to continue.

My sclerosponge

Chapter Ten

Lord Howe & Enewetak

I wish I could tell you about the South Pacific. The way it actually was. The endless ocean. The infinite specks of coral we called islands. Coconut palms waving gracefully toward the ocean. Reefs upon which waves broke into a spray, and inner lagoons, lovely beyond description.

—James A. Michener, *Tales of the South Pacific* (1948)

IN 1976, I WAS AWARDED ONE, of only two, Fulbright Scholarships for geology research. It covered travel expenses and salary for a three-month study of the Lord Howe Island coral reef. I always thought that I would return to this beautiful island someday. The University of Sydney loaned me their new thirty-one-foot research vessel *R/V Matthew Flinders* built by Charlie Phipps. I left Colorado after diving *Gamma* on the East Coast and planned to return home before Christmas. My son David, a high school senior, accompanied me, as did Don Howell, a UNC graduate student, and big John Messersmidt, a six-foot nine-inch tall associate at Woods Hole Oceanographic Institute. We rented a small house on the island.

Lord Howe looked much the same as it did during my last trip, in 1967, while working on the Tasman Sea seamounts. There were still only about 200 full time residents. We were fortunate that there was weekly air service from Sydney now. Before 1975, everyone had to arrive by ship or on antiquated flying boats that flew over from Sydney. A small landing strip was constructed on the island in late 1974.

Lord Howe Island (with the southernmost coral reef in the world)

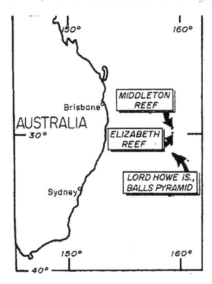

Lord Howe Is., Elizabeth, and Middleton Reefs (Slater and Phipps, 1977)

Hiking to beach for a dive, Lord Howe Island

We hiked down to the beach, about a quarter mile, from our rental house each day to dive on the fringing reef from a small rubber boat. I took underwater photos of the unique coral reef animals and plants, and we collected many sediment samples. I constructed sediment distribution maps and published several scientific articles based on this research.

Everything was going fine until two of my assistants fell in love—John for an island waitress and David for a Sydney girl. David was eager to return to Sydney, and his chance finally came after the annual sailboat race from Sydney to Lord Howe. Most boat owners flew home so they needed help in returning their yachts to the mainland—David volunteered. I was not too anxious to have my seventeen-year-old sail a yacht 400 miles back to Sydney, but I finally agreed. He had a return ride to Lord Howe on the *Matthew Flinders* with Charlie Phipps. Unhappily for David, his yacht ran into a large storm and was blown off course several hundred miles north, to where he eventually landed. The storm was terrible and several of the yacht crews were worried if they would survive—everyone did. David had little money and was 200 miles from Sydney but somehow found a way to travel down there.

He stayed at the Whale Beach Surf Club, saw his girlfriend for a few days, and then helped Charlie transport the *Matthew Flinders* over to Lord Howe Island. They hit an even larger storm, and the little research vessel started taking on water. Charlie picked up the wooden engine cover, stumbled, and mistakenly tossed it overboard. They were now in danger of sinking with water pouring into the open engine compartment. Luckily, they caught a glimpse of the floating wooden cover and managed to grab it when a large wave moved the cover close to them for a few seconds. I started to worry when they were three days late, as I was aware of the storm and had not heard from them. I kept trying to reach them on the marine radio but there was no answer. Finally, four days late, they were towed into Lord Howe by a local fisherman that found them drifting at sea with a broken radio and a dead engine. We hauled the *Flinders* up onto the beach and, in a typical Charlie operation, it fell over onto the sand. Charlie had told the local repairman the boat weighed nine tons when it actually weighed fourteen tons. We pushed it back on its cradle and the needed repairs were completed in a few days. Everyone swore they would never go back on the *Flinders* with Charlie, but of course they all did.

David leaving for Sydney

Repairing R/V Matthew Flinders

Diving from R/V Matthew Flinders

David and John with our house

Standing on north end of Lord Howe Island

After the *Matthew Flinders* was repaired, we sailed to Elizabeth and Middleton Reefs, small atolls (each about five by three miles across), 120 and 150 miles north of Lord Howe Island. We stayed for nearly four weeks; diving, mapping, and drilling to obtain cores. The atoll surfaces were usually underwater but were accessible for drilling several hours every day during low tide. The diving was spectacular; fish had rarely seen divers and were unafraid. On one dive, big John opened up his large collecting bag and a grouper swam in—easiest fishing I had ever seen. While cleaning dishes on the aft swim platform, sharks would stick their heads out of the water, fighting to grab food scraps off our plates. A few blows on the nose with a skillet usually sent them on their way. There were many sharks—a nuisance but not a serious problem.

Mapping and collecting samples, 80', Elizabeth Reef

We had a successful summer diving around Lord Howe and on Middleton and Elizabeth Reefs. I collected over 1,000 underwater photographs and several hundred samples. John married his island girlfriend, stayed in Australia, and became a Great Barrier Reef ranger. David left his Sydney girlfriend behind when we returned to Colorado.

We used the *Matthew Flinders* again, a few years later for one more, almost disastrous, trip to Elizabeth Reef. I had returned to Lord Howe for three months in 1980 to tie up a few loose ends remaining from my 1976 research. Four UNC students flew over to assist me on a new project.

The students enjoyed diving and staying on Lord Howe for a few weeks while waiting for the *Matthew Flinders* to arrive. They finally left with Charlie for Elizabeth Reef, while I returned to Sydney to meet Lois. The *Flinders* ran into a storm the first night out and was tossed around violently. First the radar went out, and then the radio went dead. Charlie ended up sick in his bunk, leaving a student to steer the boat. He tried to keep it headed into the wind and seas all night long but was terrified they would sink. When morning came, the storm was gone and when he looked around he saw Elizabeth Reef—nobody knows exactly how they got there. One of my students, Jeff Obrecht, wrote me a note about this trip and he explained what happened in great detail.

> We finally left for Middleton Reef right after dinner. Dr. Phipps was in his normal hurry up mode and did not think of the consequences after a greasy dinner that did not set well with any of us. Then the storm hit. I had never been in a boat larger than 18' and Phipps and I were the only ones that could get out of bed—everyone was throwing up in their boots, their beds and on the floor. The waves were larger than the 38' *Flinders* and it was dark with lots of lightning when Charlie said, "Jeff, keep the boat on this heading and into the waves (about the same direction) and wake me up in a couple of hours."
>
> After about 15 minutes, I learned how to gauge each wave. I gunned the engines to climb up a wave and then surfed down the backside. I kept from plowing through the wave tops and crashing down the other side. There were several times when a wave went completely over the boat. I really thought we were all going to die and nobody would have known what happened to us. After three hours, I tried to wake Charlie up but he needed more sleep so I kept going. One time I realized we had gotten sideways on a wave and the boat started to flip over but I gunned the engines and somehow we survived. By dawn the storm started to subside and I spotted the wreck on the reef. We had made it.

I joined them later and we spent several weeks diving and drilling. One of my graduate students, Don Schofield, used data from the shallow drill holes on Elizabeth Reef for his masters' thesis back in Colorado. Don enjoyed Australia so much he moved his family down under where they still live today. Lord Howe Island and Elizabeth Reef became World Heritage Sites so collecting specimens there is now forbidden.

Drilling on Elizabeth Reef   *David with Lord Howe lobster*

It was this big!

David diving off Lord Howe Island

With Charlie Phipps and Platypus, *Sydney*

WE HAD PLANNED to use a manned submersible at Lord Howe. Charlie was building a two-man submersible, *Platypus*, which he basically copied, with some modifications, after a *Nekton* submersible. Charlie kept revising and making changes, so *Platypus* was not ready when we needed it. This submersible was not very successful and now sits in an Australian museum.

A few years earlier Charlie had taken the *Matthew Flinders*, with Chris Kendall, up the east coast of Australia and around the northern tip of Queensland into the Gulf of Carpentaria. During this trip, they damaged the propeller shaft when they hit a reef. After they finally arrived in the shallow Gulf, Charlie decided to beach the boat to repair the propeller. They drove the boat onto a mud flat during high tide and then, when the tide went out, propped it up with some timber. They fixed the shaft and jumped back in the boat to await the next high tide. It never arrived; they had gone up on the highest tide of the year. An aborigine hunting party happened to wander by and was asked to help dig a ditch, using sticks, behind the boat leading out to the water. When the second highest tide of the year occurred, a day later, the boat was pushed across the mud flat using this ditch. They were very lucky that *Flinders* did not sit there for a year waiting for next year's highest tide. I never used the *Flinders* again.

JOHN WARME, a good friend and professor at Colorado School of Mines, invited me in 1978 to join him for a few weeks on Enewetak Atoll, one of the South Pacific Marshall Islands. John wanted to collect patch reef rock samples in the Enewetak lagoon. Enewetak, one of the largest coral atolls in the world, was the site of several nuclear tests in the 1950s. John was concerned with the numerous sharks. My job was to assist him with his research and to protect him from being bitten while he collected samples. He wanted to find examples of modern bioerosion similar to those we had discovered in the submarine canyons off Georges Bank.

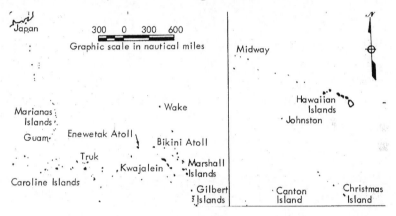

Enewetak Atoll, Marshall Islands, South Pacific

We flew to Enewetak in a C-141 Air Force plane, sitting backwards in the freight compartment—it was a free trip. There was a small military base with a store, landing strip, and a marine laboratory on one of the tiny flat atoll islands. The previous lab manager was Pat Colin, the biologist who was trapped in a Jamaica cave with me in 1972. He had built an airplane from a mail-order kit and flew it solo to New Guinea when he became manager of a marine laboratory there. The present Enewetak lab manager was ready to board our plane as John and I disembarked. He was headed to a U.S. hospital for skin grafts to cover wounds from a recent shark attack. He had been diving in the same area where we were headed.

Enewetak airport and dining hall   *Enewetak Marine Lab*

There were lots of old bicycles around the island and we would just hop on one to take us anywhere we wanted. The military dining hall was on the other side of the island, so we could ride to it from the laboratory without pedaling as the steady trade winds would blow us all the way—heading back was much more difficult. Samples were hard to obtain, but luckily, some Navy SEALs based on the island volunteered to dynamite a small lagoon patch reef for us. The blast was very successful and we collected many excellent samples. Sharks were inquisitive but never attacked. There were many World War II relics on the atoll seafloor and I recovered a belt of Japanese machine-gun bullets embedded in coral. This great souvenir sat on my back porch for many years until one day a house painter knocked it over and it shattered.

John Warme collecting samples, Enewetak Lagoon

One day John and I were resting while eating lunch on a tiny island. I suddenly remembered the large oyster I collected from the lagoon floor earlier. I had stashed it in my sample bag to save for lunch. Just as I was about to open the oyster with my divers knife, John said, "With your luck you will probably find a pearl." Incredibly, a large black pearl happened to be sitting in the middle of my lunch. Over the next few years, at Enewetak, my fellow divers collected nearly every black pearl oyster in the lagoon but no other pearls were ever found. During the same lunch, I threw down a piece of bread crust and a very large rat suddenly appeared from nowhere and grabbed it. At least we know rats survived the nuclear tests.

Black pearl oyster, 6" across (pearl just above and left of center)

MY CORAL REEF CLASS flew down to St. Croix, Virgin Islands instead of Jamaica, during the 1978 spring break. We stayed at the Farleigh Dickinson University marine laboratory.. Lois, now my fiancée, accompanied me after taking a series of scuba lessons over the winter in Colorado to surprise me. I took my class to the Frederiksted pier soon after arrival. This pier was a well-known dive site because of its unique marine life, including a large sea horse population. Lois's first ocean dive took place there, after we dragged our gear out to the end of the fifteen-foot high and very long pier. I told the group they would have to jump after putting on all of their dive equipment. Not an easy first ocean dive but Lois did well (it was better than diving in an ice covered mountain lake). We visited the *Hydro-Lab* habitat that had been moved from the Bahamas to St. Croix and was now near the laboratory in the head of a submarine canyon. The trip was successful except for one badly sunburned female student.

> [Note: *Hydro-Lab* eventually ended up in the Smithsonian Museum in Washington, D.C. with a plaque listing all the participating aquanauts. My mother took a few of her grandchildren to visit the Museum years later and was very surprised to see my name.]

I RECEIVED PERMISSION from the Dean to teach just one course during the winter quarter of 1979—twelve senior geology majors signed up. We spent the entire quarter studying modern sedimentary environments, commonly represented in ancient rocks, in the classroom and on various field trips around the country. One field trip included Carlsbad Caverns in New Mexico, where we received special permission to go back at night after the Park was closed to explore the lower portions of the cave not open to the public. A professor friend at LSU, who had dove with me in Jamaica, led the class on a study of the Mississippi Delta. We continued to the University of Alabama marine laboratory on the Gulf to observe barrier beaches, and then spent a week in the Florida mangrove swamps. The most popular part of the course was diving on modern coral reefs in Florida and Jamaica. We also traveled to Utah, New Mexico, and Texas to study ancient rocks that had been deposited in similar environments. It was a wonderful opportunity and many of these students went on to become full time geologists with major oil and coal companies. After the spring break trip to Jamaica, the students stopped in New Orleans and I returned to Colorado where Lois and I were married at her mountain home in Breckenridge.

IN THE FALL OF 1980, I was invited to New York City to appear on the initial broadcast of the TV game show *To Tell the Truth*. There were three contestants and each of us had to start by saying, "I am Richard Slater." I had to tell the truth but the others could lie. The emcee talked about my career and then it was up to the panel to choose who the real "Richard Slater" was. I wore a three-piece suit while the others were dressed for an African safari. The two fakes missed a few easy questions such as, "Where is the Woods Hole Oceanographic Institute?" All but one panelist named me so I only won $32. Margaret Trudeau, wife of the Canadian Prime Minister and one of the panelists, chose me saying, "I think he is the one but he doesn't look like a guy who did all those brave things." I'm not sure that was a compliment.

The Dean asked me to take on a third three-year term as Department Chairman and I would be tenured. I turned both down before returning, this time on my sabbatical, to Lord Howe Island. (I had been strongly disagreeing with everyone being automatically tenured over the past few years.)

I FLEW TO HOUSTON for a national geological meeting in March 1981. There was a blizzard so I left early for the airport and arrived a few hours before my flight. The girl at the airline counter asked if I wanted to take an earlier flight and I agreed. Unbeknownst to me, my scheduled flight later crashed. There was panic back at UNC until my secretary later found me that evening at my hotel—another close call. While in Houston, I ran into Jim Vernon, my former USC classmate and boss at General Oceanographics, and he asked if I would be interested in working with him at McClelland Engineers in Ventura. The pay was about triple what I was making, and after some thought, I decided this was a good opportunity. McClelland was gearing up for gathering data in Alaska because the offshore oil-leasing program was becoming active again due to the recent Arab oil embargo. I enjoyed living in Colorado, especially the skiing, but I always hoped to return to Southern California. Teaching was great but University politics were depressing. I handed in my resignation to UNC, and, Lois and I moved to California. I did not realize it at the time, but I was jumping from the frying pan into the fire. At least I was going to receive a good salary.

Don't you feel guilty diving every day and laying in the sunshine while someone else has to take your place back in the rat race?

Cartoons on my UNC office door

Slater resigning position

By LINDA KALBACH
MIRROR Staff Writer

Effective at the end of Winter quarter, the Earth Sciences Department will lose its chairman of six years, Richard Slater who will be resigning to take a position with a firm involved in off-shore exploration, said acting chairman Glen Cobb.

Slater, who is known nationally for his accomplishments in the area of oceanography research, came to the University of Northern Colorado in 1973. Since that time, Slater has had a major impact on the department of Earth Sciences and the students whom he taught Cobb said. "There were a lot of students which he literally attracted to UNC. He had a way of inspiring his students to continuing their education and career in some phase of the Earth Science," Cobb said.

Replacing Slater as professor will not be an easy task Cobb said.

"His contributions to the department will be difficult to match," he said. Finding a new professor to take over Slater's oceanography courses will take several months according to Cobb who said the department hopes to have the position filled by Fall quarter 1981.

The department of Earth Science has about 100 majors and 30 minors enrolled in its program Cobb said, many of whom enrolled in UNC specifically to take courses under Slater.

Slater was out of town and unavailable to comment on his resignation.

"UNC is losing a truly outstanding individual," Cobb said. "He had great impact, we were lucky to have had him for eight years," he added.

College of Arts and Sciences
Office of the Dean

University of Northern Colorado

Greeley, Colorado 8063
(303) 351-2707

November 12, 1980

TO: Members of the Department of Earth Sciences

Dear Earth, Sky, and Water Men:

Had Rich Slater wanted another term as chairman, he could have had it. But he's remained adamant in his conviction that six years has been enough.

I have never really been able to understand how we were able to attract Rich Slater to UNC, and to keep him here. Of course, we've not wholly succeeded in the latter—he's been the most peripatetic of our chairmen, and had he been a CSAPer, we could have had thriving programs at Wood's Hole, in the Caribbean, and on the Great Barrier Reef. Rich has added a note of urbanity, of quiet but thorough professionalism, and of widely-recognized research competence that this institution badly needs. As well, he's been a relaxed, congenial, and effective chairman of a department that is today probably as cohesive as any in the College, and one with enrollments as healthy as any. Although a good advocate, Rich has, at the same time, been among the most cooperative and understanding of chairmen, and I can't think of any time over the past six years when it's not been a pleasure to work with him.

As I write this, and after so many pleasant Indian summer weeks, the weather prediction is for a blizzard. I had not thought that the gods would react so quickly to the ascension of one of their own.

Cordially,

Robert O. Schulze, Dean

ROS:ah
cc: Drs. Bond, Barnhart and Burke
    Arts and Sciences Department Chairmen

Chapter Eleven

Alaska, *Delta* & California

Yes, I love it. The sea is everything. There is tranquility.
Ah, sir, live in the bosom of the waters! There alone is
independence. There I recognize no master! There I am free.

— Jules Verne, *20,000 Leagues under the Sea* (1869)

LOIS AND I LEFT Colorado, in April 1981, and moved to Channel Islands Harbor, just north of Los Angeles in Ventura County. We found a house, on the water with two boat docks, that we could not afford but was too nice to pass up. We bought a boat and soon enjoyed sailing in the adjoining Santa Barbara Channel. Jim Vernon introduced me to long distance running and I quickly became an addict.

I worked with the McClelland Engineers marine geologic group in Ventura. Jim had convinced McClelland on the idea of putting together geologic data packages covering potential offshore oil leases along the West Coast, including Alaska. My assignment was to manage collecting data and writing final reports. My first chore was to help mobilize the *M/V Seabird*, a converted World War II Coast Guard vessel for a six-week cruise to the Gulf of Alaska and the Bering Sea.

My crew and I flew to Yakutat and met the ship in early July. It had been eleven years since I was last there and little had changed. We started gathering geophysical data at night and collecting seafloor samples during the day by coring and dredging in depths down to 9,000 feet. The work went well and McClelland was pleased with the money we brought in.

It was decided to take *Seabird,* now renamed the *M/V McClelland Ventura,* to the Bering Sea again in 1982 to help gather geological data around the Aleutian and Pribilof Islands. Dutch Harbor, nearly 1,000 miles west of Anchorage, would be our homeport. "Dutch," as everyone called it, is actually the port for the city of Unalaska.

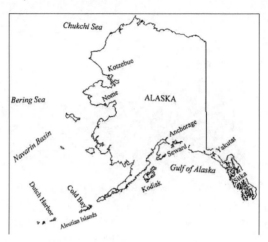

Alaska ports and areas where we worked

There were daily air flights from Anchorage to Dutch Harbor, but approximately one out of every five flights was cancelled due to bad weather. I boarded a DC-3 in Anchorage and was pleased to learn it had a new non-smoking section. Once the plane took off, a Japanese fisherman, sitting in the single seat directly opposite me, started to smoke. I asked the attendant if I was in the non-smoking section and she replied, "Yes, the left side of the plane is for smokers and the right side is for nonsmokers." Bad weather forced us to stay over in Cold Bay, a community of maybe thirty people with a large runway built by the military during WW II.

Dutch Harbor was similar to Yakutat with unpaved streets, but it had a better harbor and a Mexican restaurant. There were a few hundred residents in 1982. The military built the harbor in 1940 (the Japanese bombed it in 1942) and left a large landing strip and hundreds of empty buildings after

World War II. Dutch Harbor is the rainiest place in the United States with some precipitation falling about 300 days a year. Heavy fog obscures the harbor most days. The temperatures in August, the warmest month of the year, were in the fifties. It is the center of the Bering Sea king crab fisheries and the number one fishing port in the U.S. since 1978.

Elbow Room, Dutch Harbor

There was only one hotel, the Unisea Inn, and one other place, the Elbow Room, where you could purchase a drink. Playboy Magazine once listed the Elbow Room as the rowdiest bar in the United States. It was a place for boat crews to meet and party, including ours. I met the *McClelland Ventura* in "Dutch" the day we both arrived and gave the crew the night off, which I quickly regretted. One crewmember was arrested for carrying the Elbow Room's men's urinal down the street at 4:00 a.m. When I bailed him out of jail, he told me, "It just fell off when I was taking a piss." I found another crewmember the next morning sleeping in a ditch. We worked for six weeks in the Bering Sea and only returned to "Dutch" once, when we had to refuel. During that visit, I caught our navigator taking steaks and lobsters from our ship's freezer and selling them in the Elbow Room.

[Note: Unalaska/Dutch Harbor now has over 4,000 residents and is well known because of the TV series *Deadliest Catch*. The Elbow Room closed years ago.]

We worked in poor weather and spent many days jogging into rough seas with winds over fifty knots. However, we did collect a lot of scientific data and I headed home to write my reports. This data was sold to several oil companies and I started planning for a 1983 Alaska cruise.

IN 1982 DOUG PRIVITT, put the final touches on his new submersible. He wanted to call it *Nekton Delta* but the name *Nekton* belonged to our old company Nekton Inc.—so he just called it *Delta*. A few years later Nekton, Inc. went bankrupt. They had grown into a large company with over a hundred employees and a large San Diego facility. When the recession hit, they went under.

Doug brought *Delta* up to the Navy Lab, in Port Hueneme (near Ventura), late in 1982. They had the only pressure chamber big enough to test *Delta* on the West Coast. Doug had designed *Delta*, and the *Nektons*, so they would just fit into this chamber. I witnessed the test and watched as *Delta* was taken down successfully to 1,700 feet and was now certified by ABS to 1,200 feet—200 feet deeper than the *Nektons*. *Delta* made its first dive, late in December 1982, in the Redondo Beach Harbor. It was a big improvement over the *Nektons*.

Launching Delta *in the Redondo Beach Harbor, California, 1982*

Delta *interior looking forward from behind pilot's seat*

Delta *port interior looking aft; high-pressure air bottle, CB radio, spare CO2 absorbent containers, and pilot's control panel*

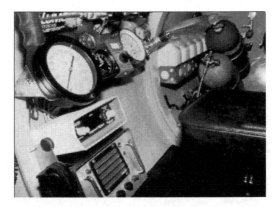

Delta *starboard interior looking aft; UQC, fathometer, depth gauge, oxygen monitor, spare CO2 absorbent containers, air and oxygen bottles*

A MCCLELLAND meeting for all employees was held early in 1983. The economy was creeping into a recession and the company needed to make cuts. Our small group was bringing in more income than any of the others so I was not overly concerned. However, when it was announced there would be no more overtime pay, I responded, "Does that include sea pay?" The answer was "Yes." Standing in the back of the room I then asked, "Do you mean that those of us who spend many weeks at sea, working over twelve hours a day, seven days a week, are going to be paid the same as those who sit behind a desk five days a week, and go home at five o'clock?" Again, "Yes" was the answer so I said, "I resign." Later, the office manager backed down and said we would still receive sea pay, but it was too late.

Three other senior scientists from our small group met with me and, after discussing our options we decided to form our own company and continue gathering offshore geologic data. We went to Jim Vernon, told him our plans, and he decided to join with us. GeoCubic, Inc. was formed with Jim as president and the four of us as vice-presidents. We each put $10,000 into an account and set up an office. For our first project, we mapped the seafloor off Point Conception, just west of Santa Barbara, using side-scan sonar and *Delta*. After combining the data into a seafloor mosaic, we sold it to ten oil companies for $15,000 each—it was a good start.

IN THE EARLY 1980s, there was oil company interest in obtaining seafloor data in two northern Alaska offshore areas, the Navarin Basin (northern Bering Sea) and the Chukchi Sea (north of the Bering Straits), where offshore oil leases were pending (and still are in 2015). These basins border the Soviet Union and were a long distance from any major Alaska port; it would be very expensive to work there. We needed financial partners, and after several meetings and intense discussions, we joined with Fugro, an engineering company from Holland, and Dames and Moore, a geological engineering company from California. Both were McClelland rivals. Fugro owned drilling equipment and a ship, the *M/V Kara Seal,* Dames and Moore provided funding, and we supplied the experience and manpower. It looked great on paper but later turned into an unworkable situation.

I had only been on one other drilling vessel. Most of my experience was in taking gravity punch cores from seafloor outcrops. To use a rotary drill rig, we needed to anchor the *Kara Seal* with four anchors, so four large winches were added to the ship in Seattle before we sailed to Alaska. My old friend Tom Crawford would be in charge of anchoring and I would be the manager of operations.

We left Dutch Harbor for the two-day trip to Navarin Basin, set the anchors, and went to work. We just started drilling the first hole when a Dutchman approached me and said we had to return to Dutch Harbor so they could switch Fugro drilling crews. I argued with him to no avail and we returned to Dutch Harbor. This added four days to the job and later Fugro tried to charge us for the four days we went over our allotted time. The hardheaded Dutchmen were impossible to deal with so we broke up our partnership in the fall. Everyone did make money on the data we gathered but we were not going to work with Fugro again. Interestingly, McClelland Engineers and Fugro merged several years later, resulting in Fugro becoming one of the world's largest geological engineering companies.

Now we needed a ship of our own. We sent Tom Crawford and several others down to New Orleans where they found the *Glorita,* a 150-foot seismic vessel we eventually bought very cheap due to a glut of available ships on the Gulf Coast in 1983. GeoCubic personnel sailed *Glorita* through the Panama Canal and up to Ventura. I quickly realized it would take a lot of elbow grease to get this ship into working condition. We spent many weekends sanding, painting, and repairing, but it never became the ship I really wanted. It was very difficult to launch *Delta* from the *Glorita,* as it had high decks with very little open space and high railings.

OUR FIRST PROJECT, aboard *Glorita,* was in January 1984 off Gaviota, just west of Santa Barbara. Exxon hired us to recover seafloor samples and to map the seafloor. We used *Delta* for mapping and *Glorita* to take shallow gravity punch cores. A gravity corer is just a large heavy weight with a pipe sticking out the bottom. It would free fall from the "A-frame" and jam into the seafloor taking a small core of the underlying rock. We recovered the corer and sample by winching it up by the connected cable and then used a hydraulic ram to squeeze out the cores from the often-bent core barrels.

Glorita *entering Port Hueneme Harbor*

Delta, *near Santa Barbara*

One day, when were anchored just behind the surf, a naked female surfer paddled out and started talking to our crew. The client representatives from Houston were amazed when I told them we were working off a nudist beach. That evening, after leaving the ship at the Gaviota pier, we saw the two Exxon representatives on top of the cliff looking down at the nudists. We honked and waved as we passed by. Later, on the same job, I climbed down a nearby cliff, with another geologist, to obtain some rock samples when we discovered a nude couple making love on the beach. They never saw us but their little dog kept sniffing us as we quietly crept by.

On another day, there was a sudden roar and a big cloud of smoke when a large rocket flew right over us. It was a missile launch from the nearby Vandenberg Base. The first stage dropped off and landed in the ocean several miles beyond us.

We used scuba and *Delta* to map the seafloor geology where we had recovered the gravity cores. I piloted *Delta* on all of the dives with one of my partners as observer. Everything was going smoothly until one dive when he started complaining about a headache and began to panic. We surfaced quickly and jumped out of the submersible onto *Glorita*. Later, he joked that I tried to kill him as I had neglected to change the carbon dioxide absorbent granules that morning. To keep air in a submersible similar to the air we breathe on the surface, we constantly add oxygen, and absorb carbon dioxide, into the submersible during a dive. Astronauts in outer space do the same thing. A headache and drowsiness were warning signals that carbon dioxide was building up. There was usually no warning if we ran low on oxygen (nine percent of less)—you would not be aware of what was happening and just pass out. *Delta* had instruments that monitored both gases. We carried a three-day supply of oxygen and carbon dioxide absorbent. If the sub ever became trapped, we would have approximately seventy-two hours to be rescued. Anytime observers asked how long we could survive underwater I explained all this to them and then added, "Of course I have a large wrench back here and if I hit you over the head, I could survive for 144 hours."

Chapter Twelve

Enewetak & Geocubic

I am not at home, nor near any city or people; I am far out in the Pacific on a desert island, sitting on the bottom of the ocean; I am deep down under the water in a place no human being has even been before; it is one of the greatest moments of my whole life; thousands of people would pay large sums, would forego much for five minutes of this!

—William Beebe, *The Arcturus Adventure* (1926)

IN THE LATE 1970s, I was part of a group that submitted a proposal to the Nuclear Defense Agency to map the Enewetak Atoll nuclear bomb craters. Our proposal was funded but I was too busy at the time to go diving. A University of Hawaii manned submersible was transported to Enewetak, but it only made a few dives over a two-month period and the craters remained unmapped. The USGS (the United States Geological Survey) decided to take up this project in 1984, ironically they called it the Pacific Enewetak Atoll Crater Experiment or PEACE Project—I was invited to participate. Geocubic was glad to get the project and to let Doug and I do all the work.

Enewetak is one of the Marshall Islands, a chain of islands formed from volcanoes that rise 15,000 feet above the ocean floor, nearly 3,000 miles southwest of Hawaii. Coral growth around the rims and the steady sinking of these volcanoes has created flat circular coral atolls with many small sandy islands surrounding large lagoons. Enewetak is the second largest atoll in the world (nearby Kwajalein is the largest).

The highest elevation on Enewetak is ten feet. The Enewetak lagoon is twenty-two miles long and fifteen miles wide with an average depth of 160 feet. Dozens of small flat sandy islands surround the lagoon. It has typical tropical weather, with constant northeasterly trade winds up to thirty knots, high temperatures, and high humidity. This does not make comfortable shallow-water submersible diving as the temperature inside a submersible would be over a hundred degrees. The lagoon dives would be tough but I was excited to return to Enewetak. Hopefully, I would have an opportunity for a deep dive on the outside of the atoll.

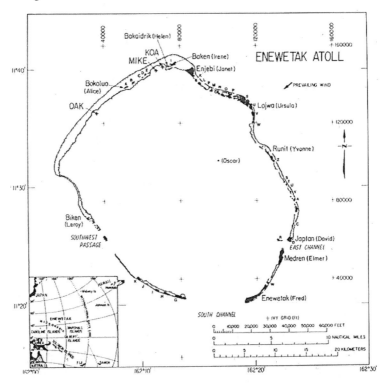

Oak, Mike, and Koa bomb craters, Enewetak Atoll (Forger, 1986)

Our mission was to map the three large craters still visible, along with other smaller craters from the forty-nine nuclear tests conducted on Enewetak in the 1950s and early 1960s.

These craters, including the three large ones named Oak, Mike, and Koa, are the only exposed nuclear craters in the world as the international test-ban treaty forced further testing underground. The first hydrogen bomb, Mike, was ignited at Enewetak in 1952. It was a ten-and-a-half-million-ton fusion device placed on an island that disappeared during the blast leaving a crater 175 feet deep and nearly a mile wide. Koa was smaller at one-and-a-half-million tons, but it destroyed three islands and left a crater 170 feet deep and 3,000 feet wide. Oak, the final surface bomb test, was placed on a landing craft anchored in the lagoon. During a storm the barge broke loose and drifted onto the reef. They set the bomb off anyway and the nine-million-ton device blew a chunk out of the reef and left a crater nearly 4,000 feet wide and 200 feet deep.

Over the years, these craters slowly filled with sediment and became larger due to slumping around the rims, caused in part by the many later and smaller nuclear tests set off on several Enewetak islands. Our instructions were to locate and measure the original dimensions of each crater. After all these nuclear tests, the government still did not know the exact size crater a weapon of known yield would produce. The Nuclear Defense Agency needed these dimensions to help place missile silos, in North America, so a single Russian missile would not destroy multiple silos. I never heard the word "bomb" from any of the government officials working with us—they just called them "devices" that caused "events" not explosions.

Before leaving for Enewetak, I teamed up with several USGS geologists on a field trip to the meteor crater in Arizona and to craters left by underground testing at Yucca Mountain, about eighty miles north of Las Vegas. A well-known USGS geologist, Gene Shoemaker, was our field leader on this trip. His specialty was impact craters on the moon. Dave Folger from Woods Hole and Gene Shin from Miami would be the USGS Enewetak project leaders. USGS geologists Bob Halley and Harold Hudson would also be diving with me. All were good friends and experienced scuba and submersible divers.

The USGS leased the converted offshore supply vessel *Egabrag II* (garbage spelled backwards) that hauled garbage from the Marshall Islands for the U.S. government. We went to San Diego to mobilize *Delta* and its support gear on *Egabrag II*, along with the USGS twenty-five-foot research boat *Halimeda* and all their diving and drilling equipment.

With Gene Shinn, Harold Hudson, and Dave Folger on Meteor Crater floor

M/V Egabrag II, *San Diego*

A month later, Doug and I flew down to Kwajalein and boarded *Egabrag II* for the two-day trip to Enewetak. The USGS chartered a plane to fly their team down and by early July, we were all ready to dive. There was concern about exposure to radiation while diving, so we were tested daily in 1984 with no positive results. The radiation technician used a Coleman lantern mantle from his wallet, to calibrate the radioactivity, because they contain thorium. He told us we received more radiation from the Coleman lantern mantle and flying over to Kwajalein at 35,000 feet than we received from the nuclear craters. During our 1985 dives, the Nuclear Defense Agency did not send a radiation technician to check on us.

Our Enewetak team totaled thirty-three people including the *Egabrag II* crew, navigators, military personnel, engineers, and geologists. We took scientists on 142 submersible dives over twenty-nine consecutive days, collected over 3,000 pounds of rock samples while recording over fifty hours of underwater videotape. I was the pilot on 108 dives, including all of the long geology transects, and quickly became exhausted from the high heat and humidity. I tried everything, even carrying ice in the submersible but it melted quickly. Every morning, I awoke with my eyes glued shut from secretion caused by sweat running into my eyes the previous dive day.

Gene and I wanted to dive on the outside of Enewetak but were ordered to stay within the lagoon. One day, when there were no officials around, we took *Egabrag II* outside the atoll. We went to the area seaward of Oak crater, as we hoped the nuclear event might have broken off a chunk of the outer reef. It had, and we got a spectacular look at a vertical wall, 60 feet back into the reef that exposed the reef framework and several caves with stalactites and stalagmites. We attempted to knock off a stalactite with *Delta's* arm but it would not budge. Finally, we backed off about a hundred feet and rammed the stalactite at full speed. There was a chance of breaking the forward port but it is located on the ballast tank, not on the pressure hull. We would have survived if it had broken. Gene and I braced ourselves when we collided with the stalactite several times but it was too solid so we never got the prized sample. Neither did we break the port or damage the submersible—except for scratches on the paint and a few small dents.

Gene's crew, using their underwater drill, recovered rock cores along the crater rims. Scuba diving along the edge of the bomb craters was amazing. There were many large fish and manta rays were common. Water visibility in the craters varied from fifty feet near rocky outcrops to just a few feet on the bottom of the muddy craters.

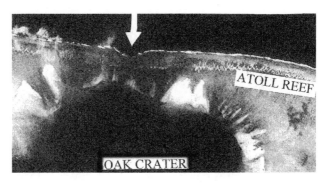

Aerial photo of Oak crater, 4,000' wide
(arrow points to area where we dove on the seaward side of the reef)

My big problem at Enewetak in 1984 was a toothache from a cracked molar caused by chewing on ice in *Delta*. I tried every painkiller on board. Government officials wanted me to fly in the tiny missionary plane over to neighboring Palau to see a dentist, but I declined. Later, I was told that dentist worked in a broken-down shack with a cardboard tooth sign outside hanging from a post. I found that biting down on a Popsicle stick throughout a dive really helped. We had problems that summer with the local dive support boat that ferried out Enewetak natives who were assisting us. It finally quit and quietly sank into the lagoon one evening.

One strange discovery was the abundance of holothurians, sea slugs, on the crater floors. Everything looks about one third larger through flat submersible view ports and these sea slugs looked much larger than normal. They were about three to four feet long but the ship's crew, after watching a few of our videotapes, was telling everyone they were thirty feet long and the nuclear tests had caused this phenomenon.

Harold Hudson, a member of Gene Shin's USGS team, later reported a surprise discovery at the 5th International Coral Reef Congress in Tahiti. He confirmed that corals had begun to grow on debris and on the crater rims within one year of the blasts and growth rates of older corals some distance away from the tests were not affected.

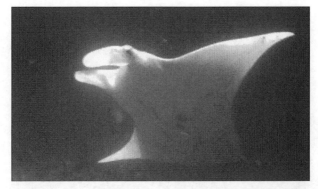

Manta ray, Enewetak

USGS geologists drilling crater rim   *Scuba diver on crater edge*

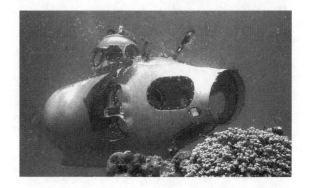

Delta *on the crater edge*
(underwater photos by Gene Shinn and his crew)

With Doug, Enewetak   *Taking a sample on the crater floor*

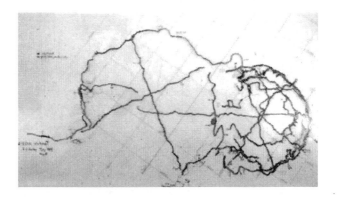

*Field map with **Delta** track lines, Mike and Koa craters*

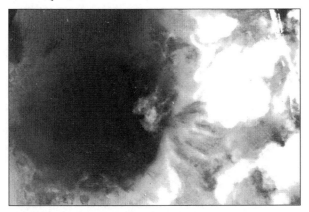

Oak Crater, atoll reef edge on the right with surf

WHEN I RETURNED to Geocubic's office from Enewetak in 1984, I found a bill on my desk. Geocubic had hired several new employees, moved to a larger office, and now the partners needed to contribute more money to help cover costs. I was not happy being the only partner working at sea, spending an exhausting month in the field earning income for Geocubic, and then finding I owed money to keep the company going.

Geocubic started a very large project to gather geophysical, geochemical, and geological data from four major northern and central California offshore geological basins: Santa Cruz, Bodega Bay, Point Arena and Eel River. All were potentially oil bearing. Exploratory drilling in these basins during the 1960s penetrated a section of oil-saturated rocks but there was not enough oil in those days to continue drilling. Since that time several giant oil fields were discovered offshore in similar basins and interest was heating up so the government put the potential oil-producing basins on their lease schedule for 1989. We used *Glorita* and *Delta* to collect data.

*Seafloor mosaic of rock outcrops from geophysical side-scan data
(collected off central California)*

Our seafloor side-scan records were assembled into very large mosaics, each one covered the floor of a large room. Towing a side scan instrument from a ship is similar to mowing a lawn or harvesting wheat. The ship just travels back and forth on predetermined lines while towing an instrument that sweeps the ocean seafloor with multiple electronic signals. The return signals are received, decoded, and recorded. The results look similar to an aerial photograph. The harder the seafloor, or any object on it, the faster the signals return and the darker the image on the printout. Later, in post-production, a seafloor map was compiled from the return analog signal records. After putting together a mosaic, we knew the best locations for *Delta* dives and where to collect the needed rock samples by coring and dredging from *Glorita*. We then used a micropaleontology laboratory in San Diego to age-date our samples. I dove in *Delta* to gather surface geological information and to collect more seafloor samples. I also captured gas from bubbling vents on the seafloor to be analyzed by a local geochemistry laboratory. We then packaged all of this data and made it available to prospective leasing companies.

Rising Geocubic expenses continued to grow, and so after several meetings, we decided to close the office. Our timing could not have been better. During the next few years, the roller-coaster offshore oil business went into another steep decline. We did not owe any money and we still had a dozen valuable data packages to sell. I was elected the Geocubic President with no employees. My only job was to sell data we had already collected. Two of my ex-partners bought my share of *Glorita*. I was greatly relieved and could now consult on my own plus earning commissions by selling Geocubic programs. In the next few months, I sold over $500,000 worth of data.

I met with Doug Privitt and, on a handshake, we agreed to form a partnership to market and dive *Delta*. I would handle the marketing, run the business, and pilot the submersible. Doug would keep the submersible in top condition, build any equipment needed, and assist me at sea when I needed help. It would be a great partnership as neither of us was very good at what the other excelled in. We decided to call our partnership "Delta Oceanographics" and it prospered for the next twenty years.

HEALTH PROBLEMS struck both my wife and me in 1985. First, in February, Lois was found to have breast cancer and was given a maximum of eighteen months to live. She fought this terrible disease for fifteen years. Almost a month later, I was diagnosed with partially blocked arteries around my heart and underwent a quadruple by-pass. Interestingly, I had run in a half-marathon race a few months before my operation and I felt fine. I was in great shape, never sick and never smoked. The last time I had a physical was in the Army. My wife read about Jim Fixx, a well-known runner and author, who had recently died while running alone along a road. His family background was similar to mine so she thought I should be tested. I could stay on a treadmill for a long time because of my running background so the tests were inconclusive, but something did not seem right. When I told the doctors that my dad had died of a heart attack at thirty-five, and that I was going to be diving in the South Pacific in a few months, they decided to operate. After my surgery, the surgeon told me that the operation was probably not necessary, as running had strengthened and enlarged capillaries near my heart and had formed my own supplemental by-pass system.

Sadly, my ICU roommate, a local rancher, died less than a year later. He had contacted HIV from a blood transfusion during his by-pass operation, which was on the same day and in the same operating room as mine. Another escape for me; I was not sure how many lives I had left.

[Note: I had another quadruple bypass in 2014;
coronary arteries around my heart had clogged up
but my supplemental by-pass was still working fine]

DOUG AND I DOVE in the Long Beach Harbor a few months after my operation to see if I could dive in *Delta* with a very sore chest. The doctors did not want me going to Enewetak but I had a quick recovery and they finally relented.

Doug and I flew to Enewetak in June 1985 to help fill in the gaps left from our 1984 efforts. This time we shipped *Delta* to Enewetak on *Egabrag II* and then mobilized it aboard a drilling ship that was being used to collect cores beneath the craters for the USGS. Diving off this large ship was very difficult; *Delta*'s location on the deck was high off the water making launch and recovery complicated. Also, the drilling mud was continually pouring overboard precisely where *Delta* was launched and recovered. *Delta* was often covered with mud when it finally got back aboard. I could not lift the sub hatch without a lot of pain so someone had to lock me in and then unlock the hatch so I could climb out. The lagoon diving was okay but my chest ached. I made two dives to 1,200 feet on the steep slope outside of the atoll with Bob Halley of the USGS (nearly a vertical wall in places). That was spectacular diving. We made fifty-five dives in fifteen days and then packed up to go home. Gene Shin and his crew arrived ready to drill and dive with us. They were surprised to see us leaving on the same plane they had just arrived on. We only had time to say hello and goodbye.

We finally calculated the original size of the bomb craters. Two discoveries that helped were; (1) roads were built out to most bombsites from nearby islands, and (2) the explosions were photographed through pipes leading directly to ground zero. I knew I was at the crater edge when I found the end of a road, cable or a pipe. Most of the roads, cables, camera pipes and support beams were instantly vaporized by the blast so finding where they still existed gave us the actual size of the original crater. Even the military observers understood that. Koa crater overlapped Mike crater, which complicated things, but Oak was easy to figure out, as it was isolated.

Drilling vessel in Enewetak Lagoon

A needed assist   *Line of sight tube on rails to bomb (1950's)*
                        (Nuclear Defense Agency photo)

Remnants of line of sight (LOS) rails and cable leading to blast site

The U.S. Congress was no longer interested in our results by the time we had finished the USGS Enewetak PEACE project and written our reports. The missile silo debate faded away when the nation turned to missile bearing nuclear submarines for protection.

Delta *on crater floor*   *Doug and I on Bikini air strip*

Doug and I flew over to nearby Bikini hoping to make a dive there but those few Enewetak dives were the only ones I made in 1985. However I was busy that year on other projects and marketing *Delta* for future work. I also traveled to many oil company headquarters marketing GeoCubic data packages. The first sell was always the hardest. Once a company bought a report, then other companies would buy so no one would have a lease bidding edge. I eventually sold another $600,000 worth of surveys to thirteen different oil companies.

Chapter Thirteen

California & Nuclear Plants

From birth, man carries the weight of gravity on his shoulders.
He is bolted to the earth. But man has only to sink beneath the
surface and he is free.

—Jacques-Yves Cousteau, *Time Magazine* (1960)

I WORKED ON several projects during the 1980s that did
not include diving with *Delta*. In 1985, I was hired to conduct
research and write a report on offshore Southern California
geology for the MMS (Minerals Management Service). MMS
protects the OCS (Outer Continental Shelf) from any adverse
effect of offshore drilling and other minerals-related activities.
For this project, I had two partners; one examined all known
shipwreck data and the other searched for potential offshore
archaeological sites. My job was to gather all known geological
and geophysical data from offshore Southern California and to
construct detailed sediment isopach (thickness) maps. Our
report helped MMS determine which areas in the future would
require archaeological resource statements prior to any mineral
exploration or development. I constructed six large detailed
isopach maps showing rock outcrops and the thickness of all
unconsolidated sediment, mainly sand and gravel, overlying
bedrock for the entire Southern California continental shelf.
This was a massive project. It took over three years to gather
and merge the geological, drilling, and geophysical data known
from the shelf that extends from the Mexican border to just
north of Point Conception and up to 50 miles offshore.

When the project was nearly completed, I visited my former USC professor with my maps and data. I carried the maps in a large mailing tube and when leaving the campus, I set the tube against the side of my car so I could open the trunk to store the large pile of data I was carrying. When I arrived home an hour later the tube with my hand drawn maps was missing. I panicked—they were my only copies—and I immediately drove back to Los Angeles and started searching. I walked up and down the streets surrounding the USC campus but it was gone. Finally, when I was climbing back into my car to return home, I saw the top of my mailing tube sticking out of a large hedge that bordered the sidewalk. Someone must have picked up the tube, decided it was worthless, and threw it into the hedge. I was greatly relieved.

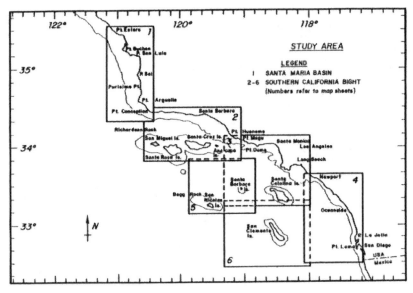

Index map for MMS sediment thickness (isopach) maps (Slater, 1987)

During the last ice age, 30,000 to 18,000 years ago, falling sea level caused the erosion of the exposed continental shelves. The lowest sea level reached was about 400 feet below today's sea surface. That is the depth of continental shelf breaks where most submarine canyon heads are located, the depth of most guyot flat tops and the base of coral reef walls. Since 18,000 years ago, the earth's climate has been generally warming, the ice sheets have been melting, and sea level has risen slowly, with minor fluctuations, until it has reached the present day shore. It will continue to rise or fall until all the earths' ice is melted or another ice age arrives.

Sediment, mainly from eroded sea cliffs and local rivers, was deposited over the Southern California continental shelf when it was exposed so it is now covered with a mixture of silt, sand, and gravel. This sediment probably covers any early man sites beyond our present shoreline. Knowing where rock is exposed, or thinly covered with sediment, gives MMS a high probability of finding possible exposed archaeological sites. We listed nearly 1,800 possible underwater archaeological sites and over 900 known shipwreck locations. Our 800-page report is classified so no one can disturb these sites.

IN 1988, I WAS involved in nearshore geological studies for California's two nuclear power plants, San Onofre* and Diablo Canyon. I clashed with environmental activists during these studies with some strange results.

Soon after the San Onofre Nuclear Plant was completed in 1974, the Marine Review Committee of the California Coastal Commission ordered Southern California Edison to fund a fourteen-year, $46 million, marine-life study off San Onofre, primarily by biological consultants from San Diego. These biologists discovered very few problems until their contract ended fourteen years later, when they asked Edison for an extension but were turned down. Their final report, issued in 1988 found, among other things, that sediment stirred up by

*The San Onofre Nuclear Generating Station is a nuclear power plant located on the beach at the northwest corner of San Diego County. Southern California Edison started construction in 1969 and operated the plant. Two more units were added in 1982 for a total building cost of around $550 million. For many years it provided nearly twenty percent of the electrical power to Southern California residents. The Station was permanently closed by Edison in 2013.

the plant cooling system blocked sunlight in the nearby San Onofre kelp beds. This retarded kelp growth by about two-thirds and caused a black ooze to appear on the seafloor, around the kelp beds, that they said could be harmful to the marine environment.

San Onofre Nuclear Plant (Southern California Edison photo)

I was part of a team hired by Edison to check the consultants' report. My job was to scuba dive, collect bottom sediment samples, and map the area offshore of the nuclear plant. A good friend, and former USC student, would analyze these samples and together we would issue a final report. A coalition of activists (many who had fought against the construction of the plant) went to court to stop Edison from further damaging the environment after the biological report was issued. Some of these activists had predicted earlier that the station's cooling system would create an ocean desert. They were wrong.

The cooling system used two large pipes. One took in ocean water to cool the reactors and the other returned it to the ocean. A million gallons of seawater were pumped through the plant every minute. The intake and diffuser ends of the two pipelines were located a few hundred yards offshore. I could not feel the warmth of returning water more than a few feet away from the diffusers. A mesh screen covering the mouth of the intake pipe keeps out everything but microscopic debris and organisms. Marine life and sediments around the distal ends of the cooling system pipes offshore were similar to that found up and down the coast.

We located all known data on the historical aerial extent of the San Onofre kelp bed and two other nearby kelp beds. The Marine Review Committee's biological report had mentioned a steady decline in kelp, and by limiting their data to the period from 1982 to 1988, they were correct. We used hundreds of aerial photographs plus data from a Cal Tech professor, to discover that all kelp beds off Southern California experienced cyclical patterns and 1982 to 1988 was a time of reduced kelp. However, a few years before, the kelp bed thrived off San Onofre and it had been spreading out again since the middle of 1988. Other nearby kelp beds followed the same pattern. Two of the San Onofre power generating units did not exist in 1977, when the kelp density off San Onofre and other nearby kelp forests declined to practically zero. In our preliminary report concerning the kelp beds, we concluded:

> To assume that a similar decline around 1984 is attributable only to the power generating plant simply because it was there at that time is a perversion of the data—in fact, it is a flagrant abuse of science.

I collected sediment cores in and around the kelp beds by pushing and sometimes hammering two-inch plastic pipes into the seafloor. The sticky "black ooze," now called the "black mayonnaise," which biologists suggested had resulted from the breakdown of kelp killed by the nuclear plant cooling system, was never found. The Marine Review Committee reported that this "weird" cohesive sediment cover was a grave danger to kelp forest biota. Their description of this black sediment came from visual observations by the diving biologists. Our laboratory analyses proved that the sediment around the San Onofre kelp bed was similar to sediment found around other

Southern California kelp beds, was not cohesive, and even had a lower organic content than most nearby areas. The only black sediment found was near the bottom of several cores and it was composed of dark minerals weathered from nearby rock outcrops. The biologists had stated that the kelp beds were being smothered by very fine sediment stirred up by the Nuclear Plants cooling system. I found no evidence of this. We age-dated several cores to confirm the sediment settling rates off San Onofre were similar to those we found elsewhere along the California coast. The rates of sediment accumulation stated in the Marine Review Committee's report were greater than the rates off the Amazon River! I asked the biologists who discovered the black ooze to show me exactly where this phenomenon was observed. During a full day of diving they could not point out any black ooze while claiming it was still there. Our report stated:

> Thus, we can only conclude, unfortunately, that the motif in the Marine Review Committee reports was not one of providing an objective interpretation derived from a solid base of facts. Instead, it embodies a series of inconsistent arguments used whenever or wherever it is convenient to justify the overall goal of trying to implicate the local power plant as a detriment to the marine environment offshore of San Onofre. It is embarrassing to see such machinations under any condition but to think that they were formulated under the aegis of a state governmental agency is particularly repugnant.
>
> All of the evidence from an extensive investigation of the shelf domain off the San Onofre Plant indicates that natural conditions dominate sedimentologic processes in that area. There are no indications that the power plant has altered those processes and we were unable to verify one assertion or speculation outlined in the Marine Review Committee reports. Moreover, the evidence shows that a considerable portion of the conclusions, assertions, and speculations in those documents are erroneous. In the final analysis, one might wonder how such a situation developed. Perhaps

there are many reasons, but one condition appears to be a fundamental factor. A group of investigators with poor qualifications in sedimentology persisted in working on a problem that bewildered them. The inherent problems that presumably were not corrected because these investigators were working under the supervision of a political appointee with no evident background in marine science.

We gave testimony at several environmental hearings and left with the feeling that we had nailed the case shut. However, a year later, I read in the Los Angeles Times that Southern California Edison admitted their guilt and they agreed to keep paying the biologists that had tried to pin the environmental damages on them. They also agreed to construct a 150-acre artificial reef, help restore kelp beds, and to protect several wetlands along the Southern California coast. Activists cheered the report and immediately went to court to force Edison to pay for damages they had caused. The statewide director of the Sierra Club called the plant "the most destructive marine industrial facility ever built." This statement astonished me and I could not keep from wondering how many dives he had made off the San Onofre plant.

[Note: A May 8, 2011 front-page article in the Sunday Los Angeles Times described how kelp forests, found off the San Onofre Nuclear Plant, during the 1990s and early 2000s experienced the greatest resurgence of giant kelp growth since the 1950s. In 2011 it was one the two largest kelp beds found along the Southern California coast.]

I called my contact with Edison and was amazed when he told me that the $400 million settlement was the easy way out. If they admitted their guilt and kept paying their consulting marine biologists, they could continue to operate their nuclear facility. He added, "Anyone that reads a newspaper or watches TV news thought we were guilty anyway."

A year later, in 1989, I was involved with a similar project concerning the Diablo Canyon Nuclear Plant located about 200 miles northwest of Los Angeles. This time a consulting group from San Francisco hired me. Diablo Canyon is owned and managed by Northern California's PG&E (Pacific Gas & Electric). A group of environmental activists were trying to shut down the nuclear plant because they thought it was sitting on an active earthquake fault (in 2014 they were going to court again for the same reason). My job was to map the area off the Plant and several miles down the coast. First, I checked the cooling system's pipelines; and discovered similar sediments and marine life around the seaward ends of the pipes that I had found off San Onofre. Then, I spent several weeks diving on every nearby underwater rock outcrop taking samples and mapping the strike and dip of each bed. I gave all the samples and my map to the consulting company and they incorporated my data into their report, which also featured cores from holes they drilled onshore. Our work proved that the plant was not on an active fault and PG&E was allowed to continue running their facility.

Diving off Diablo Canyon with sextant for navigation

Chapter Fourteen

New England & New York

There are only two great wildernesses left: outer space and the deep ocean. Space is a dusty void full of the wreckage of defunct satellites. We justify the expense of escaping from gravity by claiming we are heading for the stars, but really we are only peering at lifeless planets. Only one percent of the ocean has been explored and its dark floor twinkles with just as many stars as the heavens, but all of these are luminescent winks of unknown creatures of wondrous design and mysterious behavior. You can keep the dead expanse above our heads, given a choice of which stars to explore, I would go down to the living illuminations beneath the sea. Who knows what aliens await discovery?

—Trevor Norton, *Underwater to Get Out of the Rain* (2004)

THE TWELVE YEARS from 1986 through 1997 were the golden years for *Delta* diving. *Delta* made nearly 4,000 dives during that time with a record 550 dives in 1991. Doug was hard at work in his shop and I needed help at sea. David, now a teacher living near Seattle, was hired to assist me in the summer of 1986. A few years later, he was working full time. By 1995, David and other employees were carrying most of the at sea workload. I cut back diving and managing at-sea operations, while taking care of *Delta* business. However, from 1986 to 1997 I was extremely busy diving on *Delta* projects.

Dick Cooper, my old diving buddy, came out to Southern California from Connecticut in April 1986 with several other scientists to check out *Delta*. We must have impressed them as we received a contract for six weeks of work starting in May.

NOAA designated the University of Connecticut as their Marine Center for New England and Dick was hired from Woods Hole NMF to manage that office. NOAA's primary goals were to fund diving research to help manage a three-billion-dollar New England fishery, to study environmental concerns, and to map sea floor geology around New England. In 1986, Dick received forty-nine proposals from scientists for support off New England and funded thirty-five. *Delta* was chosen for the four manned submersible projects. I chartered the *Atlantic Twin* in New Jersey, this time with a better crane, to support us. An employee and I drove a rental truck, with *Delta,* to New Jersey and mobilized the ship. Every time we stopped for gas or a meal, we were surrounded by inquisitive faces asking what that yellow machine was for. "Treasure hunting" I would usually say and they went away happy.

We finally got rid of the tethered red ball we had towed for years when we purchased a new electronic tracking system in 1986. This unit, a Trackpoint II, had a video screen similar to a radar screen that displayed both the direction and distance the submersible was located from the support ship at all times. *Delta* now carried a transponder* that sent out rapid signals to a large transducer hanging from the support ship. The new Trackpoint II made diving much safer and navigation more accurate. We eventually added GPS (Global Positing Service) to our navigation system. GPS and Trackpoint II data were entered into our shipboard computer allowing us to save the exact location, latitude, longitude, and depth of *Delta* on the seafloor every few seconds. We plotted each submersible track with the time of every navigation fix and the location of every photograph and sample collected on a seafloor map.

---

*A transponder sends out a signal in response to a signal it has received. A pinger emits a timed signal at a set frequency. The Trackpoint II could receive multiple signals using different frequencies. This allowed us to place a pinger at a work site and later redirect *Delta,* with its transponder, back to that site using our Trackpoint II navigation system.

Trackpoint II ad with Delta

Shipboard navigation center for Delta
(Trackpoint II next to TV monitor)

OUR FIRST NEW ENGLAND project, in 1986, was a sand wave study in Long Island Sound for scientists from Boston University. This was an area of shallow water with very swift tidal currents resulting in poor visibility and tricky diving. On one dive, I could hear the steady beat of a large propeller as it drew closer. I finally called the *Atlantic Twin* and asked if there was a large ship in the area. The answer was, "Yes, it is the *QE II*." After a few seconds, I asked what the draft was on that large ocean liner, as we were diving in very shallow water. The *QE II* sounded like it was right on top of us. I visualized a large propeller coming straight at me, but it was at least a quarter of a mile away.

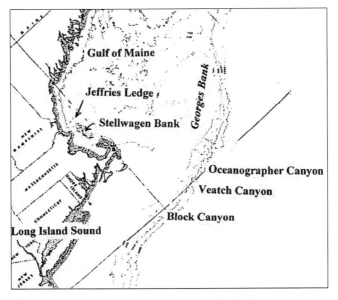

Delta *dive areas, New England*

We then traveled east to the Block Submarine Canyon, south of Rhode Island, for dives with Woods Hole USGS geologists. We searched for tilefish and mapped the distribution of their burrows located on the outer edge of the continental shelf. Some of the burrows were up to six feet across. These large beautiful turquoise fish can weigh up to fifty pounds and some were nearly six feet long. Unfortunately for them, they are very good to eat. As we moved along the continental shelf edge, we would occasionally observe a tilefish resting on the seafloor ahead of us. When *Delta* came within twenty feet, the fish would suddenly dive into its burrow leaving behind a large cloud of sediment. Tilefish locations were leaked to the local fishing fleet and the fish were nearly exterminated over the next few years. I rarely saw a large tilefish in the 1990s where they were common in 1986.

Diving under QE II

5' tilefish entering burrow, 690'

Scientists and Delta *crew, Long Island Sound*
(David on far left, I am in front, Doug is behind me)

Next was a stop at one of my favorite ports of call, Woods Hole, on Cape Cod. Visiting old friends, restaurants, and the aquarium made a port day there always enjoyable, although we were busy working during most port days. One scientific party would be collecting their gear and samples to disembark, while another excited group would be coming aboard with their equipment to be mobilized. I usually gave the *Delta* crew the afternoon off to enjoy some shore time.

We sailed into the Gulf of Maine to study the effects of "ghost" gill nets on marine life at Stellwagen Bank and Jeffries Ledge. Conflict between gill net fishermen and recreational fishermen had recently intensified off New England. New and improved gear for bottom draggers (commercial fishermen that drag a large net over the seafloor) forced the gill-netters (fishermen that set nets along the seafloor to catch passing fish) to move into less productive fishing areas where they conflicted with recreational fishermen. Many gill nets were lost when they became tangled in rocks and others were torn apart by bottom draggers and storms. Nets deserted or lost on the seafloor are called "ghost" nets. Many continue to trap and kill fish, crab, and lobster.

Dead shark in a "ghost" gill net   *Knife on* Delta *for cutting nets*

Our job was to figure out ghost net longevity, fishing potential and their effectiveness in capturing crustaceans and fish. We found that they were very effective over a long time. It was difficult to see monofilament nets underwater and occasionally I would run right into one with the potential to entangle us. There were a few close calls but we always managed to escape. New England gillnets usually ranged in length from a few hundred to several thousand feet in length and up to forty feet high. They were connected to the seafloor with weights and were hanging from small floats attached along their upper edge. These nets were set to intercept fish that would be trapped by their gills when they swam into the net. The size of the mesh depended on what they were fishing for. Small fish swam right through the nets while large fish and whales often destroyed them. We photographed and plotted many "ghost" net locations, and planned to return over the next few years for further observations.

Our next stop was Provincetown, a small village located near the far tip of Cape Cod, the home base of many artists and eccentrics. We took several local newspaper reporters to sea while we observed the local lobster population. My crew had never seen a place like "P-town"—everyone had an interesting time ashore. One employee brought a girl back to the ship and when I checked *Delta* that evening, I discovered them inside in a compromising position, much to their embarrassment. We docked the *Atlantic Twin* at the Provincetown Coast Guard dock, (we were on government-funded projects). For the next ten years, we often used excellent Coast Guard docks around the United States, including Alaska, during many of our port days. We often tied up at the Coast Guard Academy dock in Groton, Connecticut. Once, when we arrived late at night, we put our trash bags on the dock planning to get rid of them in the morning. Seagulls pounced on the bags spreading trash all over the adjoining field where graduation was to take place in a few hours. The Coast Guard officers were not happy.

A group of biologists from the University of Rhode Island came on board in Provincetown to search for local migrating right whales. They hired a small airplane to spot whales and when they located one, we would rush to the area, a scientist would throw a Frisbee onto the whale (for scale), and then we would dive. It is very difficult to approach a whale underwater. They like to keep their distance and it was daunting being close to something moving that was much larger than we were. Usually, all I saw was a large dark moving shadow. The singing from whales blasted over *Delta's* UQC speaker making it difficult to communicate with the *Atlantic Twin*. The chief scientist told me that whales had different accents and he could tell which ones came up from Puerto Rico from those that stayed in the north Atlantic. Dolphins chatter while most whales wail. When both were nearby, it sounded like a large orchestra playing loudly off key.

We studied whales during twenty-two day and night dives between Cape Cod and Georges Bank. *Delta* was not the proper tool for chasing whales and I never made another dive to study whales. However, *Delta* was great for collecting and photographing plankton and to determine the distribution and abundance of zooplankton—whale food. We used a suction pump to sample water and zooplankton at different depths around the clock, which meant we dove day and night. Night dives were interesting. From the ship you could see a ball of bright green light deep in the water that grew bigger and brighter as the submersible neared the surface. I always turned all of the submersible lights on when surfacing at night to entertain everyone on the support vessel.

After chasing whales, we traveled to Boothbay Harbor, Maine. This was the first of many port days in Boothbay. It is a delightful spot and I always enjoyed a visit. It is the only place I ever ate lobster pizza. Geologists from the University of Maine joined us for a week in the Gulf of Maine, collecting rock samples and mapping the seafloor geology. We placed sediment traps on the seafloor to measure sediment settlement rates down to a depth of 800 feet and planned to collect the traps the next summer. I enjoyed working with geologists—we spoke the same language and I usually knew exactly what they needed during a dive.

On the last leg of the 1986 New England cruise, still in the Gulf of Maine, we worked on several scallop projects. We dove on Stellwagen Bank to collect scallops and to map their distribution. Scallops normally lie on the sea floor but they are capable of swimming up into the water column for short bursts by quickly opening and closing their shells. When *Delta* cruised by they would scatter, many crashing into the sub and several flying over us. Sometimes there were so many in the water, it looked like we were surrounded by butterflies. On several dives, we filled the sample bag with dozens of scallops, some as large as ten inches across. We would eat them raw or they ended up in the galley for dinner after scientists were through analyzing them.

Sediment traps   *Bagged scallops caught with* Delta

Several very shallow dives near Boothbay Harbor checking lobster trap lines were next on our agenda. Nearly everyone in Maine sets traps for lobster and their surface buoys can be so close together it is difficult to maneuver through them. It is a colorful scene; everyone has his or her own buoy designs.

Diving nearshore off Maine   *Working in the rain*

DOUG REFURBISHED *Delta* during our 1986-87 winter break—it looked great with a shiny new coat of yellow paint. The color Doug chose was school bus yellow, which made submersibles easier to locate on the ocean surface. Doug was painting his submersibles yellow before the Beatles wrote their song. Interestingly, Tasmanian lobster fisherman used black flags and buoys so they could spot them against the horizon; colored flags blend into the sea or sky.

1987 was another busy year, starting in early May off South Carolina and finishing in the Bahamas in late October. We made nearly 400 dives in seventy-nine dive days without a day lost due to weather or equipment failure. We needed a larger support vessel for our 1987 work on the East Coast so I leased the *R/V J.W. Powell,* a 150-foot oil field supply ship, out of Louisiana. We rented a mobile crane, to launch and recover *Delta,* and secured it on the deck of the *J.W. Powell. Delta* was mobilized at West Palm Beach, Florida, before we headed to South Carolina. The Carolina project was for the Smithsonian and Harbor Branch Institutes (owners of the *Johnston Sea-Link* submersibles). Smithsonian scientists wanted slit-shells for their aquarium in Washington, D.C. In three days of diving, as deep as 1,200 feet, we picked up ninety slit-shells along the upper continental slope. We probably wrecked the shell collectors market for slit-shells.

R/V J.W. Powell

Next, we mapped the offshore clam population along the New Jersey continental shelf. We worked alongside clam boats to observe how efficient their fishing techniques were—they were very efficient. This was shallow diving in murky water, not a lot of fun. On one dive, I was asked to retrieve a fish trap in 140 feet of water that had been placed earlier by lowering it from the surface. It was positioned near a large shipwreck (for protection from trawlers) thirty-five miles off New Jersey. The wreck was the *M/T Varanger*, a 469 foot Norwegian oil tanker* torpedoed by a German U-boat in late January 1942. There are over 4,000 shipwrecks off New Jersey but the chance of running across one is almost zero. In all my years of diving, I never came across a shipwreck that I was not searching for.

Delta was inching along on the seafloor in very low visibility when suddenly my observer spotted his fish trap. I moved the submersible over and he grabbed his trap with the arm. I then decided to go straight up to the surface because I could see that it was all clear above me and I did not want to become entangled in the wreck. The visibility started clearing as the submersible lifted off the seafloor and I suddenly realized we were passing through the middle of the ship. We narrowly squeezed through a large hatch, and then went by the *Varinger* wheelhouse as *Delta* continued to head for the surface. We had unknowingly entered into the bowels of the wreck through the large crack where it had been torpedoed.

We then moved north to continue our sand wave studies in Long Island Sound. The *QE II* was not passing by this time but we still had poor visibility and strong currents making the dives difficult. Moving farther east, Dick Cooper brought out a group of scientists to see what *Delta* was capable of. They observed many lobsters on the continental shelf south of Rhode Island. Shelf lobsters dig shallow depressions in the soft sediment and hunker down to hide from predators. I

---

*The *Varanger* was one of the first, but over 171 merchant ships were torpedoed and sunk by U-boats in the next five months between New York and Florida.

could usually drive right up to one and grab it with *Delta's* arm. These lobsters migrate every spring from the outer continental shelf into the warmer shallow coastal waters and then return to deep cooler waters during the fall.

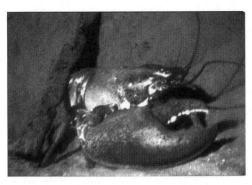

Lobster in depression, ≈180'

DELTA HAD ALREADY made 100 dives on NURP's* 1987 schedule and it was only the end of May. Our new suction sampler proved to be a valuable tool for collecting sediment and biological samples. Doug's innovative collection box could hold four different samples from each dive. The Mystic and Boston aquariums used the suction sampler and Doug's collection box to gather specimens for their displays.

For six days, we studied right-whale food for University of Rhode Island scientists. This time we concentrated on all types of zooplankton through several twenty-four-hour periods. Many zooplankton are bioluminescent and emit a green glow when agitated, making night dives quite spectacular. We often left a long bright green glowing cloud trailing behind *Delta*. Plankton rise up near the ocean surface at night to feed when predators have difficulty seeing them. By morning, they are back in deep water or on the seafloor for protection during the day. We filtered a known amount of seawater at different

---

*NURP was the National Undersea Research Program under NOAA. It was a new name for the old MUST (Manned Undersea Science and Technology) office. This office was in charge of all federal diving programs. NURP was zeroed out for fiscal year 2013 funding and no longer exists.

depths to collect plankton every few hours. A special camera was mounted on *Delta* to take mid-water plankton photos.

Rigged for plankton photography   *Suction collection box*

After a port day in Booth Bay Harbor, we visited Ammen Rock, a large seafloor outcrop in the Gulf of Maine. I dove many times over several years on this undersea mountain and knew my way around it like the back of my hand. This year, we took several biologists diving from the University of Maine, to set up long-term experiments. We also dove around nearby Mohegan Island, located about ten miles off the coast of Maine, where we went ashore to observe many types of sea birds including puffins. One early morning, while waiting for the fog to lift so we could dive, I heard a voice and suddenly a kayak appeared nearby. The kayaker asked which way was land and we pointed him in the right direction. He must have been at least thirty miles offshore with no compass. We made 143 scientific dives in forty-six dive days around the Gulf of Maine. A personal highlight was my submersible dive #1,000 with Dick Cooper as observer. It was also *Delta*'s dive #600. We continued diving around the Gulf of Maine for many years and became very familiar with the local geology and marine animals. The New England scientists were some of the most enthusiastic and fun people to be with at sea—I have lots of great memories.

With Dick Cooper and Doug after my #1,000 submersible dive

BEFORE WE MOVED south, there was a NOAA open house for *Johnston Sea-Link* and *Delta*. Both submersibles and their support ships were docked at the Submarine Memorial Dock in Groton, Connecticut, next to the Nuclear Submarine facility. *Delta* looked very small next to her big brother Navy submarines. The *Johnson Sea-Link* was left suspended from its A-frame while *Delta* was used on all demonstration dives as we could launch and retrieve a submersible much quicker than they could. We had a big crowd that included Senator, and later governor, Lowell Weicker, a strong backer of NURP programs. Senator Weicker asked me if I would be interested in bringing *Delta* down to Cuba for a dive with Fidel Castro. The U.S. government was not communicating with the Cuban government in 1987, and Weicker thought he was the man who could bring the two countries together for talks. I could not travel to Cuba and the Cuban representatives, who were trying to put this program together, could not travel to the United States. We ended up having meetings in the Bahamas and Mexico City during the winter and everything was looking good for a series of dives around the Isle of Pines off the southern Cuban coast. I only asked that Castro not smoke his cigar in the submersible. Near the end of the 1988 summer, just before we were to leave for Cuba, a couple of Weicker's aides requested he cancel the trip. His re-election that fall was going to be close and the trip could cost him votes. The trip was cancelled and Weicker lost the November election anyway to Joe Lieberman. This was my third disappointment involving Senator Lowell Weicker. Earlier, when I was an aquanaut in the Bahamas, I was to dive down the "wall" in the front sphere of the *Johnson Sea-Link* to select my lockout site. At the last moment Weicker, who showed up unexpectedly, bumped me and I rode in the back sphere with its limited visibility. The other disappointment was when Weicker told us he was going to bring out Vice-president George Bush for a dive off Maine, but fog kept their helicopter on the ground and we went ahead and dove without them.

On the way south for our next project, in Long Island Sound, we took a shortcut through the Cape Cod Canal that separates Cape Cod from the mainland. We sailed through at night and I was awakened from a deep sleep by a loud crash when the *J.W. Powell* took a wrong turn and entered a local yacht harbor at full speed. Luckily, we hit a large pylon before we could plow into several very expensive looking yachts. This accident damaged our over-the-side navigation transducer and scraped paint off the side of the ship, but no one was injured. There were, however, a few red faces up on the bridge.

The EPA (Environmental Protection Agency) hired us for an environmental project off New York City in 1987. For over 100 years the continental shelf off New York City was used for ocean disposal of various city wastes, including building materials and sewage sludge. Waste building materials had raised the seafloor over thirty feet at one near-shore dumpsite. Since 1924, New York City had used a site twelve miles from shore to dump treated sewage sludge. Environmentalists were campaigning to move this dumpsite further offshore during the time when the city was nearly broke and could not afford the extra barges and ship time. Some New York City waste was being shipped to other states, and even to a country in Africa that was paid to accept it.

Rumors abounded that the twelve-mile dumpsite seafloor was covered with black organic ooze (the "black mayonnaise" again) and, as it piled up from further dumping, this ooze was moving toward beaches along Long Island and New Jersey. Jacques Cousteau was seen on local television with black ooze dripping from his hands. (Later, I discovered he was up the Hudson River off a sewage outfall.) Our EPA project was to map the extent of this black silty ooze around the dumpsite.

New York City's fourteen sewage treatment plants were dumping about four million tons of wet sludge annually at the twelve-mile offshore site. A local newspaper editorial cartoon highlighted the black ooze as a wave chasing sunbathers up the beach. Rumors of black ooze on beaches were common even though there was no evidence of the ooze ever reaching any shore. Several nearby beach communities publicized that the water was the cleanest it had been for years—but people did not listen. Tourist facilities were losing millions of dollars.

We arrived over the dump site and I was the pilot on the first dive. As *Delta* settled on the seafloor, I was surprised to see white sand, starfish, and other common continental shelf animals. We continued to dive for several days and never found any black ooze. We also could not find any ooze along the shoreline or on the beaches. The EPA scientists working with us wrote in their report that the sludge dumping did not disturb the seafloor and did not seem to have any impact on nearby human health. What happened to the sludge? Sand covered seafloors are found in high-energy zones whereas mud occupies low energy areas—this dumpsite was definitely in a high-energy zone. The dumped treated sewage was about ninety-seven percent water and the Gulf Stream diluted the sludge even more. This fast moving current also moved the diluted sludge out to sea before it ever reached the seafloor.

Three months later, the EPA ordered New York City to move their dumpsite 106 miles offshore to an area on the slope around 6,000 feet deep. Individual sewage charges were raised about $13 per year for New York residents and the city had to buy new barges and tugs. I called the EPA and talked to one of the scientists that had accompanied us on our dumpsite dives. I asked, "What happened? I thought we proved that the sludge dumpsite wasn't really a problem." He then replied that the final decision was strictly political. A Congressman from Long Island had blocked the release of our report because he felt that the public would probably think the government was involved in a cover-up (this was only a few years after Watergate). It seemed to be politically advantageous just to move the dumpsite, and then everyone would think the government had fixed the problem even though, as we had proved, there was no problem to start with.

Lobster depression in clam bed, 175', New Jersey

After working off New York, we dove off New Jersey for a week while following a clam fishing boat around and again found it to be very efficient. They used GPS for navigation and a huge vacuum pump and hose to suck up the sandy overburden along with the live clams. They shucked the clams at sea and threw the empty shells overboard. The seafloor was covered with discarded clamshells.

My son David made his first dive as pilot in August 1987 off New Jersey. I started a training program so he would be able to pilot *Delta* full-time by the next summer. Doug wanted to spend more time in his shop so I needed another pilot. I also needed a third person to assist us, as our dive operations were becoming much more sophisticated. Over the next few years, I hired several young men who had recently graduated from a local college marine technical program, and eventually had good luck with two employees. Four people were needed on deck, plus the crane operator, to help us launch and retrieve *Delta*. David and I started alternating piloting and running our navigation/communication center on the support ship bridge. This meant the two of us were working during every dive. A third person gave us a little relief with navigation duties plus assisting us on deck.

IN 1988, WE TRAVELED back to Atlantic City to continue our research projects from 1987. We dove on the remains of a Texas Tower—once an offshore platform located near the edge of the continental shelf. It had totally collapsed during a hurricane in 1961, with a loss of twenty-eight men. This Tower was originally an Air Force early warning radar platform and once looked like a three-deck offshore drilling rig, except for the three large radar domes on top. The bottom deck of the tower stood sixty feet above the sea. In 1988, it was a tangled jumble lying in 180 feet of water sixty miles off New Jersey. Diving was difficult with strong currents and lots of tangled fishing lines and nets. Biologists wanted to observe how many and what kinds of fish were using the ruins. There were a lot of fish but we could not get very close because of the lines and nets.

We sailed up to Stellwagen Bank off Massachusetts for a series of High School Aquanaut day trips. This was a chance for qualified students to participate in real undersea research around the Gulf of Maine. We completed fifty dives in five days including a record eighteen dives one day. The kids had a great time and they each captured a lobster or a few scallops. The plan was to expand this program but funding problems limited it to just two seasons.

From mid-June until mid-July, we dove around the Gulf of Maine and in the submarine canyons south of Georges Bank. These dives were for continuing projects from earlier years and we collected more data, photographs, and samples.

Next dives were made on the shallower section of the new 106-mile dumpsite off New York for the EPA. The results were the same as those at the twelve-mile site—no sewage on the seafloor. We again concluded that the sewage sludge rarely, if ever, fell to the seafloor and it did not drift to the inner shelf or seashore. Animals residing nearby on the continental shelf and slope, even those living directly under the dumpsite, showed no evidence of adverse impact from the sludge. There was very little current on the sea floor between 500 and 900 feet but there was a strong current in mid-water—the Gulf Stream. We even dove while they dumped sewage on top of us—none reached the seafloor but we carefully washed *Delta* after each dive. Dumping at this site was stopped in 1992. It was the same story; environmentalists saying that it continued to harm the environment even though several government reports, including ours, said otherwise.

IN 1990, I WAS BACK with Dick Cooper's scientific party for dives on Pigeon Hill off Gloucester, Massachusetts. We retrieved several experiments that we had left the year before and replaced them with some new ones. I needed to make travel arrangements for the rest of the year so David, for the first time, managed the next project. He and a newly trained pilot took High School aquanauts diving off Massachusetts before they moved up to Maine where I joined them again to investigate some strange seafloor craters. There are over 7,000 craters in Belfast Bay; one is 600 feet across and another one is over 100 feet deep. Their origin is unknown but escaping gas or fresh water seeps possibly formed them. No seeps or gas bubbles were observed but it was interesting diving.

Returning to Pigeon Hill, we spent a week trying to trap wolf fish. These ferocious looking fish can be up to five-feet long and weigh over forty pounds. They are sometimes called wolf eels, which is the common name for their Pacific cousins. The biologists constructed large traps that we placed in strategic places on the seafloor with *Delta*. We tried to stun wolf fish with poison we pumped out by reversing our suction gun. Sometimes we put the nozzle within a few inches of a wolf fish; the poison did not seem to faze them. Nothing worked but we got some great photographs. *Delta* made 176 dives along the East Coast during four weeks in August.

We had made nearly 1,000 dives in *Delta* off New England and I was sorry we could not continue there in the future. We had a lot work lined up along the West Coast and Alaska and it was difficult to dive off both coasts during the busy summer dive season. I was pilot on over 1,000 submersible dives in those five years including my 2,000th dive in 1991, with Dick Cooper as my observer. I ended up making more dives off New England than in any other area in the world during my career.

With Dick Cooper after my 2,000ᵗʰ dive   *Wolf fish trap on* Delta

Wolf fish off New England (photos by Peter Auster)

Chapter Fifteen

Florida & Bahamas

There comes a time in every boy's life when he has a raging
desire to go somewhere and dig for hidden treasure.

—Mark Twain, *The Adventures of Tom Sawyer* (1876)

IN THE SPRING of 1986, we trucked *Delta* and its support
systems to Miami for two weeks of diving. This study was a
cooperative effort between the Caribbean Marine Research
Center, the John Perry Foundation, the United States National
Park Service, and the United States Geological Survey. Most of
the work concerned fresh water seeps located seaward of the
Florida Key's living reefs. Geologists wanted to discover what
types of rocks formed in this environment and biologists
searched for seep effects on coral and fish distribution. We
used John Perry's sixty-five-foot private yacht, *Undersea Hunter,*
to support *Delta.* This was the same ship I was aboard many
years before, in the Bahamas, trying to film a TV documentary
on sharks. A total of forty-eight dives were made in ten days,
the shallowest (and the hottest) was thirty feet and the deepest
was over 1,000 feet. We surveyed over thirty-two miles of the
continental shelf east of Biscayne National Park.

An added benefit was discovering and mapping locations of
eighty-two "ghost" fish and lobster traps. All were abandoned
and twelve were still actively catching fish. Visibility was good
in this area known for clear water. On one dive, while sitting
on the seafloor at 270 feet, I looked up and could see the tiny
support ship moving along on the surface. We also dove on
sixteen wrecks, some old and some recently sunk in or near
the Park for the purpose of enhancing fish stocks and sports

fishing. All these shipwrecks, now called artificial reefs, were in depths of 100 to 400 feet. The newer wrecks, placed away from fresh water seeps, had extensive marine growths and supported lots of fish. Those located close to the seeps were virtually barren of life.

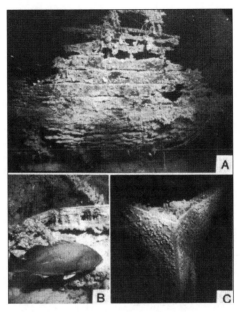

A. Wooden minesweeper, 190'   B. Large grouper on minesweeper, 190'
C. Bow of Liberty ship, 390'
Biscayne Bay National Park, Florida (Shinn and Wicklund, 1989)

WE LEFT FLORIDA for a short trip over to the Bahamas to meet Bob Ginsburg and his scientific team. The Bahamas are a collection of over 700 islands located just east of Florida. These were my first deep dives on Bahamian coral reefs and I would continue to dive there for many years. Most of our dives were along the walls of TOTO, "Tongue of the Ocean," a trench over 6,000 feet deep located in the center of the Bahamas. We made over forty dives in two weeks using the same sampling techniques, including dynamite, which worked so well in Belize and Jamaica. I was the pilot on most of the dives with Doug and David's support.

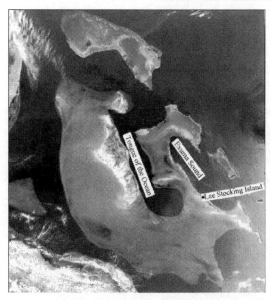

Satellite photo of the Bahamas

Our next destination was John Perry's Lee Stocking Island. The Caribbean Marine Research Center was located there and it would become the center of our Bahama dive operations over the next twelve years. Lee Stocking Island is a very small island on the east side of the Bahamas, and on the western edge of Exuma Sound, with a typical modern reef with a steep drop off. To the west, it is separated from TOTO by a twenty-mile wide shallow bar of coral sand and rock. The normal route to Lee Stocking from TOTO is around Nassau, to the north several hundred miles. We gambled and tried to shortcut across the shallow bar. Bad decision; we ran the *Undersea Hunter* aground and were stuck for nearly twenty-four hours!

Lee Stocking Island has a private airstrip but no facilities other than a few Research Center buildings and John Perry's private home. There was drug trafficking around the Bahamas during this time and bales of marijuana would occasionally wash up on island beaches. One night, a plane running low on fuel, and loaded with drugs, landed on the primitive Lee Stocking airstrip. Scientists held the pilot until the police from Exuma Island finally came over and arrested him.

There is a well-known blue-hole that divers enjoyed diving in on nearby Norman Island. Blue-holes are roughly circular, steep-walled vertical caves that look dark blue from the air against the lighter blue of the reef. Newly arrived divers to Lee Stocking were often taken to Norman Island for a spectacular blue-hole dive. A scientist brought a human skeleton he had "borrowed" from a University anatomy laboratory and hung the skeleton about fifty feet down in the blue-hole. It was hard to see on the way down but when returning to the surface, this skeleton was backlighted and startled anyone who did not know it was there. Several years later, a hurricane decimated Haiti and many bodies floated up on Bahamian shores. Police went around the islands in a small boat collecting bodies. When they landed on Norman Island, someone told them there was a body in the blue hole. They removed the skeleton and buried it in a common grave along with other bodies they collected. That was the end of the blue-hole skeleton diver.

Lee Stocking Island   *Looking up at blue-hole skeleton*
                               (photo by Bob Halley)

Ready to dive   *Algal stromatolites, 3 to 4 feet high*
Lee Stocking Island (Awramik, 2006)

A USC DIVING buddy of mine, Bob Dill, made an important geologic discovery when he found living algal stromatolites, up to six feet high, in a channel just north of Lee Stocking Island. There were dozens of these ovoid humps surrounded by loose sediment in the shallow tidal channel between islands. The scene looked like something out of prehistoric time. During my stay in Australia, I had traveled to Shark Bay in northern Western Australia to see newly discovered stromatolites. They were the first living stromatolites ever discovered; the Lee Stocking ones were only the second. Living algal and bacteria organisms bind sand particles together to build stromatolites. Mats of algae in tidal areas sometimes, under ideal conditions, form algal heads. Large stromatolites were common in ancient seas but very rare these days. I was fortunate to see the only two stromatolite areas that are known to exist today. A noted scientist wrote,

> These strange, dark humps on the floor of a Bahamian tidal channel are a kind of Loch Ness monster, survivors of an ancient age, hidden from view until their discovery in the early 1980s, and now offering scientists a glimpse into an ancient world that has been mostly erased from the face of the planet.

Lois's only submersible dive

Lois flew over to Nassau and came aboard the *Undersea Hunter* before we left for Lee Stocking. She was excited to be on John Perry's private yacht in the Bahamas, until she found out it was a workboat with typical smells, noises, and movements. We were accustomed to it but it was not to her liking. She was not impressed with our navigation either when we were stuck on the sandbar for a day after we took the shortcut. However, she did enjoy scuba diving around Lee Stocking and made her first, and only, *Delta* dive during her last day on the island. We descended down the "wall" and fore-reef slope to 1,000 feet. On returning toward the surface, I observed a strange dirty cloud in the water near the base of the "wall" at 400 feet and moved over to investigate. There were two turtles mating and paying no attention to us. Earlier, I had mentioned that Jacque Cousteau and his wife held the world record for having sex at a depth of several hundred feet. She was not interested in breaking the record as there was too much to see and do in the short time we were diving. She thought I was showing her the turtles to remind her that we could still set a world record. The turtles continued having a good time.

One of Gene Shinn's former assistants was working on Cousteau's ship *Calypso* in 1986 and wrote Gene the following note while we were diving in the Bahamas:

Thanks to you I'll now be able to judge other submersible operation against the *Delta* sub. The *Calypso* is still using that old, round saucer thing from about twenty-five years ago. It's rated to 2,000 meters and they spend hours and hours on the damn thing just for one dive. In anything other than pure flat calm seas, they can't do anything with it. They put a diver on top of the thing when lifting and putting the sub into the water and someone is going to be very badly hurt one of these days. Just putting the thing in the water takes about six people and a crane, and lifting the thing out takes another four. If Doug Privitt and Rich Slater would send me the specifications to their sub I could show it to Captain Cousteau.

Cousteau already knew about *Delta*. He was always very complimentary when asked about our operations.

EVEN THOUGH we were not spending much time off the East Coast now, we were still diving in the Caribbean and Florida during the winter. In 1987, we closely followed our 1986 Caribbean schedule, starting with dives on the wrecks and other artificial reefs off the Florida Keys with Gene Shinn and other USGS geologists. We then sailed over to Nassau on the R/V *J.W. Powell* and took government officials, including the British High Commissioner, for dives. We dove outside the Nassau harbor and were amazed to discover champagne bottles covering the seafloor. Cruise ships pass over this area and bottles had accumulated over many years.

We then traveled to TOTO with Bob Ginsburg and his group of scientists from the University of Miami. We had planned to continue down to Lee Stocking Island but a large hurricane quickly altered our plans, and we headed back to Florida losing out on two weeks of work. This unexpected break allowed me to travel during the early fall to market the last GeoCubic programs to oil companies. This was my last chance to sell these programs. In the next few years, almost all scheduled offshore lease auctions were cancelled.

Nassau Grouper, Bahamas

From left, Doug, Bob Ginsburg and me with University of Miami scientists

WE RETURNED to the Bahamas in 1988; this was the first year Doug did not accompany me on any *Delta* dive trip. He was now full time in his shop manufacturing new tools and parts for *Delta*. I trained another young man, Bob Wicklund Jr., and together with David, I now had two assistants to help me at sea. David and Bob both would pilot during busy days. After 1988, the three of us rotated the positions of pilot, navigator, and deck hand.

Fish biologists really wanted to observe the Nassau Grouper mating gathering during the full moon in early January 1988. Using the *J.W. Powell,* we headed to Lee Stocking Island on New Year's Day. One biologist on board was Pat Collin, the scientist stuck in the Jamaica cave with me in 1972.

We made sixty dives in three weeks including *Delta's* #1,000. The large grouper schools were fantastic. There were hundreds of large groupers swimming around during several dives that included an exciting spawning session late one night. Marine biologists caught several groupers, in large fish traps that we had placed on the seafloor, and placed them in salt-water-filled troughs on the *J.W. Powell*. Most fish can slowly adjust the air in their bladders so they can float at any given depth, similar to what we do with *Delta*. However, when you bring fish up quickly from depth, the air in their bladders expands rapidly due to the changes in pressure. A needle was used to extract the excess swim bladder air, enabling the fish to swim upright.

Sharks were very common in this area, including the largest fish in the world, a whale shark. Whale sharks are very slow moving and this one allowed *Delta* to move in very close. The other various species of sharks were there to feed on groupers that were old or injured during mating. It was a feeding frenzy, and we were right in the middle of it. It was especially exciting to see this during night dives.

Our last Bahamian dives were near Nassau searching for evidence of sea level changes. Chris Kendall, Bob Ginsburg, Bob Dill, and Gene Shinn, all old friends, were along for these dives. Bob Dill usually wore a Captain America wet suit and was an expert on submarine canyons. He once estimated the rate of sand moving down the Cabo San Lucas Submarine Canyon in Baja California by collecting beer-cans at different depths on the sloping canyon seafloor. Mexican fishermen and tourists fished over the head of the canyon and threw lots of beer cans overboard. Sand carried these cans as it crept down the canyon floor into deeper water. Bob identified the cans and the year of their manufacture. The old metal cans were in deepest water, then the old pop open cans, then aluminum cans, until finally the beer cans in shallowest water were the aluminum pop-top cans. There had been no sudden emptying of the canyon by a turbidity current for some time now so his technique worked well.

DELTA WAS LEFT in Florida and I returned to California for several months. Meanwhile, the *J.W. Powell* was used as a prop in a James Bond movie. One scene had Bond shooting the bad guys on the *J.W. Powell,* and then diving overboard to escape. The only problem; the actor playing Bond could not swim and he wanted to do the scene himself. It was hilarious to see several of our crewmembers diving overboard to save James Bond from drowning. This was my second connection with a James Bond movie, *Dr. No* was filmed by the Discovery Bay Research Laboratory in Jamaica. We were asked to be in several Bond movies being filmed in California, but there was always some reason it never worked out.

IN MAY 1989, we again returned to the Bahama Islands on board the University of Miami's *R/V Columbus Iselin* with Bob Ginsburg. He had been working on a very important problem concerning deep coral reefs. Bob wondered why the sides of present day atolls and coral reefs were so steep. Could it be erosional, sea cliffs formed at the time of low stands of sea level during the last ice age? Or could it be possible they were created by accretion with holes in the reef filled with marine cementation? Deep coral reefs can be divided into three zones that are similar around the world. The deep-reef slants about forty-five degrees from shallow water down to around 100 feet. It consists of a series of ridges and grooves covered with modern day coral growth that decreases with depth. This zone is well known to scuba divers. Next is the "wall," ranging from around 100 feet down to about 400 feet. It is nearly vertical with ledges, overhangs, and caves. The "wall" and the slope below is submersible territory where we made most of our dives. The "wall" is partially covered with sponges, both soft and hard calcareous ones. Below the "wall" is the deep-reef slope, sometimes called the island slope that dips about 50 degrees and is covered with sediment, debris, and occasional large blocks of rock, all fallen down from above. This steep sediment-covered slope continues into very deep water.

Setting explosives, deep reef, 820' (notice primacord leading to TNT)

Picking up blast samples with Delta's arm and sample bag, 410"

We discovered that the "wall" is actually growing in places from samples we obtained by blasting. Coral and hard sponge skeletons form the reef frame and fine carbonate sediment fills in the cracks and crevices. Much of this sediment is cemented underwater, as our "genesis" rock from Belize confirmed. Most of the modern upper reef slope limestone surface is composed of recently cemented sediment. Rock samples from this area were dated at about 7,000 years. The almost vertical "wall" was definitely wave-cut during the last rapid rise of sea level from 18,000 to 10,000 years ago. The base of the present day "wall" marks the last low stand of sea level, about 18,000 years ago. There is some modern growth on the "wall" today. The answer to Bob's question, "Why are the sides of present day atolls and coral reefs so steep?" Because erosion during lower sea levels and growth by cementation have probably both contributed to the present day "wall."

While working with Bob in the Bahamas, we were troubled by more than the usual number of sharks. Finally, one of Bob's graduate students, who handled the explosive primacord line during our dives, spotted the cook throwing garbage overboard. He was doing this every morning and the sharks were gathering for their daily feed. We quickly put an end to that chore.

I RECEIVED MANY inquiries over the years asking us to search for sunken treasure. The problem was, treasure seekers usually had no money, thought they knew the exact location of a long missing shipwreck, understood it contained a lot of treasure (usually gold), and wanted us to take a percentage of anything we found instead of paying our daily rate. I told many people over the years that I owned more percentages of wreck treasure worth zero than anyone. I never received a dime.

A message was waiting for me when I returned to California, from the Bahamas, concerning a treasure hunt near the Dry Tortugas off the southern tip of Florida. I began working on this project with a group of treasure hunters from Berkeley, California, in early 1990. An early seventeenth century Spanish galleon lost about ninety miles west of Key West was their target. They were nice guys, not the typical treasure hunters, but sadly were in over their heads. They would not let me see their side-scan sonar records (electronic maps of the seafloor) they said contained proof of the sunken Spanish galleon. The records were so good, according to the treasure hunters, that they could see cannons, ballast piles, and an anchor lying on the seafloor. Cannons, anchors, treasure and piles of ballast rocks are usually the only things left after a wooden ship rots away. When you ever find a pile of granite or other hard rock cobbles in a coral reef environment, you know they are not natural but were left there by humans. Sailing ships carried rocks in their holds for stability—finding a pile of ballast rocks with cannons and an anchor lying around is a certain sign of an old shipwreck site.

The Berkeley treasure hunters formed a company, Treasure Ventures, and invested $5 million to dive on their four major targets. One wreck supposedly carried $300 million in gold plus an estimated $300 million in jewels and other cargo. Our job was to search a designated four square mile area of the seafloor, in international waters, down to a depth of 350 feet. Any treasure recovered would be taken directly over to the Cayman Islands. I accepted one percent equity in the venture in exchange for lowering our daily *Delta* rate. One percent could be worth $6 million if we found the right wreck.

It took one day in Miami to mobilize the 130-foot *Beacon,* a treasure-hunting equipped ship, to support dive operations. The ship, our clients, *Delta,* and crews then set sail for the two-day trip to the planned first dive site, about twenty miles west of the Dry Tortugas. I still had not seen any of their research data.

The side-scan records were finally unrolled the first evening at sea and the targets pointed out. I kept looking at several "ballast piles" and finally asked, "Are you sure these are not holes instead of rock piles?" There was stunned silence until someone said, "What do you mean?" I then explained that features found in aerial photographs and on side-scan records can be interpreted as positive or negative images. Hills can sometimes look like large holes and holes can look like mounds depending on the way you hold the photograph or the side-scan record. Someone asked, "Why would there be holes out there?" I explained that we had seen tilefish along the eastern continental shelf dig and live in large holes. I had also witnessed groupers doing the same thing off Florida. This made everyone a bit nervous but we continued on.

On the first dive, at their most important site, I quickly found a large, twenty-foot wide, grouper hole in the seafloor. We continued to dive for six more days but only found more grouper holes. If they had only let me review their records in California, I could have saved them a lot of money. My one percent was added to the other percent's I owned of nothing.

Interestingly, we saw another treasure ship working, at the same time, a few miles seaward of us in deeper water. They were using an unmanned ROV (a tethered remotely operated vehicle carrying a video-camera) instead of a manned sub. It was nice to know a rescue vehicle was nearby in case of an emergency. This group discovered a 1622 Spanish galleon in 1,500 feet of water the same day we found the first grouper hole. They recovered an extremely rare type of gold ingot that appeared to have come from a convoy of gold-bearing ships destroyed when a hurricane sank nine of a twenty-eight ship Spanish fleet. These were probably the same ships we were looking for. I felt sorry for our treasure seekers—they were really nice guys and deserved better but treasure hunting is not for amateurs.

DELTA WAS LEFT in Miami where we would return in a few weeks to make our annual jaunt to the Bahamas. David and Bob Wicklund were now my experienced assistants and they helped me by piloting and keeping operations running smoothly. In early June we mobilized the *J.W. Powell* at Perry's marine facility on the inland waterway near West Palm Beach before setting off for Grand Bahama Bank. While docked at the Marine facility, the Captain put the ship in gear while it was still tied to the dock to rev up the engines. The current from the propellers undercut Perry's parking lot and a large chunk of it fell into the waterway. Perry's people were not happy with us and there were several red faces on board the *J.W. Powell.*

We headed east to investigate the morphology, biota, and sediments of the Grand Bahama Bank rocky slope between 160 and 600 feet. This was an effort to discover if the slope was erosional or accretional for geologists from Woods Hole and the USGS, the same problem Bob Ginsburg was working on, We completed forty-four scientific dives in six days at various sites around TOTO.

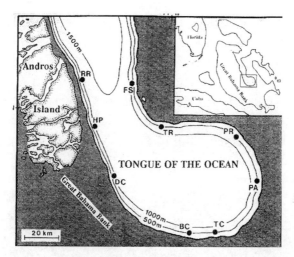

Delta *dive stations around* TOTO

One of the geologists kept complaining about water dripping on him during a dive. We occasionally had very small leaks around the hatch and hull penetrators when diving in shallow water, but they almost always sealed tightly at depth—at least Bahamian water was warm. However, most observers were not comfortable getting water splashed on them or getting squirted in their face during their first dives. The interior of *Delta* was always wet, especially when diving in warm tropical water, due to the walls sweating from temperature changes, occupants sweating, and condensation from our breathing. A thin jet of water would sometimes squirt out from around the ball holding the arm when it was used at depth. Water drops continually ran down the submersible walls and into the bilges located under the floorboard where the accumulated water sometimes sloshed back and forth during a dive. When too much water collected, it would occasionally splash out onto the observer. After each dive, a *Delta* crewmember would crawl into the submersible, pump the bilges, and wipe down the submersible walls. To help dry and cool the submersible, we ran a four-inch air conditioner hose from our shipping container into *Delta* between dives and we carried frozen ice packs and a fan while diving. Unfortunately, the cold air and ice quickly disappeared. The fan inside the submersible helped circulate the air but the interior was always hot and steamy unless we were diving deep. Usually after a few dives, most observers ignored the sloshing and dripping water and I would not have to hear any further complaints. Everyone diving lost a few pounds on a shallow warm water dive. We did not have these problems when diving in cold water—there the problem was keeping warm.

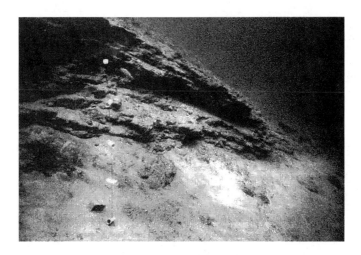

Interior of TOTO deep-reef slope exposed by slump, 525'
(photo by Bob Ginsburg)   (18" cement block for scale)

We dove again in the Tongue of the Ocean (TOTO) in 1990 with Ginsburg's team. Bob was not with us as his wife was terminally ill. Forty dives were accomplished in five days and we collected a ton of data. There had been three major *Delta* diving expeditions in the past few years to TOTO with some interesting and dramatic results starting to appear in print. The surrounding coral platform, and the slope below, provided new evidence of sea level changes during the last 18,000 years. We took several natural light, high-speed, black and white photographs in 500 feet of water and deeper. These were a first, and provided scientific researchers with visual evidence to support some of their theories.

One of my more unforgettable dives took place along the southern wall of TOTO in early 1990. We had been studying this 800-foot high, nearly-vertical, sea cliff for several years. Geologists were interested in what happened to any sediment pushed over the top of this wall by surface currents and storms. One objective in 1990 was to collect sediment traps we had deployed at different depths up and down this scarp the year before—they were missing. We searched everywhere and finally found one about 300 feet deeper than its original position. This was puzzling until Bob Halley, one of the USGS geologists, and I made a dive to collect samples at the base of the wall. We had started to surface when, at about 600 feet, something started to push us down. It was a strong vertical current carrying loose sediment over the wall, an underwater waterfall. I quickly compensated by putting more air in the ballast tanks and we gradually came to a stop. When I added more air, we started to rise up again while still being pelted by sand, gravel, and shells. *Delta* then shot to the surface after we escaped the grip of the downward current. Bob later said, "We broke the surface like a breaching whale." This was amazing and made us realize this powerful process, caused mainly by changing tides, was very influential in moving shallow TOTO reef sediments, and warm water, into deeper cooler water— similar to what we found later on the Great Barrier Reef.

DOUG CUSTOMIZED a yellow shipping container for us to transport *Delta* and its support equipment. After *Delta* was removed, we could convert it into a work area. We developed film, watched videos, and repaired equipment in this container while we were at sea. It was also a place we could get away from the rest of the ship and other people on board. In 1990, we added two laser beams to *Delta's* externally mounted video camera to provide a visible scale on all underwater video. Doug built the lasers in his shop from used parts he removed from an old Xerox machine he found in the dump.

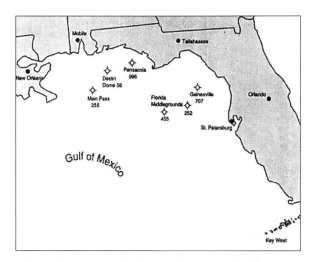

Dive locations on offshore drill sites, Gulf of Mexico

WE TRAVELED to Florida in 1991 for a Gene Shinn-managed USGS project. Gene wanted to dive in the Gulf of Mexico on six abandoned exploratory oil well drill sites, in 70 to 500 feet of water. We used the University of South Florida's research vessel, *R/V Suncoaster* for support. Public concern over offshore drilling had risen steadily since the early 1970s, even though several studies had shown offshore drilling was much less likely to cause an oil spill than an oil tanker. There was also concern about the condition of the seafloor around the old drilling sites. We dove on all the sites, photographed them, and collected nearby seafloor samples. The areas around each drill hole contained some cuttings from drilling but these were spread out and did not appear to have any impact on the local biota. There were also a few lost drilling tools lying on the seafloor. Large groupers had enlarged many of the small pits left from drilling—now we knew where to fish if we came back in the future. It was concluded in Gene's report:

> From a biological perspective, the impacts observed are minimal compared to the known impacts caused by nets and trawls dragged along the bottom.

*USGS-*Delta *crews. I am on the left, Gene Shinn is standing in the middle, and David is in the front row, far right*

Delta *on* R/V Suncoaster

AFTER WORKING with Gene, we traveled a few hundred miles to the deep drop off south of the Dry Tortugas (near the treasure hunter fish holes). We dove with University of South Florida geologists looking for deep drowned reefs and old shorelines. When sea level was much lower during the ice ages, shallow reefs and shorelines formed and then later submerged. We were going to search for these features along the Pourtales Terrace in over 800 feet of water. By studying rock samples from this Terrace, scientists hoped to learn more about the last rise of sea level. A 1992 article in Earth magazine detailed this expedition and the spectacular diving in this very clear water. *Delta's* lights illuminated large sections of the sediment-draped cliffs that were crawling with fish and crabs.

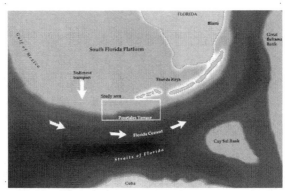

Pourtales Terrace with dive area in the box

*Painting and article on Pourtales Terrace dives
(from* Earth *magazine, Mallinson, 1992)*

We brought along a well-known Southern California undersea filmmaker, Earl Richmond, to take underwater photos and to take underwater video of *Delta*, we knew the water clarity would be fantastic. Earl used this video footage to make a demonstration tape for us. It turned out, even though he was a very experienced scuba diver, he was not NOAA certified and unfortunately for him this was a NOAA project. NOAA rules required a safety diver to be in the water with him at all times.

The safety diver chosen to accompany Earl was a very young female in a bright red bikini, Earl was concerned that the red bikini would end up in the background of his *Delta* video and photographs. Earl later said, "Everything turned out okay because *Delta* moved very fast." First we launched *Delta*, and then Earl jumped into the water and followed us down for a minute, filming all the way. By the time he finished shooting, the submersible continued to sink deeper while the red bikini clad diver was finally ready to dive. Greatly relieved he said, "I vividly remember looking up as I came off the sub conning tower at about 150 feet and saw a bright red bikini entering the water far above. It was then, in those final moments, I felt safe knowing we would get the images I wanted."

THAT SAME SUMMER, I saw a newspaper headline in a Miami grocery store. It said we were operating a secret Navy submersible off the Bahamas and we had discovered the skull of a thirty-foot man on the seafloor. Interesting article, but unfortunately, for us, it was not true.

WE HAD OUR BUSIEST diving year in 1991. *Delta* made 553 dives, in 107 dive days, with 247 different observers. I was the pilot on only fifty-four dives, as the younger pilots were making most of the dives now. I was searching for support vessels, filling out proposals, marketing, and making travel plans for everyone. This kept me busy. The *Delta* crew flew over 40,000 miles without leaving the United States in 1991.

Working for the government became tougher each year with more rules and regulations. Sometimes it would take several weeks to write a bid proposal. Using different support vessels on the East, West, and Gulf coasts was difficult as each vessel had to pass Coast Guard inspection and we had to install equipment on board that many lacked. I usually flew ahead to future ports to make reservations for docking, to arrange for fuel and groceries and to welcome the support ship and *Delta*.

Miami newsstand tabloid featuring Nekton Beta

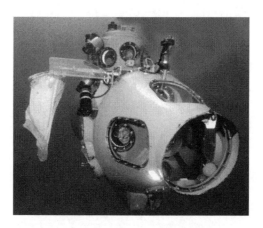

Diving Delta *off Pourtales Terrace*
(photo by Earl Richmond)

Chapter Sixteen

Middle East & Africa

Things are so confused out there they ought to
call it the Muddle East.

—Robert Orben

I WAS INVOLVED in several adventures in the late 1980s
that did not involve *Delta*. One took place when I was invited
to visit the Persian Gulf in 1987 with Chris Kendall and Gene
Shinn. They both had worked in this area during the 1960s
and wanted to re-visit old study sites and their friends while
we attended a World Sedimentology Conference in Kuwait.
We drove a four-wheel-drive vehicle along the Persian Gulf
from Oman to Kuwait traveling through Abu Dhabi, Dubai,
Qatar, and Saudi Arabia. I saw my first car phone (a very large
one) when an Arab called the United States from the middle
of the desert.

One evening, we were sitting on a carpet under a tent in the
desert with about thirty Arabs while servants kept bringing out
platters of food. As visitors, we were offered the choicest
pieces and I was concerned, after being warned, about having
to eat a sheep eyeball. I already tried spleen and it was not my
favorite dish. All of a sudden, a platter with a cooked sheep's
head was placed in front of me. While trying to get Chris's
attention across the carpet, someone reached over and plucked
out the eyeball and swallowed it whole. I was greatly reliefed.

With Arab host and Gene Shinn, Dubai   *Visit to Abu Dhabi*

A Qatar University geology professor and a graduate student traveled with us. There was always commotion in roadside restaurants every time we stopped to eat as the student was a soccer star and a national hero (he is now a high government official in Qatar). Often, he would stay in the car to avoid the crowds. While in Kuwait, we participated in a field trip to the Euphrates/Tigris delta in southern Iraq near Basra. At night, we could see and hear the artillery barrages from the ongoing Iran-Iraq war. Three years later, Iraq invaded Kuwait and the city was nearly destroyed. My friend Ana Gunatilaka, a geology professor from the University of Kuwait, had his equipment and records stolen, or destroyed, during the invasion including his two computers with the only copies of a book manuscript detailing twenty years of his Persian Gulf research.

DICK COOPER WAS involved in a cooperative study with several African scientists planning to dive in the African Great Lakes (Lake Victoria, Lake Tanganyika, and Lake Malawi). He invited me along for a scouting trip in late 1987 to determine how and if *Delta* could be used in these lakes.

Lois and I flew to Nairobi, rented a small four-wheel drive jeep, and drove west about 200 miles to Kisumu, a small town on the eastern shore of Lake Victoria. The highway was in good condition and we enjoyed the interesting drive. I found Lois a room in the only hotel in town. She was the only white person at the hotel (and in the entire town) where she was left alone while I traveled with Dick to check out Lake Victoria. The locals were very nice and she enjoyed her stay. Dick and I met with Kenyan scientists and they were excited about the possibility of a submersible diving in their lake. After our meetings, I told Dick I would meet him in Malawi next week.

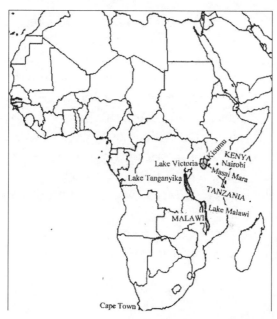

Great Lakes of Africa

With Lois in Kenya

Near Lake Malawi

Lois and I then went on safari in Kenya. Our trip was to start at the Masai Mara Game Reserve, about 100 miles southeast of Kisumu on the Tanzania border. There was no direct road and it was a long trek back through Nairobi. I found an old Shell Oil map showing a track heading south from Kisumu toward Masai Mara, and I decided to try it. The trip started off okay, but the dirt road gradually became a rough path through high grass with no road signs. We stopped in a very small village where I went into an unlit store to purchase a cold drink. The natives in the store took one look at me and fled. I left a few dollars on the counter. We later stopped to take a picture of a boy herding cattle. He posed for the picture but when I tried to take a picture of his cows he started screaming and shaking his stick at me. You must not be allowed to photograph cows in Kenya. After nearly five hours of bouncing along in a dust cloud, we finally arrived at the edge of the great East African Escarpment.

The game park was a thousand feet below and there seemed to be no way to descend the steep cliff. Finally, I discovered a narrow rutted road, more like a goat path, covered with loose rocks. I asked Lois to walk down the steepest parts while I rolled off rocks and drove our small four-wheel drive jeep slowly along the so-called road to the base of the cliff. After reaching the bottom we stopped by a river to relax and wash up. We watched hippos feeding, for a few minutes, before continuing on to our safari camp. Later, we were told no one was allowed to leave a vehicle along that river because it was extremely dangerous.

We finally arrived at our safari camp in the early evening after the all-day, hot and dusty, rough ride. The camp manager did not believe we came from the west. No guests had ever arrived from that direction before and they thought it was very unlikely anyone could get down the escarpment. Nearly all of the other guests had flown in on private airplanes. Lois was not happy when she opened her suitcase and found it full of red dust. We ended up having a great week of watching animals and even went on a spectacular hot air balloon ride one morning. This was one of two wild road trips* that Lois survived with me. She did not enjoy either drive but was a good sport.

We enjoyed game watching, great meals and just relaxing. At the end of the week, we drove north back to Nairobi on the main paved highway to catch the plane to Malawi. The camp manager asked if we would take a very elegant Masai woman, in full native costume, with us. I stopped at a small bridge and asked Lois to drive across it so I could video both of them together. When Lois got into the driver's seat the Masai started making all kinds of strange noises—she obviously did not want Lois to drive. It all finally worked out and I got my video. After a short flight south, we landed in Lilongwe, the capital of Malawi, where we caught up with Dick Cooper while checking into a local hotel with a registration area full of flying termites.

Lake Malawi had an active fishery and I attended several meetings with local fishermen and scientists. Dick hired a bus to take us to a tourist camp at Monkey Bay, near the south end of Lake Malawi where, again, I had to leave Lois for a few days while I joined the scientific party exploring the Lake. The first night after we left she heard something in her tent, turned on a light, and discovered hundreds of flying insects. She spent a few hours sitting on the beach in her nightgown while several natives fought the insects. She did enjoy the rest of her stay for the few days I was away.

---

*The other wild trip was a few years earlier, in Morocco, when I decided to take a rental car from Fez to Tangiers over the Rif Mountains. We were told we could not travel that way by the rental agency; it was considered way too dangerous. However, I wanted to see the spectacular geology. As we started down a very steep windy road I noticed several motorcycles following us. Suddenly they came alongside with young men yelling and pointing for us to pull over. I sped up and the chase began. We were taking sharp curves at a very high speed with Lois down on the floor begging me to slow down. It lasted for about thirty minutes until we reached the valley floor and entered a small village. The motorcycles turned back at that point. I think they represented several drug dealers and they wanted to make a deal with a gringo. The Rif Mountain area is known for having some of the best marijuana in the world. It was like the Wild West and even today considered extremely dangerous for outsiders.

Dick had brought a small ROV to film the bottom of Lake Malawi. We used a fishing boat for support and delighted the locals with underwater views of their lake and fish. Later, we stopped for lunch at a small hut with a "Food" sign out in front. When we asked what was on the menu, the answer was "chicken." We said okay and the lady then chased a chicken around the dirt floor in the stifling hot, humid, dark, one-room restaurant until she caught it. She chopped off the chicken's head and went outside to prepare it. The ROV pilot turned and handed me his wallet while telling me he was going to pass out, which he did. We hauled him outside and revived him, but he did not eat any lunch. I was excited to be involved with this project but it never came to fulfillment. Not sure exactly why, but money and politics were the usual suspects.

Chapter Seventeen

New Guinea & Great Barrier Reef

Nanbawan bot igo insait long salwara
(Number one boat he go inside deep seawater)

—Papua New Guinean's Pidgin English name for *Delta*

IN APRIL 1989, AN American scientist, Jim Prescott, who was working in Papua New Guinea (PNG) contacted me about bringing *Delta* down to assist him on a study of local lobster migration patterns. He had discovered that there was American government money available in PNG for American companies to work on various local projects. Pat Colin, now managing a PNG marine laboratory after flying there in his homemade airplane from Enewetak, had told Jim about *Delta*.

PNG is an independent nation with a population of over six million people—the most populous island nation in the South Pacific. It covers the eastern half of the island of New Guinea, located just north of Australia, and is one of the world's least explored, most primitive and less traveled to countries. It was, and still is, considered a dangerous place for foreigners. The national capital is Port Moresby where the only international airport is also located. There were well over forty-five political parties in their usually unruly parliament and tension between the many tribes occasionally broke out in warfare. PNG has roughly 850 indigenous languages spoken by over a thousand different cultural groups. English is the official language but most natives speak Pidgin English.

Study area and lobster migration path, Papua New Guinea (PNG)

Prescott had spent five years conducting research on spiny lobsters along the 300-mile breeding migration that three- and four-year-old lobsters take across the Gulf of Papua from Torres Strait to just north of Port Moresby. There seemed to be no return migration. In some years, nearly a million lobsters migrated along this route. This lobster migration takes place from November to late January, so we were invited down at that time. There was a chance we could make a few dives off the Great Barrier Reef and around Eastern Fields, an atoll in the Coral Sea. I jumped at the opportunity.

R/V Kulasi

PNG lobster

Delta, along with its support equipment, was shipped in our yellow container to Port Moresby. We flew down in mid-November via Hawaii and Guam. Our support vessel would be the fairly new sixty-foot PNG fisheries research vessel *R/V Kulasi.* This was one trip I kept a detailed log and it illustrates the frustrations of working in a third world country. It was definitely the longest mobilization I was ever involved with.

Thursday, Nov. 16: Met Bob Wicklund and Chris Ijames at LAX and we flew to Hawaii. I sat next to a person with terrible body odor that permeated the entire plane. From Hawaii to Guam, I was sitting next to a native girl that kept chewing something and was constantly spitting it into a bag. Crossed the International Dateline; lost a day.

Saturday, Nov. 18: Three-hour flight from Guam to Port Moresby. Dark and stormy over PNG mountains. Met Jim Prescott at the airport and he drove us to our support ship. *Delta* container, with sub and equipment, locked in customs. We were given a four-man room, tight quarters but comfortable. Ship looked new but not very clean.

Sunday, Nov. 19: Cannot retrieve our container because customs is closed on Sundays. Met Captain Knut from New Zealand, Engineer Rob from Australia, and the entire six-man native New Guinea crew. Three Australian government fish biologists are also on board. They will surely make the trip entertaining; Australians are usually great shipmates. We were invited to a Mu-Mu, a Papua New Guinea feast, at Jim Prescott's home in the evening. Dinner was chicken and pork with bananas, yams, and other vegetables wrapped in banana leaves. These stuffed leaves had spent the day on top of hot stones in a pit. It was a delicious dinner with lots of beer and storytelling, a great start for our trip. One of my crew passed out—we carried him back to the boat.

Monday, Nov. 20: Ran errands around the busy city of Port Moresby. You have to be careful where you walk as the locals chew beetle nut and spit red juice everywhere. You can buy one betel nut with lye and a mustard bean for thirty toya (about forty cents). The locals mix these together and chew it for about thirty minutes while constantly spitting red juice. This makes one very mellow and laid back. One of my crew tried to buy a rubber snake at the local grocery store for a potential practical joke. The cashier freaked out and would not ring it up—he left the store empty handed. Papua New Guineans are deathly afraid of snakes.

The *Kulasi* did not have a crane so Jim purchased one and had it shipped up from Australia. Building the simple crane base plate took all day. I walked over to our container, which was finally being cleared by customs. They wanted the submersible removed so they could check our support equipment. We had no way to move the submersible so the officials had to climb over *Delta*. There was loud, continuing argument between our shipping agent and customs officials before we were finally cleared. I walked back to the ship to ask the Captain to move the *Kulasi* over to pick up our equipment but he had left for the day. The boat crew and many volunteers then unloaded our container, except for *Delta*, and moved our equipment, most of it on their heads, a few hundred yards across the docks to the *Kulasi*. There was great excitement with onlookers shouting instructions. Everyone was having a good time, I was concerned some equipment might be stolen—it wasn't.

Bosco, the assistant engineer, was a hard worker and most helpful. He was always barefoot. I watched him hold the crane's metal base-plates with his toes while welding the plates to the deck. He later stepped on a nail from one of our crates and it just bent over leaving him unharmed. We worked until 10:00 p.m. cutting and welding a pipe to hang over the side for our Trackpoint II underwater navigation transponder. First dinner on board, the cook Newman was new but served a decent meal. He was small, polite, very dark, and rugged looking. The crew is trying very hard to please us but they have never been around Americans or on a diving trip.

Tuesday, Nov. 21: Raining hard this morning so we covered our crates but everything got soaked. Ship's crew still working on the crane base-plate. Food for the trip was brought on board. I went to visit Prescott's office for an appointment to sign our contract. Fisheries manager did not show; he was out of town. We ate lunch at a private club mainly used by Australian expats. They served great cold beer. While there I met an environmentalist working on a gold mining project at Misima, an island off the far eastern tip of PNG. She asked if we could dive on several waste pipelines to observe if mine discharge was damaging local coral reefs. She would fly us there to meet the *Kulasi*. Sounded like a good idea and I agreed.

I spent over an hour in several shops trying to buy basic supplies but will have to return tomorrow. Visited the US AID office at the American Embassy; they were paying for our project. It looked like a CIA front to me. I met the director, a nice guy, who told me they were funding a huge grant to study malaria, PNG has more types of malaria than anywhere in the world. None of us had brought any malaria medicine. The crane was finally lifted onto the base-plate in the evening. It normally takes about half a day to mobilize a ship and this was our fourth day.

Bosco, PNG engineer, in Delta   *Newman, PNG cook*

Wednesday, Nov. 22: Major problem discovered this morning. Crane motor runs on 240V 3-phase power and the Kulasi has none—the crane will not work. After driving around several hours we finally located a shop that could convert the crane motor. They said it would be ready at 10:00 a.m. tomorrow. I finally signed our contract at the Fisheries office and visited another PNG government office to have our PNG visas renewed so we can make multiple entries.

Visited a few furniture stores, they have beautiful hardwood handmade furniture in Port Moresby but I did not buy any. After lunch we finally succeeded in getting our navigation Trackpoint II system up and running. We are now ready to dive but the crane problem is holding us up. Submersible still in the container, we cannot bring it on board without the crane. Dinner served at 9:00 p.m. I will have to get Newman to serve dinner earlier. Visited the local yacht club for a few beers.

PAPUA NEW GUINEA

Post-Courier

56 Pages   THURSDAY, DECEMBER 14 1989

US sub on marine surveys in our waters

AN American submarine is currently working on a PNG fisheries project. A USA fisheries group has carried out two surveys on behalf of our Fisheries Department since last month.

The first assignment, trying to locate the route of the tropical rock lobster that breeds and moves from Torres Strait to Yule Island, was not successful.

Tomorrow, the group moves to Misima where it will carry out an environment research on mine wastes. The assignment is to locate where the wastes rest after flowing 160 metres and to see what effects it has on the mine surroundings.

ABOVE: ROBYN Sels gets a feel of the submarine mounted on MV Kulasi at the government wharf in Port Moresby yesterday. *Picture by AUHI EVA*

Port Moresby newspaper article

Thursday, Nov 23: Thanksgiving. The fifth day of our mobilization and more bad news, the crane motor cannot be fixed for another three to five days. Big storm hit this morning forcing us to move the ship away from the dock. These storms last only a few hours but can cause a lot of damage. Went back to town with Jim to buy a $2,000 crane motor after we were finally told the first one couldn't be converted.

I had asked one of the Australian scientists to bring us a frozen turkey from Australia. It arrived this morning and I handed it to Newman to cook for dinner tonight. I told him it was for an American holiday. He had never seen a turkey and thought we wanted to eat a cassowary, a large emu type bird in PNG, which he considered uneatable.

We installed a microwave oven in Newman's galley. It was the first one he had ever seen and I found him lighting matches trying to start it. I explained to him how it worked. We left for the afternoon; I told Newman we would be back for dinner at 8:00 p.m. While we were gone he cooked the turkey in the microwave all afternoon. It looked funny, was tough, but okay to eat. The first course was French onion soup. Bob Wicklund thought it tasted strange and when one of the Australians pulled a large cockroach out of his bowl Bob ran to the door after climbing over the table—he missed Thanksgiving dinner. Lots of cockroaches and they caused great discomfort for my crew. Caught the Captain smoking pot on the bridge.

Friday, Nov. 24: Checked out *Delta* which is still in our container—it seemed okay. Waiting for crane motor. I asked the ship's crew, "Please do not spit around our equipment" and they all agreed. Newman is scrubbing our shower and toilet, not a very pleasant sight. Motor arrived in the afternoon and we assembled the crane. It finally worked but kept blowing hydraulic lines, causing oil spills into the harbor. No one seemed to care about the harbor.

Saturday, Nov. 25: Seventh day of mobilization. Crane still blowing hoses, called the manufacturer in the States and they instructed us to tighten down the hose clamps. We did, and the crane finally worked. Moved the ship over to the loading wharf to retrieve *Delta* from our container just when it was announced, "timeout for a Smoko," which is a PNG/Australian coffee break. Nearly everyone smokes home rolled cigarettes in PNG. They use local newspaper and their cigarettes look like big fat cigars. A few years ago the local newspaper changed print paper and no one bought any newspapers until they went back to the old paper.

A large group of onlookers yelled encouragements

when we finally pulled *Delta* out of the container and lifted it onto the ship. We moved the *Kulasi* away from the pier for a test dive in the harbor where we discovered that the crane could not lift the submersible over the ship's railing. We spent several hours cutting the railing off. Went to bed late and very tired.

Sunday, Nov 26: Another typical tropical hot humid day. Everyone grumpy as we finally finished testing *Delta* and its support equipment. Returned to the pier to unload the pipe railing cut off yesterday. After a one-week delay we finally set sail for Torres Straits in the evening. I was last there when I visited Thursday Island in 1968 during the Great Barrier Reef project. (This was the end of my diary)

PNG participants, 1st row: David, Newman; 2nd row: Jim Prescott on left; 3rd row: Doug in middle of Australians

We arrived at our first dive site off Yule Island around 10:00 a.m. and made three one-hour dives. Water visibility was near zero—not a good start. This was not typical tropical diving I was accustomed to, no lobsters either. The scientists placed pingers on two lobsters, brought from Port Moresby, and we tried to track them all night but kept going in circles. Turned out the mate had been tracking the ships echo-sounder signal. We went aboard a Japanese fishing boat working nearby. They were hauling in a large amount of lobsters and prawns, plus assorted fish, which they stored in large freezers. They gave us a tour of their ship including the top of the bridge where I hit a few golf balls from their driving range.

Jim caught a very poisonous six-foot sea snake that swam by the *Kulasi* during the night and placed it in a plastic garbage can. I showed it to Newman and he went berserk and ran back into the ship. I felt bad and went to apologize. Later, one of the crew told me that Newman had just been released from an Australian jail where he had been sentenced to two years for murdering a friend. The friend threw a dead snake at him so he used a machete to cut his friend's head off as they were walking through the jungle.

Several more dives were made, with water visibility starting to improve the farther we moved away from land. There were lots of hammerhead and white-tip sharks in this area. Bob Wicklund wanted to go home; he did not care for the ship or the people on it.

We continued to dive for another week and finally settled into a routine. The weather was very warm and the seas flat calm, making for easy diving. Fresh fish and lobster for dinner every night seemed to soothe my crew and there was little talk now of going home. The only problem was, we still could not locate the migrating lobsters. Jim's wife drove my son David over from Port Moresby in early December and he joined us for the remainder of the project. We celebrated with a large lobster/fish bake on the beach while we read mail from home.

One of our dive sites was a reef just off a coastal village. We needed permission from the local chief to dive on his reef so we headed to shore and landed on a black sand beach after running our rubber boat through the surf. The sand was very hot and we were hopping around, much to the amusement of the local villagers who had come out to welcome us. We scrambled up to a delightful and very clean village where we sat in a circle on the ground with village elders, while young girls served us coconut and cool drinks. After negotiations through an interpreter, we received permission to dive on their reef. We finally located a few lobsters with *Delta* but had more success while scuba diving. I cut my leg on some coral while diving and it soon became infected.

Villagers welcoming us   *Meeting in the village*

During the next week, we dove in front of the Great Barrier Reef—this was spectacular diving. Everything looked very familiar from my Caribbean deep-reef dives. There were lots of fish and plenty of sharks swimming around. We caught and cooked a 150-pound tuna. My infected leg seemed to be worse but I still dove every day (the wound eventually scabbed over and the pain subsided around Christmas when I was leaving PNG).

One morning we saw a ship off in the distance, first ship we had seen for ten days. They contacted us on the marine radio and asked what we were doing. When the Captain said we were diving a small submersible someone, asked if Rich Slater was on board. He said he knew me and I had once promised him a day of skiing in Colorado. He mentioned that he was a friend of Charlie Phipps. I never did figure out who he was. After a few more days of diving, everyone was getting grumpy. Having sixteen people living close together on a cockroach infested sixty-four foot boat is really pushing it, especially in the steamy tropics during bad weather. After an eighteen-hour rough riding trip, with high seas and strong winds, we returned to Port Moresby.

My plan for the Christmas break was to fly the *Delta* crew to Sydney to meet their wives for a short vacation while I flew home. When I went to reconfirm our tickets, I discovered the airline had canceled my ticket home and the crew's flight did not exist. Luckily Jim, experienced with travel in and out of PNG, had double booked us.

We checked into the Travelodge, the most luxurious hotel in Port Moresby, while the *Kulasi* sailed off for the Misima gold mine giving us a needed three-day break. The next day, Jim Prescott drove us up for a visit to the famous Kokoda Trail, the site of tremendous fighting during World War II. Later, I spent two more fruitless hours in the QANTAS office. The U.S. ambassador invited me to a dinner party at his house that evening. It was a beautiful setting overlooking the ocean with about fifty people enjoying drinks and food. Most of the American Embassy staff and many ex-pats were there.

Arriving at Misima, PNG

On December 15th, we flew in a small chartered plane to Misima. Everyone and everything we carried was carefully weighed before we could leave. It was over an hour before we were cleared to fly. The flight took two-and-a-half hours and crossed over the Owen Stanley Mountains with many peaks over 10,000 feet. The mine supervisor met our plane and drove us around the large open-pit Canadian gold mine. Our objective was to validate the predictions made in a report on the behavior of the mine tailings following their discharge into the ocean. The next morning we were ready to meet the *Kulasi* but it did not appear until noon.

We made five *Delta* dives that afternoon on the two six-foot diameter slurry-waste pipes in very murky water. The mine supervisor asked us to cut off two large buoys that were left connected to one of the waste pipes when it was laid down, but we could not locate the buoys in the complete blackout. *Delta's* lights could only penetrate the water a few inches as the mine slurry left a thick cloud of suspended fine red sediment. Jim Prescott, using scuba, dove to 200 feet in zero visibility and cut off the buoys. This was very gutsy and impressive. David was his support diver and waited for him at 140 feet, dizzy from nitrogen narcosis. Finally, after a few days with the slurry line turned off, the water cleared enough so we could take photos of the large pipelines. We made fifteen dives in four days. On December 20th, we flew back to Port Moresby with a fuel stop at the World War II airstrip in Milne Bay (this is where Amelia Earhart left to cross the Pacific).

We flew down to Sydney the next day. I flew the crew's wives in from California so they joined their husbands for Christmas while I continued my trip home. David, Bob, and Chris handled the next two weeks of PNG diving off Daru and the Fly River delta as operations moved further to the west. David took the opportunity to venture up the Fly River in a dugout canoe (near where a Rockefeller had disappeared a few years before).

I returned to PNG with Doug Privitt, on January 22nd, and briefly saw Bob and Chris in Guam on their way home. Doug, David, and I would finish the PNG diving. We ran several transits up the Fly River delta and continued to dive for a week in this area with good weather, until a storm hit us on February 1st. I woke up early that morning when I heard a loud cracking sound—the anchor line had parted. Winds were up to forty miles per hour so we ran for shelter up the Fly River.

One of the deck hands dislocated his shoulder but kept working without complaint. Finally, someone helped him pop it back. David only drank water from a large metal canister containing boiled water for tea. One day, when the tap became clogged, he opened the lid and saw hundreds of cockroaches inside. He only drank bottled juice and beer after that.

We finally found a large group of migrating lobster just when the ship's generator failed and then the second engineer received an emergency phone call while making repairs. His five-year-old daughter had pulled a pot of boiling water off the stove and was in very serious condition in Port Moresby. We immediately sailed for Daru and dropped the engineer off at 4:00 a.m. That was the end of our chasing lobster off PNG.

Helping to navigate, Great Barrier Reef   Delta *on the Great Barrier Reef*

We headed south to finish our surveys on the Great Barrier Reef. We would be diving in very strong currents this time, caused by some of the biggest tides of the year. We started near the northern end of the Reef. The scientists and *Delta* crew sat on top of the bridge to help navigate the *Kulasi* through the patch reefs. The weather was clear, calm, and very hot. The full moon spring tide occurred on the 9th and when we dove that day we were in for a surprise.

Delta was hovering on "the wall" in 380 feet of water while we were photographing a lobster, when suddenly *Delta* started to move and the seafloor just below us exploded. We were caught in a swirling cloud of sediment, rocks, and shells. The submersible was twisting and turning as I purged the ballast tanks of water so we could quickly rise toward the surface. Instead, we were driven down into deeper water until we hit the seafloor hard while spinning around. It felt like we were ascending but we were under a torrential underwater waterfall that kept pushing us down. We quickly sank down to 480 feet. Normally, at this depth, Great Barrier Reef water temperature is approximately sixty-six degrees but it was now over eighty degrees. This was Torres Strait surface water coming over the reef and plunging down, at least 500 feet, while also scouring the seafloor. When we finally surfaced, the sea was boiling and the *Kulasi* could not maneuver toward us. We were nearly a mile off the reef. I had to run over to the ship while crossing a very rough turbulent sea.

We decided to head for Eastern Fields, a large atoll in the middle of the Coral Sea. It is a reef complex far from the outer margins of the Great Barrier Reef and a marine wonderland. Located in the middle of the Gulf of Papua, about a hundred miles south of Port Moresby, it had some of the clearest water I had ever seen. Very few divers had been there and, as far as I knew, no submersible had ever visited. We made outstanding dives around the atoll. While scuba diving, we could just relax, forget about tracking lobster, and let the strong current carry us around the atoll. There were hundreds of tame fish, many sharks, and some very large grouper.

It was a great way to end our PNG project. We never did locate the large masses of migrating lobsters but recorded enough data to keep scientists busy for years. We logged 162 dives in forty-nine diving days with thirty different observers, including fourteen Papua New Guineans. We flew home on Valentine's Day for a well-deserved rest.

With David and filming off Eastern Fields, Coral Sea

Chapter Eighteen

West Coast, Fish & Crabs

The best way to observe a fish is to become a fish.

Dan Yaccarino—*The Fantastic Undersea Life of Jacques Cousteau* (2009)

THERE WAS PRESSURE from many scientists and several government agencies to dive along both East and West Coasts every summer. We tried in 1988 and met with some success. The 106-foot *William A. McGaw* was leased for our West Coast operations. It was small and crowded but proved to be more than an adequate support vessel. *Delta* was used successfully from the *McGaw* for several years diving along the West Coast, and around Alaska.

Delta *and* M/V William A. McGaw, *Alaska*

Our first West Coast stop in 1988 was Sitka, the old Alaska state capital. Sitka is on an island located just south of Juneau, the present state capital. Sitka would be homeport for many of our summer projects over the next few years, as the Alaskan Department of Fish and Game main office is located there. It is a pleasant town and we always looked forward to Sitka port days. Most of our Alaska dives, for State and Federal Fishery biologists, involved counting ground fish. We ran one mile transects across the seafloor while identifying and counting every fish seen on our starboard side. This data helped fishery biologists set catch limits and choose areas where fishermen would be allowed to fish each year. I liked Alaskans; they have a great love for the outdoors and most of our trips up there were usually great, except for the weather. We were often tied up for days waiting for calmer seas or the fog to lift.

Fish photos taken off Alaska from Delta

Delta *ready to dive off Oregon*   *With Chris and David going ashore*

AFTER DIVING OFF SITKA, we headed south to Oregon where the maritime weather was sometimes even worse. We worked with many biologists and geologists from Oregon State University and biologists from NMF. The biologists were mostly fish scientists. Geologists wanted to explore, map, and sample several large offshore banks. No one had dove on these deep-water banks before—it was exciting to be first as you never knew what you might come across.

On several offshore banks we collected methane gas, which escaped through seafloor vents that were connected to frozen methane beds located well below the seafloor. Many gas vents were discovered by first seeing the bleached white sediment surrounding them. This snow white sediment was cemented close to the vents forming rocks, exposed by current erosion, which resembled white cement birdbaths or stacks of white tires similar to the Michelin Man. When rich methane fluids encounter very cold seawater, they often precipitate out as carbonates around the vent rims. Gas bubble collection was important, as was obtaining seafloor samples especially near these vents.

Biologists wanted to identify and count bottom fish. These counts were difficult when we drove through large schools of thousands. After hundreds of fish dives, I became somewhat of an expert on fish identification and sometimes assisted by pointing out certain species. Most scientists were delighted to have an extra pair of eyes in the submersible especially since, as the pilot, I had a better view of distant objects.

During my entire career, there was only one scientist who asked me not to help. This was the biology professor who we had met on the East Coast the previous year. He was not the most popular person on board our ship. On one dive, he asked me to stop the sub and said, "I am the scientist and you are the pilot. I do not tell you how to pilot your submersible so do not tell me about my fish." After that I never mentioned any fish to him including once when I spotted a rare fish he was searching for and never found. My crew disliked this guy, my son David even banned him from the bridge navigation station one day during the 1988 expedition. On a previous Bahama project, Doug woke me up in the middle of the night to tell me this same guy was demanding he cut a hole in the submersible ballast tank so he could take better photographs. It took a while to cool Doug down. A month or so after this professor's 1988 dives, I was told his wife had left him and he was blaming it on my crew. He called me wanting to know who had put a pair of sexy red panties and bra in his suitcase before he left the ship. I knew nothing about it. I asked my crew who pleaded they had no knowledge of the incident. Several years later, the *McGaw* female cook asked what ever happened to that Oregon State professor. I asked why and she said, "That jerk complained about my cooking all the time so I put a pair of my sexiest panties and bra in his suitcase before he got off."

He left Oregon State soon after diving with us and went to work for NURP in Washington D.C. This was not good; we now had a guy who didn't like us working for the organization that funded much of our work. Several sources told me he was bad mouthing *Delta* and I am sure we lost several projects. The other Oregon State fish scientists were some of the finest shipmates I ever sailed with—I enjoyed their company and projects over many seasons.

One highlight of fish surveys was that most fish biologists like to fish during a cruise to obtain specimens for research and to take home for their freezers. We usually volunteered to catch fish and the fish biologists always knew the best fishing spots. The support ship carried large salt-water tanks on deck to keep fish alive for further research. There were usually enough fish left over so we ate fresh fish for dinner on many evenings. Newport was our homeport in Oregon and a good town for a day off. Entering most ports along the Oregon-Washington coast can be very dangerous. There are many shallow sand bars stretching across most entrances and very large waves and rough water often occur in these areas. It was always exciting to enter an Oregon port city; our large support ship frequently surfed in over the sand bars.

AFTER TWO WEEKS of diving off Oregon, we headed south to Monterey Bay. This time, we were studying Pacific hagfish, probably the most disgusting of all fish. These small eel-like primitive fish evolved hundreds of millions of years ago. They feed by burrowing into bodies of dead fish and then eat their way out. They also secrete buckets of slime when caught. Sometimes they are called "slime eels" but are not true eels. They are pink, about eighteen inches long, and can tie themselves into a knot. To capture them, we lowered a net bag full of rotten meat from *Delta,* and when they attacked we slurped them up with a suction hose. It took hours to clean the slime out of our pump, hoses, and bags.

Pacific hagfish

FROM MONTEREY, we headed home to find a lost current meter array off Ventura. Recovery of this equipment, a set of sophisticated current meters with "irreplaceable data," was of utmost concern to the Department of Energy and University of Washington scientists who were in charge of the study. This episode began in 1986 when their new current meter array first disappeared. They thought the equipment was still lying on the seafloor, close to its original site in Santa Monica Bay. The government hired *Alvin* for a search but all they found was a three-foot gouge along the seafloor where the 3,500-pound anchor dragged. How could 4,000 pounds of gear disappear with a pinger and a surface buoy to mark its location? Then, some Navy personnel telephoned the scientists a few months later, and said they found the surface buoy but could not pull up what it was attached to, so they cut the line. They did not mention that the buoy was off Anacapa Island so a lot of time was wasted. Finally, in 1988, scientists discovered that the final buoy location was fifty miles from the original site. That is when we were called and, on our second dive off Anacapa Island, we found the array in 1,010 feet of water. There was a problem; the equipment was tangled in a large fishing net with a fifty-foot whale-shark skeleton.

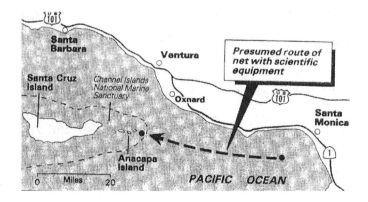

*Current array drift (*Ventura Star *newspaper, 1988)*

It was later determined that a fishing vessel snagged a very large basking or whale shark in its nets off Santa Monica. The fishermen could not pull the huge animal in as they drifted to the west, and it eventually became tangled with the current meter array. Finally, they cut their net loose forming a large pile of net, cables, fish, scientific equipment, and debris on the seafloor. It was impossible to electronically release the current meter trapped in the net.

While I maneuvered around the pile taking photos of the current meter, net and whale shark skeleton, *Delta's* propeller inadvertently sucked up a piece of the net. I was lucky because when I reversed the propeller the net spun off. This saved me from having to drop *Delta's* tail assembly if the propeller had remained tangled in the net, and make an uncontrolled ascent. The wind strengthened by the time we surfaced and a very rough sea slammed us around. My observer said later he thought he was going to die when his head kept banging against the submersible hull. We finally got aboard the *McGaw* and I called off the mission—too dangerous for another dive.

We returned a few days later. I carried down a cable, being played out from the *McGaw*, and snapped the end hook into the mess. After *Delta* was safely aboard, the large winch on the *McGaw* slowly reeled in the pile of debris. The 800 feet of pink fishing net with the large skeleton and current meters appeared near the surface an hour later. It took another hour to cut away the net so scientists could finally recover their current meters. We had saved an important government study.

 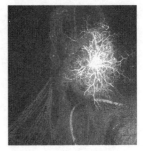

Net, current meter, and skeleton, 1,010', near Anacapa Island

DELTA UNDERWENT its annual overhaul in Doug's shop during the winter of 1988-1989. Again, as every year, *Delta* looked brand new before our first dive in 1989. After a few dives, the paint and ports usually became scratched and some dents would appear in the thin ballast tanks. We also added a new updated Trackpoint II navigation system and film-developing equipment so we could now develop 35mm film on the ship at night. Scientists would no longer have to return to shore to see photographs taken during their dives. They also received instant maps after each dive with photograph and sample locations plotted with dates and time along the sub track. It was important to keep everything up to date with the latest best equipment and software. Doug and I formed a new company, "Delta Oceanographics," in May. We could no longer work on a handshake or as independents. Government agencies would now only issue contracts to insured companies or corporations working on federal projects. We leased the building next door to Doug's shop in Torrance for our new submersible research and development facility, and I would continue to run the business out of my home office. After a six months break from diving, everyone was ready to return to sea in June, when we cruised to Alaska on the *William A. McGaw*. Doug stayed in the shop so Bob Wicklund, David and I would now be the *Delta* pilots.

OUR FIRST TASK in 1989 was an NMF king crab survey near Juneau. These large crabs look spectacular underwater and move very fast over the seafloor. A graduate student brought out his newly typed dissertation for his professor who was on board our ship. He tied his small boat alongside us and climbed aboard over our tire-mat. The captain, not knowing the boat was there, took off to follow *Delta*. The boat was swamped and hundreds of dissertation pages were soon seen floating on the bay. We spent over an hour picking up waterlogged pages that, unfortunately, were part of his only copy.

Alaska King Crabs

Holy cow! That was a bovine endeadeus!

By David Hulen
McClatchy News Service

ANCHORAGE, Alaska — What happens when people spend a week in a tiny submarine on the ocean floor, looking out a little window to count fish and identify seaweed species?

They start seeing things. Strange, wondrous things.

Things like cows.

A marine biologist and the pilot of a two-person research submarine were 20 miles off the southeast Alaska coast last week, creeping along the silty floor of the Gulf of Alaska to peer out at things as part of a study of Pacific perch populations.

In the inky underwater darkness at 690 feet below the surface, their peering yielded something neither fish nor fern — a full-grown bovine, lying on its side amid the silt and seawhips.

It looked to be a Holstein.

Tory O'Connell, a marine biologist for the state Department of Fish and Game, and sub pilot David Slater looked at each other. They surfaced a little while later, and as they climbed out of the sub, the people waiting on the deck of the research ship asked what they usually ask when the sub comes up, O'Connell said.

"They said, 'What did you see down there?'

"David said, 'Well, we saw a bovine endeadeus.'"

Someone asked him what that was.

"He said 'A dead cow.'"

Nobody could believe it until they saw the videotape.

When the ship got back to Sitka a couple of days later, after a week of doing daily surveys on a section of ocean bottom, the sunken cow instantly became the talk of the boat harbor. The Sitka Sentinel sent a reporter to view the tape, and he reported that, sure enough, the thing looked like a dead cow.

The submarine was cruising along a flat, relatively barren section of sea bottom, O'Connell said. As the sub passed along the floor, different things came into view in its harsh spotlight — a halibut here, a couple of pollock there, an occasional starfish, she said.

The Sitka newspaper reported that O'Connell's voice can be heard on the tape, counting off fish species. Suddenly, a black and white cow fills the screen, its back to the sub.

"What the heck is that?" asks Slater, the pilot.

O'Connell suggests it looks like a horse. Slater says it looks like a sheep. Then he says, no, it's a cow.

"Holy cow!" O'Connell replies.

The sub kept moving along, and after a couple of seconds the cow vanished. "We couldn't stop or it would have thrown our grid all off," she said. "It would have spoiled what we'd done that day."

O'Connell and marine scientists on the research ship don't have a clue how a cow wound up on the ocean floor 20 miles offshore. Neither does anybody else in Sitka.

1989 Sitka newspaper article

A WEEK LATER, we were making our first dives off Sitka for Tory O'Connell from Alaska Fish and Game. She would use *Delta* for the next twenty years on her Alaskan rockfish projects. Tory is remembered that summer for her discovery of a cow lying on the seafloor 700 feet below the surface and twenty miles from the Alaskan coastline. She was counting fish when David, the pilot, said, "What is that?" Tory can be heard on the videotape saying "Holy cow," when a black and white cow appeared on the seafloor near *Delta*. When we returned to Sitka nearly a week later, the seafloor cow instantly became the talk of the town and the story went nationwide on TV and newspapers. We had no idea how the cow got there. Probably fell or was pushed off a ship passing the area. One person suggested lust-crazed walruses had abducted it.

FROM SITKA, WE traveled up to Prince William Sound, where an oil spill had occurred in the spring. This was not just any oil spill but the largest, up to that time, in North American history. In March 1989, the *Exxon Valdez* hit a shallow reef and spilled eleven million gallons of crude oil into one of the most beautiful places in the world. When we arrived in early June, the Sound looked pristine and you could not tell there had been an oil spill except for crowds of workers on several of the hardest hit beaches.

NMF requested we make the first dives after the spill. *Delta* was used on seventy-one Prince William Sound dives. We did not find one drop of oil in the over 200 seafloor samples we collected—we proved that oil floats. The long-term results of this spill were very controversial, with both sides publishing self-serving data. The entire month of June had a real circus-like atmosphere with thousands of people trying to grab some of the money Exxon was throwing around. Valdez, the main town in the Sound, was overrun with lawyers and prostitutes. Small boats came alongside our vessel, mistaking us for an Exxon ship, with people jumping onboard asking for free fuel and food. Many local natives and fishermen, already living in poverty, were claiming their lives were ruined. Exxon spent several billion dollars on the cleanup and compensation for damages.

Diving near shore on Prince William Sound oil spill (notice oil-stained rocks)

I believe Exxon caused more damage to the environment than the spill did by cleaning the beaches with chemicals and hot steam. Most of the Sound's 3,000 miles of shoreline were not touched by the oil spill but several small areas were hit hard. One beach was not cleaned so it could be used to demonstrate the damage to a steady stream of VIPs who flew in on floatplanes to see the spill. I was glad to leave this carnival at the end of the month for the Bering Sea.

NURP FINALLY OPENED a University of Alaska office in Fairbanks to cover West Coast diving. In 1989, we were awarded eight Alaska, and one Oregon project. After Prince William Sound, we worked our way north along the West Coast of Alaska, diving for NURP projects around several Bering Sea Islands. Near one island, we discovered a graveyard of walrus bones. While we were anchored during bad weather, we explored several islands and met some of the local natives. Several dives were on, or near, the USSR/USA border.

The small isolated city of Nome on the Bering Sea, only two degrees south of the Arctic Circle, was our next port stop. We exchanged personnel and purchased fuel and groceries there. My memories of Nome are wooden sidewalks, muddy streets, drunken natives, the Iditarod Dog Sled Race finish line, and the difficulty getting into and back out of the port. In the mid-1970s, the Corp of Engineers built a rock jetty and a fortified sea wall that now protects Nome from Bering Sea storms. This wall allows small boats to anchor in the resulting small man-made harbor. We anchored the *McGaw* offshore and took our small rubber boat into this harbor to visit Nome. It was always a thrill, equivalent to the best ride at Disneyland, to ride a series of very large waves rushing down the narrow channel between the two rock jetties until we reached the harbor. Nome is icebound for most of the year so our dive season was limited to just a few summer months.

For our next port call, we anchored off the very small native village of Teller, a former reindeer station, about ninety miles north of Nome. It was necessary to ride our rubber boat through the surf to land there. A *McGaw* crewmember was attaching the outboard motor to our rubber boat when he dropped it into the ocean. I had to make a thirty-foot dive in *Delta* to recover the motor. After a rinsing with fresh water, it was as good as new. I stopped by the only store in Teller and found the shelves almost completely bare, except for a few Eskimo Pie ice cream bars left in the freezer. I hitched a ride back to Nome with a local native and flew home to attend to business while *Delta* continued north into the Chukchi Sea and the Arctic Ocean. Sixteen dives were above the Arctic Circle. The *McGaw* then headed back to Sitka, where I came aboard, and we resumed Gulf of Alaska fish counts with Alaska State biologists. *Delta* made over 200 dives off Alaska in 1989.

After diving off Oregon, we trucked *Delta* to the East Coast for a month of diving. I could now leave *Delta* operations for a week or two and feel comfortable that my crew would do a good job. This was the first year that neither Doug nor I were on board for every dive. Working at sea is a young man's job. It takes strength and agility to labor on a rolling wet ship deck and I was realizing I could not do it all anymore. However, I had several exciting future projects lined up that I did not want to miss.

IN 1990, WE AGAIN dove off Sitka with Tory O'Connell and her biological team. Several dives were on the "pinnacle," one of the most spectacular dive sites in the Gulf of Alaska. It is an underwater seamount that rises up about 300 feet from the seafloor to less than 100 feet from the ocean surface and supports thousands of fish. Lingcod up to five feet long were sometimes stacked on top of each other. Tory later had this area declared a fishing reserve. Just north of the "pinnacle" is Mt. Edgecombe, an inactive volcano. One April Fools' Day, someone hauled tires to the top with a helicopter and set them on fire. Local residents thought the volcano was erupting.

Diving on pinnacle off Mt. Edgecombe

Lingcod stacked up on pinnacle, 225'

Yelloweye near Delta

THE *WILLIAM A. MCGAW* sailed south to Oregon where we dove with scientists from Oregon State again. Our mission was to obtain more vent sediment and to collect gas samples. Our biggest problem was the very poor water visibility caused by erupting gas stirring up fine surface sediment. We used some elaborate submersible sampling equipment designed and built by Oregon State scientists to help on this mission. Their boomerang sampler allowed us to drop a box-corer from *Delta* onto a very small target, such as a gas vent. We then released a series of buoys that lifted the corer and sample back to the surface where they were recovered. A large funnel-like device, attached to *Delta,* was used to capture gases that were analyzed in a laboratory on board. We collected sediment, rock, and gas samples during forty dives in seven days.

Gas capturing device on Delta   *Boomerang corer*

Oregon State University onboard Geochemistry Laboratory and geologists

1990 AND 1991 WERE record-breakers for *Delta* diving and were very profitable for Delta Oceanographics. We could now afford to continually upgrade our dive systems plus Doug and I took home some nice paychecks. During 1989-1991, *Delta* was used on 1,576 dives along both USA coasts and off the Bahamas, Australia, and Papua New Guinea. We were now diving on the second and third year of many projects. Once a scientist used a certain tool to obtain data he does not want to change, it could skew his data. We were locked in, or so we thought. NURP offices on both coasts wanted more of our summer season and it became obvious we had to choose one over the other. Sadly, this was to be our last year for NURP projects on the East Coast. California, Alaska, and Oregon projects were too big to give up. It was also the first year we used Buccaneer Marine, from Ventura, for support. Their oil field supply boats were ideal and they were our west coast support vessels for many years.

WE CONTINUED TO upgrade *Delta*. In 1991, we installed all new digital gauges, bought a new sonar system and, most importantly, added a new robotic hydraulic arm designed and built by Doug. This arm worked at any depth, unlike the old mechanical arm that needed a lot of manpower in depths over a few hundred feet. I replaced Bob Wicklund, who wanted to be closer to his home in Florida, with Chris Ijames, who had been working as our deckhand for the past three years.

After conferring with Alaska NURP director's office, they announced we would be awarded a 149-day work schedule from Ventura to Alaska and return in 1991. This would be our first million-dollar contract.

We started off Alaska in April on a Kodiak Bay tanner crab study with Brad Stevens from NMF. This was one of the most interesting projects I was ever involved with. During forty-one dives in *Delta,* we searched for crabs and collected mating pairs. Yes, we had to collect them in the act with the male still attached to the female. A surprising result was to discover over

100,000 sexually mature crabs aggregated into a very small area with the females piled up in mounds of up to 500 crabs each. There were over 200 mounds covering a small part of Kodiak Bay, with each mound covering ten to twenty square yards of the seafloor. These female crab mounds were only a few yards apart with one or two male crabs located near each mound. The major factor limiting our filming and collecting crabs was water clarity. The crabs kept the water just above the seafloor stirred up with suspended fine sediment. It was fascinating to watch a male crab dash into a pile, grab a female, and then hold her over his head showing her off to the other males that had no mate. The female biologist on this expedition did not think this was very funny. A scientist named our research the "Coitus Interruptus Project." Brad sent a letter to the NURP office saying without *Delta*, he would not have been able to find and captured mating pairs. He wrote:

> I have a high opinion of *Delta*, and of Rich Slater and his crew. They are highly competent, very professional, and dedicated to the conduct of good science. The sub was highly maneuverable, allowing us to literally spin on its axis to capture crabs. It is a relatively simple system and all of its major components are mechanical, so there was very little that could go wrong. In that sense it is a very safe operation. It had adequate visibility and was quite comfortable to work in. The only mechanical problem was a slight leak in the propeller shaft.

No one liked the "slight leak" from around the propeller shaft so we would replace the shaft packing to stop the leak whenever it became a steady flow. The submersible electric motor was inside the hull, so the drive shaft had to penetrate the hull. Packing around the shaft allowed the shaft to spin while at the same time it kept the water out. As the packing wore down, it would start to allow a little water in. It only took a few hours to change the packing while the sub was on deck.

A large male Tanner crab holding the smaller adult female in his right chela. Such behavior may precede mating by up to ten days; while the male waits for the female to become ready to mate, he uses his free claw to fend off competitors.

Mating Tanner crabs (Stevens, 1997)

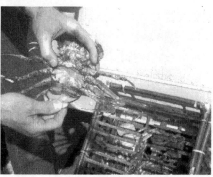

Pile of Tanner crabs (Stevens, 1997)   Delta *crab basket*

We also made several dives on an EPA designated dumpsite in Kodiak Bay. It was a Kodiak cannery fish waste disposal area in 600 feet of water. We observed fish waste on the seafloor in several stages of decomposition. When the waste was first dumped, thousands of seagulls consumed a large portion of the more buoyant materials. Heavier parts (heads and whole fish) sank quickly to the seafloor. Medium size parts drifted down in about thirty minutes as a "snow-storm" of flakes. The smallest pieces took an hour to settle, during which currents spread them over half of a mile. This debris covered the entire seafloor and fish moved in immediately after a dump. Other predators, an octopus and sea stars, were observed eating debris at least several days old. Sand fleas cleaned up the rest. Within six months all of the waste material was gone. The initial conclusion was the dumping does not seem to impact the bay adversely. I made one dive when they dumped all the waste detritus right above us so we could measure the settling rates. Tiny fish debris was stuck on *Delta* for weeks.

We arrived at the tiny Kodiak airport for the trip home and passed time watching a Seattle Supersonic NBA playoff game. This was David's favorite team, and he wanted to watch the entire game so he decided to wait for the next plane that was to leave a few hours later. Bad decision, the fog moved in and David spent three days in Kodiak sleeping on the airport floor.

SOMETIMES OUR GOVERENMENT dive schedule did not make much sense and 1991 was one of them. After leaving Kodiak, we spent two weeks traveling to Monterey to dive five days for more slimy hagfish research. Then it was ten days back to Sitka to continue on Tory's rockfish surveys for eight days. This time the weather was very poor and we lost three days of diving. On the other days, we dove into a confused sea with six to twelve-foot swells and winds blowing over thirty knots. The month of May is usually too early to work in the Gulf of Alaska unless you are in protective waters.

Fish biologists had a continuing problem estimating the size of a fish and the distance a fish was from *Delta*. Our two-laser beams helped measure the size, as they put two dots a known distance apart on a fish. For a few years, on the East Coast, we used a chain suspended from the submersible bow plane for distance. This technique did not work in Alaska, the chain would tangle in the rocky seafloor.

Tory O'Connell suggested using a hand-held laser beam with a digital read-out for distance from the device to a laser dot on an object. The problem was it kept reading the distance from the observer to *Delta's* port. To solve that we tied a small water balloon around the front end of the device and then pressed it against the port. Now the beam was traveling through water and Plexiglas, not air. The next concern was where to get more balloons. Tory, who was seven months pregnant, went into a local pharmacy and bought several dozen prophylactics. The druggist took one look at her and said, "Lady, they will not do you any good in your condition."

Tory was a good sport but riding in *Delta* that year was very uncomfortable for her. She was also woozy on the support ship where rough seas normally did not bother her. However, she continued to count rockfish, the basis for an important Alaskan commercial fishery, including the popular Yellow-eye Rockfish, commonly called Pacific Red Snapper.

Pregnant Tory with measuring device   *With Tory and Dave Carlisle*

David on a rare nice day in the Gulf of Alaska

NEXT WE DOVE for a few days up and down the Alaskan Inside Passage counting sea cucumbers. Someone wanted to start a sea cucumber fishery—they are considered a delicacy in Asia. We had to determine if there were enough cucumbers to support a fishery. Sea cucumbers live on the steep rocky walls on either side of the Inside Passage. I do not know whether a fishery ever got started but we found a lot of sea cucumbers. While diving there, we ran into treasure hunters who had no money but wanted us to search for a sunken ship. We had a contract to fulfill so I declined their offer.

Hunting for sea cucumbers, Inside Passage

Delta *off Alaska*

Pacific Ocean Perch (POP)

One large 1991 project was for NMF. They were responsible for monitoring the commercial stocks of POP, Pacific Ocean Perch, in the Gulf of Alaska. Their fish estimates were based on previous bottom trawl samples even though the trawlable seafloor comprised less than ten percent of available POP habitat. The fish biologists needed *Delta* to observe POP abundance in nontrawlable areas, and to observe POP vertical migration in the water column while feeding on plankton both day and night.

Delta was used off Juneau to search for several sonic-tagged King Crabs again. We did find an active tag inside a King Crab trap but there was no crab attached. At least we proved that we could find and follow a signal. That study was followed by a ten-day transit back to Nome. We anchored outside again and took our small rubber boat, with an outboard, through the wave-tossed rock jetty channel. It was exhilarating to make it through without ending up soaked with cold water. This time, Nome's dirt main street had about six inches of mud on top making travel around town very difficult. Using the wooden sidewalks did not help much either—drunks sleeping off the night before usually occupied them. The new Alaska NURP director celebrated his 50th birthday at sea with us off Nome and we decorated the galley with blown up prophylactics left over from Tory's cruise. We made 229 dives off Alaska during fifty-six dive days before the Ventura based support ship, *M/V Pirateer* left for Seattle.

WE RETURNED TO Newport, Oregon to again collect gas samples and map several offshore banks. Using sidescan sonar at night, scientist's located surface expressions of earthquake faults previously identified with Oregon State seismic profilers. We used *Delta* during the day to map their fault scarp targets. The Oregon chief scientist wrote in his report:

> The combination of using sidescan and *Delta* was highly successful, allowing us to confirm that the faults are recently active which was our primary hypothesis.

We then helped biologists complete their four-year rockfish study off Oregon. The rocky Oregon offshore banks were quite different, both physically and in the type of fish they supported. These banks are a critical part of the commercial marine fisheries off Oregon and our results helped conclude that each bank needed to be managed separately. Scientists had enough data for several manuscripts from the combined sub surveys and day-night comparisons. Diving late in the year off Oregon was risky because of foul weather, but we lost only one-and-a-half days of diving and even had time to recover another lost current meter off Washington for University of Washington scientists.

AFTER OREGON, we sailed to California and made nine dives off Anacapa Island in one day, taking several prospective clients on their first dives. This island is near the Navy missile range and we discovered several missile nose cones, some still attached to parachutes, lying on the seafloor. I even came across a large torpedo. During one of the deeper dives, I found a Navy two-ton truck sitting upright on the seafloor covered with thousands of crabs. The truck must have rolled off a ship heading out to the navy base on San Nicolas Island.

Richard Slater inside the Delta, which has logged more than 2,700 deep-sea dives since 19

Los Angeles Times *photos*

DIVING IN *DELTA* was generating a lot of publicity in the local press and on television. Several articles appeared in the *Los Angeles Times*. A French advertising agency contacted me in 1992 and asked to use *Delta* in a new candy bar advertisement. We filmed the ad while anchored off Santa Barbara—it looks similar to the south coast of France. My job was to "pilot" the submersible from my hiding place while an actor acted as the pilot. The candy bar was similar to a Baby Ruth. When *Delta* was brought on board, after a "dive", the actor opened the hatch, stood on the pilot's seat, tore off the candy bar cover, and took a big bite. They filmed this episode over and over so the actor had to spit out his bite over the ship's railing each time the director yelled "cut." The candy bar chunks made a trail as they floated along the side of the ship and the ship's engineer panicked thinking his holding tank had overflowed.

I always requested a copy any time we were featured on a television show or when a reporter wrote an article about us. The people involved always agreed but rarely did I see a final production. I looked up the French advertisement company on a visit to Paris later in the year and they gave me a copy of the candy bar ad but it was in the wrong format. I never did see the final cut.

Filming Delta *for candy bar ad*

IN OCTOBER, 1989, the Underwater Society of America announced I was the recipient of their 1989 "diver of the year" NOGI science award. I was honored and presented with their statuette during the OCEANS '89 Convention in Seattle. This award is given annually to the individual who has exemplified himself as a leader and a major contributor to marine science. Previous recipients included Jacques Cousteau, Bob Ballard, and my friends Gene Shinn and Dick Cooper. On the way home, I was stopped in airport security by an excited female who thought my bubble-wrapped statuette going through the x-ray machine was an Emmy award and they wondered who I was. I think they were disappointed.

My 1989 NOGI award for Science

Chapter Nineteen

Ireland & *Lusitania*

No schoolboy going for his first airplane ride was more excited
than I was as I prepared for my first dive in *Delta.*

—Bob Ballard, *Exploring the* Lusitania (1995)

IN 1993, I DOVE with Bob Ballard for *National Geographic* to
observe and photograph the *R.M.S. Lusitania,* a British luxury
liner built by Cunard in 1906 and sunk by a German U-Boat
off southern Ireland on May 7, 1915. It was the largest (762-
feet long), fastest (twenty-five knots), most luxurious ship of
its time, and nearly 1,200 people drowned, including 128
Americans, when it sank. This sinking provoked a massive
outcry in the United States, even though the Germans claimed
the *Lusitania* was carrying munitions and weapons—therefore
a valid target. This incident contributed to the deterioration in
U.S./German relations that eventually led the United States to
enter World War I.

The liner's remains lie in 293 feet of water about eleven
miles southwest of the Irish port of Cobb. Our goal was to
find any contraband munitions evidence and proof of why the
Lusitania sank, after being torpedoed, in less than twelve
minutes. During twenty-one dives, we recorded more than
eighty hours of video and took hundreds of photographs.
Considerable amounts of our footage was used in a *National
Geographic* television special, a book by Ballard and an article in
the *National Geographic* monthly magazine.

We shipped *Delta* to Ireland and then flew over to meet the film crew in Cork. Several underwater vehicles were used on this project besides *Delta,* including *Jason,* a very large ROV (remotely operated vehicle) owned by the Woods Hole Oceanographic Institute, and *Homer,* a small mini-ROV owned by the Harbor Branch Oceanographic Institute in Florida. There were four vans and twenty-eight people, plus the ship's crew, on board the 240-foot support ship, the *M/V Northern Horizon,* a dynamically positioned vessel from England. This ship could hover over the wreck and would move as little as one meter in any direction upon request. Talking to *Lusitania* experts while off Ireland, I found they thought the constant ship movement, the drone of the generators, and most of all, the smell of diesel fumes were very annoying. To the *Delta* crew it felt like an ocean liner compared to most ships we had worked on. A full galley with hot meals and large staterooms with great accommodations were more than welcomed.

Container ready for shipping and after removing Delta

M/V Northern Horizon *and* Delta   *Launching* Jason

Our biggest problem turned out to be launching and retrieving *Delta* from the *Northern Horizon* as it was about thirty feet from the main deck to the ocean surface. This necessitated using several of our crew in a rubber boat to unhook *Delta* once it landed on the sea surface and to hook it up during retrieval. It also meant *Delta* would be swinging free during launch and recovery with the pilot and observer in the submersible during the entire time. Not our normal way of working but after a little practice, everything went smoothly.

I was the pilot on the first dive as we slowly approached the *Lusitania* in very murky water. It was massive, and I was in awe alongside a wall of steel with water visibility only ten to fifteen feet. There was little sea life around the wreck but lots of ship debris on the seafloor. The ship was in disarray with rivets missing, pieces hanging loose, and wreckage everywhere. The *Lusitania* had broken in half when it hit the seafloor, with the stern section landing upright. The forward half of the ship was now leaning over about forty-five degrees. At one time the wreck was over a hundred feet high but only about forty feet now as pressure, gravity, and time has caused the wreck to completely collapse. The entire superstructure had slid off to the seafloor and was lying in a big jumble. We discovered many interesting objects including the ship's whistle, a bathtub and shower, and the elevator car. There were no bodies and we did not expect any. Shoes were common and when there were two together a body was probably once lying there.

Bob Ballard and his support team from Woods Hole were impressive. They were very professional and had studied the wreck in great detail before we made a dive. We had meetings each evening to discuss results from our dives and to plan new dives for the next day. Every dive had a purpose. There were two working models of the *Lusitania* on board the support vessel, one of the original ship and the other of the wreck. A *National Geographic* artist and a *Lusitania* historian kept bringing the wreck model up to date by viewing photos and videos after each dive.

Delta *and* R.M.S. Lusitania *(paintings by Ken Marschall)*

Several scuba divers had been on the *Lusitania* before our dives. There were rumors that British Navy divers dove in the 1950s to remove any evidence of articles of war and then set off charges to destroy the hulk. In the 1960s, an American scuba diver reached the wreck but only stayed about ten minutes. A deep-sea diving company successfully retrieved three propellers in the 1980s, turning one into golf clubs.

Numerous fishing nets, draped over the wreck, were a real problem for all the underwater vehicles. These clear nylon monofilament nets were very strong. Local fishermen said whenever they had an old net at the end of the fishing season, they would make a pass over the wreck and either make a big haul of codfish or lose their net on the wreck. The artist Ken Marschall eliminated most of the nets in his paintings—they would obscure the wreck. One problem with "ghost" nets is they still catch fish. The *Lusitania* nets were full of live and dead fish in various states of decomposition.

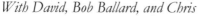

With David, Bob Ballard, and Chris   *Ballard's* Lusitania *Book*

Usually, *Delta* carried a single observer but during one *Lusitania* dive there were two observers, the artist and the historian. They were cruising around the wreck when *Delta's* propeller sucked up a fishing net from below and the propeller became entangled. I was managing the navigation station and told Bob about our predicament. He said to do whatever was necessary. I contacted Chris, the *Delta* pilot, and told him I would direct *Jason* over and use its hydraulic arm to cut *Delta* free. Chris answered that he was dropping the tail and would be on the surface shortly. It was not necessary to drop the tail but I thought the two observers were probably freaking out and Chris realized the quicker he surfaced the better. Doug had designed *Delta's* tail assembly so it could be released in an emergency. We had practiced dropping it in training but never during a working dive. Chris unscrewed the tail from within the submersible and *Delta* rapidly floated to the surface. The *Delta* crew was standing by in the rubber boat and towed the submersible over to the support vessel where it was lifted onboard. I was very concerned as the observers climbed out. Fortunately, they had a great time as the entanglement enabled them to stay down longer on the wreck with a great overview. Everyone was calm and there had been no panic. Chris turned the sub lights off to save power and after a few moments, when the observer's eyes adjusted to the darkness, visibility from the surface light increased. The historian told me, "The visibility, although dim, was perhaps forty to fifty feet, double what we could see with the lights on. The artist added, "The ambient light is amazing. It was a deep Christmas green. I've always used blues before. But it's not blue and pretty. It's green and creepy!" Later that day he produced several sketches and when he returned to California, his paintings included green seawater. However, the editors of the *National Geographic* "*Lusitania*" book did not care for the green water and ordered him to change the color back to blue so all the underwater paintings in the book have the inaccurate blue seawater.

Northern Horizon *crew with dropped tail and painting by Ken Marschall)*

Navigation room for tracking vehicles on the Northern Horizon

I found *Delta's* tail on the next dive and David salvaged it a day later with the fishing net full of fish. *Jason* became tangled in nets several times. Once, when *Jason* was caught, two divers went down and freed it after it was pulled part way up to the surface. Another time, the crew pulled on its tether until *Jason* broke loose, severing all the fiber-optic cables, which resulted in *Jason* being unavailable for the last few days.

The operator/pilot of *Jason* celebrated his 40th birthday while we were at sea. During one dive, on the big day, when *Jason* was filming *Delta* in the *Lusitania* dining room, we put a sign in a *Delta* porthole saying "Happy 40th Martin." When

Jason's TV camera zoomed in on *Delta's* conning tower the sign filled the screen. Martin who was piloting *Jason* was completely surprised. It was the first, and probably the last, birthday party in the dining room since the *Lusitania* sank.

One day, an official-looking boat came bearing down on us and it looked like we might be in trouble with local authorities. It was an Irish Fish and Game boat; they thought we were fishing over the wreck without a license. Another day, Walt Disney's nephew, Roy Disney, made a dive after he came out for a visit from his nearby castle.

It is difficult for me to understand why the *Lusitania* has not received the attention the *Titanic* has. The *Lusitania* story is much more interesting and a mystery as well. The wreck is in a very advanced state of decay, so we asked Bob if we could recover some artifacts for the nearby *Lusitania* museum but he thought, as it was a gravesite, we should not remove anything. Because of the ship's position on the seafloor, and her poor condition, it is unlikely that anyone will ever know exactly what happened that day in 1915. We could not see the area where the torpedo hit; it lies under the wreck. It is common knowledge that there was a second explosion just after the torpedo hit the *Lusitania*. The second explosion probably caused the ship to sink as her sister ship was torpedoed four times during World War I and never sank. Did unauthorized explosives stowed on board cause the second explosion? Some experts on board came up with the idea the second explosion was caused by coal dust but this was later discounted. We did find several hedgehogs (mines), unexploded mortars, and many percussion caps around the wreck, making every dive somewhat hazardous. The hedgehogs and mortars were from World War II when the British used the wreck for target practice. The percussion fuses could be from the wreck itself and would prove there were munitions on board. It was a little unsettling to be sitting next to a bomb on the seafloor.

With Bob Ballard and Explorer Club flag

Bob and I made a dive together to take the Explorer Club flag down to the *Lusitania*. This flag had been to both Poles and on top of Mt. Everest, among other places, and after our dive it was returned to New York for display. Bob and I planned a few other adventures together but Bob only used ROV's and never dove in a manned submersible again.

Project group (I am in Delta *next to David who is above Chris)*

Chapter Twenty

Taiwan, Iran, & Italy

The world is a book; those who do not travel read only
one page.

—Attributed to Saint Augustine in Thomas Fielding's
Selected Proverbs for All Nations (1824)

LATE IN 1992, TWO VISITORS met with Doug and me in
our submersible facility in Torrance. They were Taiwanese and
were interested in using *Delta* for various projects in the South
China Sea and around Taiwan. I flew down to Taiwan in early
1993 to search for a possible support vessel while presenting a
lecture at the annual Chinese Undersea Technology meeting in
Taipei. I also met with several potential customers from local
Taiwanese Universities, the Taiwanese Government, and a few
private industry research groups. Dr. Frank Wu, a Taiwanese,
was my main contact. He had a Stanford education and now
lived in Los Angeles. Frank arranged for me to give a few
presentations concerning *Delta* to high-level administrators and
government agencies while I was in Taiwan. My lectures were
well received and it appeared we would have plenty of work
here in the future. One evening, Frank took me to Taipei's
Snake Alley, a place where every kind of food imaginable was
sold. Most popular was the blood of a live snake squirted into
a glass and then mixed with some snake venom to form a
popular drink—I did not try it. I later reached an agreement
with Frank; we would ship *Delta* to Taiwan after our North
American dive season was completed in the fall of 1993.

Delta was flown from Los Angeles to Kaohsiung, a major port city in southern Taiwan, in early December 1993. Dan Wang, a local engineer, was our contact in Kaohsiung. There were many potential projects including dumpsite surveys, cable and pipeline inspections and work for the Taiwanese Navy.

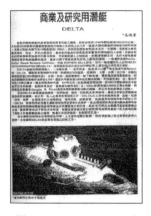

Taipei newspaper article

Ready to go diving off Kaohsiung

Dan Wang and Frank Wu

The support ship Frank had arranged for us was a disaster. There was no room for our van, the crane operator could not see *Delta* during launch or recovery, and the ship's Captain could not speak English. Any order we gave the bridge in English first had to be translated into Chinese and then into the local Taiwanese dialect before the boat would move.

We went ahead, mobilized, and prepared to dive. The weather was very poor when Frank and I made the first dive off Kaohsiung. Everything went okay until the ship came to recover *Delta* and ran over us. I remember seeing the ship's propeller spinning very close as we were banging along the bottom of the ship. *Delta's* tail was smashed so I could not maneuver the submersible. David dove in, fully clothed, and attached a line that saved us. After another dive, I canceled further operations—it was too dangerous. Those were two very expensive and hazardous dives. At least we stayed in a nice hotel with great food. Later, I received a letter from Frank:

> Thank you very much for all your effort contributing to the development of undersea technology in the Republic of China, Taiwan. We had two successful dives and we should celebrate!

Water Taxi in Kaohsiung   *Heading to dive site*

We tried again in 1996, shipping our yellow container with *Delta* to Taiwan in February. Ten days of diving were scheduled off southern Taiwan and we would again work out of Kaohsiung. I flew down from Los Angeles and switched planes in Taipei. Waiting for my plane, I joined a nicely dressed group of Chinese and was glad I was not going with that rowdy, poorly dressed, chain smoking, collection of Asians who I saw walking in the pouring rain to board their plane. When I checked in, I was told my plane was leaving so I ran across the tarmac in the rain to join the rowdy smoking group. I ended up in a middle seat on a very bumpy one-hour ride through a large storm. The nicely dressed crowd was heading to the United States.

The Taiwanese government had requested that we dive in the Formosa Straits between Taiwan and the mainland, but China had recently made threats against Taiwan so we were not allowed to go near the border area. The Chinese threats coincided with the upcoming Taiwanese national election. There were colorful flags and posters everywhere and loudspeakers on trucks blasting campaign propaganda.

We rushed *Delta* through customs in one day—in 1993 it had taken over a week. The container lock was missing but all our equipment was still there. The new support ship that Frank had found was small but adequate. Mobilization only took one day with lots of help from the friendly locals. The hardest worker on the little support ship was the captain but he broke his ankle jumping off our truck and could not sail with us. A very old woman drove the forklift and did a good job of getting *Delta* out of the van and onto the ship. The heat and humidity were both close to a hundred.

A problem soon arose. There was no generator on the boat, how would we charge *Delta's* batteries at night? One of the deck hands came up with a great solution by using a very long extension cord. He ran the cord across the ship, across the dock, across a busy street, and up the side of building three stories to his apartment where he plugged it into a wall outlet. He had to check it several times during the night to make sure the cord was not unplugged or that a circuit breaker had tripped. His ingenious idea worked quite well.

Everything was ready to go the next day at 7:00 a.m. when we arrived onboard. Unfortunately, the immigration officer did not show up until noon. Anytime we left the harbor, we had to officially leave Taiwan and reenter upon our return. We cruised around the harbor practicing launches and retrievals while waiting for immigration.

The harbor at Kaohsiung was polluted with oil, trash, and bloated dead dogs. Some Taiwanese must have thought the proper place for a dead dog is in the harbor. During a practice session, a tire mat line caught in the support ship's propeller and we were drifting toward a rock jetty. I motioned to the deckhand to dive in and cut the line loose. No one moved, so I grabbed a knife and dove in to free the ship. Everyone thought I would catch some weird disease but I was fine. At last we sailed out to sea to survey the local sewer outfall. Our practice launches and retrievals helped and everything went smoothly. Our new skipper, a very young lad, had a name that sounded like "Shinn" so that is what we called him.

Delta, *support boat, and apartment building used to charge submersible at night*   *Attaching tire mat*

Pollution, Kaohsiung Harbor

That evening we had dinner at a nice hotel with our clients and several professors from Sun-Yat-Sen University. We sat around a large round table with waiters serving us plates of delicious food. After dinner, everyone made toasts with some kind of 100-proof Chinese liquor. One drink was enough for me but the others kept knocking them down. The next day we sailed at 7:30 a.m. and whisked through immigration in one hour. We were diving by 10:00 a.m. and completed a sewer pipeline survey before returning to port. That evening, we had another great dinner with more toasting with the firewater.

The next day, we headed south to survey an offshore dumpsite. The wind freshened some and we had a difficult time returning to port. The surf was too heavy to enter the harbor so we waited outside for several hours while jogging into the weather. While waiting, we witnessed the port police capturing a crowd of illegal Chinese trying to enter Taiwan. I begged off dinner that night and ate in a fast food restaurant.

Frank bought our lunches daily at a local market. They were in Styrofoam boxes held together with a rubber band. We called them mystery meals. You never knew what was inside and every day was different. We could usually eat about half of the food and did not try the unidentifiable items. The crew kept throwing trash overboard, including our mystery meal boxes, until we insisted on having a trash barrel onboard.

The next to last day of diving got off to a bad start when we arrived at immigration early that morning. Our immigration officer was late to work and while we were waiting, we heard a loud argument from inside the building. His boss was chewing him out for being late and because he had not cleared us properly the last few days. We had not notified the military tower when we left and when we returned. The boss said both David and I were illegal immigrants; we had been entering the country without proper papers. A few hours later, it was finally settled and we proceeded to our dive site where the wind was blowing over twenty-five knots and the sea was very rough, making diving almost impossible. We searched for the pipeline dive site with no compass, no depth sounder, no radio, no radar, no anchor, and usually no power because the engine kept stalling. Finally, some local fishermen led us to the spot, as sewer diffuser output always provides really good fishing. A couple of dives were completed under very extremely stressful conditions but it was better to be underwater in *Delta* than riding the little bucking bronco support boat.

On the last day we arrived at the boat around 6:30 a.m., raced through immigration and the military tower by 8:00 a.m., and made four dives to collect rocks and slag from the local steel mill dumpsite. The wind blew up before noon forcing us to head in early. As we tied up at immigration, the deckhand dropped our official papers overboard and we had to collect them with a boat hook while they were floating out to sea. As we were leaving the boat for the last time, I looked back and saw our valiant crew emptying the trash barrel into Kaohsiung Harbor.

Delta had been used for eight dives in six days. Not up to our usual standards, but given the circumstances, the very windy weather, and the poor support boat, we did okay. *Delta* never returned to Taiwan but I look back on our trips there with fond memories of good friends, excellent dinners, poor support vessels, dead dogs in the harbor, and lots of powerful liquor.

IN AUGUST 1992, I received a fax message from the Iran Media Co. Ltd. in Tehran. This was a company that claimed to be involved with Iranian scientific instruments, especially oceanographic dive equipment. They had recently received an inquiry from a fishery research center for a small submersible to use on a few Persian Gulf underwater biological research projects. They asked if we could help. I was a bit skeptical; Iran wasn't one of the safest places in the world, with religious zealots running the country. There was no way I would ship *Delta* to Iran. I did contact the CIA, however, and they were interested in having me follow up to discover what was behind the request. I eventually sent a fax nine months later and said I would meet with their company representatives somewhere outside of Iran.

Late in 1993, I received a letter from a Subsea Research and Development Center professor at Isfahan University in Iran. He was also interested in using *Delta* for Persian Gulf studies. The Persian Gulf War was over but I was still not interested in diving there.

In September 1994, I was invited by IFREMER, the French Research Institute for the Exploration of the Sea, to give a talk at the Third International Submersible Rescue Symposium in Toulon, France. I spoke on *Delta's* safety features and how they were used on the *Lusitania* when the submersible became entangled in the fishnet. I had suggested to the Iranians we meet in France during this Symposium and gave them the dates and hotels where I would be staying. A letter came back from Iran, written in French, setting up several meetings. I waited at the requested times and places but no one appeared. Later, a message caught up with me in Paris apologizing for missing our appointments and asking for a new date but I was leaving France and declined. I did not hear from the Iranians again.

The Agency did not want me to drop my contact with Iran, even though I was still not interested in working with them. In 1995, my handlers came up with a plan. No one from the USA had been inside the Iranian Embassy in Rome. They wanted to know what was in there and they wanted me to find out. Since I lost contact with the professor from Isfahan University, I thought someone in the Iranian Rome Embassy might assist me in locating him. I mailed a letter to the Iranian Defense Attaché in Rome and a meeting was set up for late November 1995.

My youngest son, Stephen, accompanied me to Italy and we planned to travel around after my meeting. His trip highlight was running into the Pope twice, once only a few feet away. The lowlight of the trip occurred when we were in northern

Italy. I had to attend a meeting so I asked Stephen to fill up the rental car at a service station just down the street. He made a wrong turn and became lost. Later, when I was walking down a deserted street after dark trying to figure out how I could contact him, he suddenly came driving down the street by sheer luck. He had been driving around the surrounding farm area for over three hours, mainly on dirt roads, looking for me. How he found me was a miracle. He had no cell phone, addresses, or telephone numbers, they were all in my briefcase.

We had a very nice hotel suite in Rome. After a few days of sightseeing and warding off pickpockets, I finally received my instructions to meet someone at 10:30 a.m. the next morning. I was to walk clockwise around the oft-visited tourist stop, Trajan's Column, carrying a Time magazine. When I spotted someone walking around the Column counterclockwise with a new Sports Illustrated, I was to ask if he was Mike and identify myself as Todd and we would then exchange magazines which happened. I followed my instructions and was motioned to follow "Mike" to a nearby coffee shop in a back alley. The guy even had on a trench coat and dark glasses. He briefed me on the next day's plans. At 10:00 a.m. a taxi would pick me up at my hotel and take me to the Iranian Embassy where I was to meet with the Iranian Military Attaché. During this meeting, I could ask the Attaché about my lost Iranian contacts while observing everything.

The next morning, I jumped into a taxi and traveled to an upscale residential area on the outskirts of Rome. The Iranians had bought a beautiful estate and transformed the big house into their Embassy. I climbed out of the taxi at the Embassy gate and was immediately surrounded by press, police, and others wondering who I was and why I was going into the Iranian Embassy. I checked in at the front gate with a startled sentry. He phoned someone and then let me in while pointing to the big house. After walking a few hundred feet through beautiful gardens, I arrived at the front door, knocked, and was let in by a secretary who motioned for me to wait in a nearby chair. Looking around I noticed the house was basically stripped of furniture and wall hangings except for a very large picture of the Ayatollah Khomeini who seemed to be staring at me. I was ushered into a large room, also bare of trappings, and met the young handsome military attaché sitting behind a large desk. He seemed a bit suspicious when speaking to me in broken English while asking me many questions about my contacts in Iran. After ten minutes, he ushered me out and said he would be in touch and would try to locate my contacts.

I returned to my hotel and while going up in the elevator I realized that "Mike" was beside me. He did not say anything but followed me to my room where he debriefed me. I never heard from the military attaché or the professor in Iran again.

I did get to visit several friends and associates in the Italian submersible business which made this trip worthwhile. One company was building heavily armed mini-subs for the North Korea and I was able to inspect one waiting for delivery. I also learned the Iranians owned only one submersible, in very poor condition, and recently had been shopping around for a new one. The owner of an Italian submersible company said he would help me if I traveled to Iran. He thought the Iranians were very confused on exactly what they needed and what they wanted. The Italians have been building military mini-submersibles since before World War II. They build an excellent product and were willing to sell to anyone.

Chapter Twenty-One

Admiral Sampson & Brother Jonathan

There are few things as powerful as treasure
once it fastens itself upon the mind.

—Joseph Conrad, *Heart of Darkness* (1902)

WE BEGAN OUR 1992 season by diving with several long-time clients. Many biologists were now relying on *Delta* as a tool to help observe and count marine animals. We hopefully had found our role. There was little competition; many sub research proposals, sent to NURP, at NOAA, by scientists, were written with *Delta* in mind.

In early April, we sailed north to Sitka, Alaska, aboard the 130-foot supply vessel *Jolly Roger,* an excellent support ship as were its Ventura sister ships, *Cavalier, Pirateer,* and *Buccaneer.* We used all of these ships up and down the west coast for many years. After more sea cucumber surveys in the Inside Passage, we counted lingcod on the "Pinnacle" off Sitka and filmed tanner crabs off Kodiak Island. We were in the Gulf of Alaska by June checking long-line fishing arrays.

Long-line fishermen put out miles of fishing lines, each with thousands of hooks, along the seafloor. *Delta* was used to run transects along these long-lines so we could video anything caught. Occasionally, a hooked large halibut would lunge up into the water column. Halibut, some appearing to be nearly as large as the submersible, normally lay still until we moved very close. Then they exploded off the seafloor, flipping over and heading in the reverse direction with awesome speed.

Rockfish caught on a long-line   *Lingcod with fish on a long-line*

THERE WERE SEVERAL new adventures waiting for us in
Puget Sound, near Seattle, when we arrived in late June 1992
aboard the *Jolly Roger*. Kent Barnard, a Seattle businessman and
diver, had recently started up Argonaut Resources to search
for shipwrecks along the Oregon and Washington coasts. He
created an extensive computerized database and was a leading
expert on American northwest shipwrecks. He was addicted to
searching for shipwrecks after a 1972 scuba class, and he had
spent a lot of money and time on various underwater projects
since then. Kent first approached me in 1991 to help find and
salvage two major wrecks in Puget Sound. He wanted to locate
the steam-powered ocean liner *Admiral Sampson* that sank in
1914 and the small coastal freighter *Coaster* that sank in 1938.
Kent had obtained exclusive salvage rights to both wrecks
from the federal court and was eager to recover anything of
value from them.

Coaster was a Canadian ship that was towing a barge carrying
large bags of ore concentrate from a British Columbia gold
mine. She was rammed by another vessel in the early morning
Puget Sound fog—her eight-man crew was saved. We found
what was left of the *Coaster* and its barge in 200 feet of water.
However, we did not salvage any gold ore as it was widely
spread over the seafloor. Later, Kent sent scuba divers down
to collect some ore concentrate around the wreck but currents
and storms had reworked the remaining ore with the seafloor
sediments. There was very little concentrated gold ore left.

Admiral Sampson

The *Admiral Sampson* is the deepest known shipwreck in Puget Sound. She was a luxury ocean liner constructed in 1898 and was traveling to Alaska from Seattle in 1914 when she collided with another vessel in early morning fog. Aboard were sixty registered passengers and a crew of sixty-five. Eight people, including the captain and two passengers, drowned when the ship sank in just seven minutes. Kent used side-scan sonar to locate the vessel in 320 feet of water off Point No Point, a few miles north of downtown Seattle. He then photographed the 208-foot liner with a video camera. Kent hired several ROVs to pick up artifacts but the strong currents made maneuvering around the wreck nearly impossible and they became tangled in their own support lines. One ROV was lost on the wreck so they sent down a diver in a one-atmosphere armored diving suit worn like a suit of medieval armor. His umbilical cord tangled and he became pinned against the wreck. Six hours later, during slack tide, another diver, on mixed-gas, descended and freed the entangled diver.

After these escapades, we were hired in 1992. Our job was to recover artifacts estimated to be worth over $2 million with possibly a collection of diamonds in the safe. The following sketch is not very exact as the entire forward main deck has collapsed into the ship and *Delta* is about three times too big.

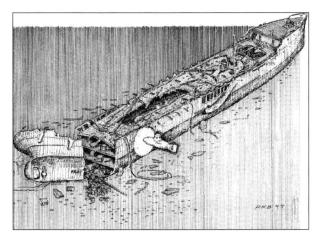

Sketch of Admiral Sampson *wreck with* Delta
(drawing by Ronald Burke in consultation with Kent Barnard)

This magnificent wreck is sitting upright on the seafloor. She is covered with large, white, sea anemones and is home to schools of fish, including snapper and lingcod. There was a large octopus living in one stateroom. We made many dives over three years and became very familiar with this ship. At 320 feet it is usually pitch dark in these waters but we had about forty-foot visibility with submersible lights illuminating the wreck. The two upper decks had collapsed onto the main deck and there was a gaping big hole where the collision occurred. Exploring the forward part of the ship was similar to diving in a giant bucket with the remains of the wooden decks lying on the bottom. Aft, near the galley, we found silverware, crystal, and plates stacked in their bins. The stern lay askew; it had broken off when the ship hit the seafloor. A jumble of ore cars, wheels, and axles had tumbled out of the broken ship onto the seafloor. There were large brass letters from the ship's name and over a hundred portholes lying nearby. Our support ship almost ended up on top of the wreck when a large freighter headed in our direction early one morning and apparently could not see us in the fog. Everyone jumped up and down trying to arouse attention until the ship suddenly changed direction at the very last moment.

Admiral Sampson *anemones and fish*

Admiral Sampson *whistle, brass letters,*   *With recovered brass "S"*
cup, ceramic bowls, and porthole

Delta proved powerful enough to handle the strong currents sweeping the wreck. We retrieved many artifacts, including the eighty-pound bronze steam whistle. Unfortunately, the safe fell down into the hull when the wooden decks collapsed and was never recovered. I salvaged a large bronze letter "S" from the ship's name that had fallen off the stern. Over all, more than one hundred items were recovered and eventually put up for sale at auction. Every item sold except for a few that Kent donated to a local museum. I wanted my letter "S" but it sold for a bit more than I had offered to pay and I was out of the country during the auction. After diving in Puget Sound, we headed north to the San Juan Islands to take scientists from local universities and government agencies diving. These were enjoyable dives for me. Most scientists had never been in a submersible and to give them an opportunity to observe the undersea environment was always fun and exciting.

OUR OPERATIONS then moved south to continue diving with Oregon State geologists, using sidescan sonar to identify offshore faults. We mapped fault scarps prominent on the seafloor and collected more seafloor gases and sediments. There were also dives for biologists to observe local fish.

After the Oregon dives we sailed down to California where biologists dove in *Delta* to assess fish assemblages and habitat types at four sites around Soquel Submarine Canyon near Monterey. Doug's parallel lasers were installed on either side of *Delta's* external video camera to help estimate fish size. The laser beams cut through the water and placed two dots a known distance apart on objects we were filming. Biological observations demonstrated the utility of submersibles for evaluating fish populations associated with deep-water rocky areas that were unavailable using other methods of evaluation. Monterey scientists reported:

> *Delta* provided us with a superior field of view to directly quantify abundance and size, and identify difficult species when compared with surfaced-based or ROV techniques.

In 1993, we traveled to Ireland and Taiwan in addition to our regular West Coast projects. The year started off searching for another lost current meter. This one belonged to the Scripps Institute. We found it during our first dive in 335 feet of water off San Miguel Island, the westernmost Santa Barbara Channel Island. After we had recovered the equipment, we attached a new transponder and set it back in position. *Delta* then went to Seattle for a week of diving on *Coaster* and *Admiral Sampson* before being shipped to Ireland. It was a month before *Delta* returned to the West Coast. We again mobilized in Ventura on the *Cavalier* and sailed north to start diving off Oregon in early September for biologists (fish counts) and geologists (mapping fault scarps). After fifty-five dives in three weeks we headed south to Monterey to continue running fish transects. This was a very busy year for *Delta*.

ON OUR WAY TO Monterey, we stopped for two days near Crescent City just south of the Oregon border to search for a famous shipwreck. This was an interesting project as several treasure hunters had approached us over the years wanting to find the *Brother Jonathan*. Many attempts had been made but the wreck remained elusive to all searchers. *Brother Jonathan* was a nineteenth century steamship that became a twentieth century quest for treasure hunters. She was a 220-foot wooden side-wheel steamer built in 1850 on the Hudson River in New York—originally owned by Cornelius Vanderbilt. She carried 365 passengers, later altered to carry 750. By 1861, she was based in San Francisco and was known as one of the finest and fastest steamships on the West Coast.

Brother Jonathan

In July 1865, she was fully loaded in San Francisco, probably overloaded, with mining equipment bound for Vancouver, British Columbia. There were 240 passengers and crew on board when she sailed out the Golden Gate into a northerly gale and very rough seas. Prominent passengers included a U.S. Army paymaster with a $200,000 payroll for troops at Fort Vancouver, the Northwest Government Indian Agent with money for annual treaty payments, a well-known Civil War General, the Governor of the Washington Territory (a close personal friend of Abraham Lincoln's), the editor of a San Francisco newspaper, and a well-known San Francisco madam with seven attractive young females. Other cargo included 300 barrels of whiskey, two horses, and two camels.

The storm kept building as they headed north past Crescent City, when the Captain decided to turn and head for shelter. The ship hit an unknown reef around 1:00 p.m. and began to sink. Lifeboats were lowered but all were swamped except for one with five women, three children, and ten crewmembers who were the only survivors. The wreck became famous as it was, and still is, the largest maritime disaster in West Coast history. It was thought there might be as much as $50 million in gold on board. Over a hundred expeditions were launched during the past 125 years to find the *Brother Jonathan*. None were successful.

In 1988, a local investment group, Deep Sea Research, or DSR, received permission from the California State Lands Commission to search for the *Brother Jonathan*. A few years later, the president of DSR contacted us and asked if we could help. We were working off Oregon at the time and would be passing by Crescent City on our way south, so we agreed to stop for a few days to dive on targets found during a recent side-scan sonar survey. Doug and I reviewed their side-scan records while DSR directors pointed out the locations of the anchor, side-wheel, safe, and other objects. Everything was on the rocky reef where the ship floundered. Treasure hunters had been diving on that reef for many years. Why hadn't someone found the wreck if it was there? I informed DSR that we needed to be paid for this job; they tried to convince us to take a percentage of anything we found. We finally agreed they would pay our operating costs, and we would receive six percent of anything we found. Six percent of $50 million would be $3 million.

Delta *and* Snooper *on* Cavalier

DSR hired two submersibles, *Delta* and *Snooper*, for two days of diving around the reef off Crescent City in October 1993. *Snooper* was a one-man submersible from Los Angeles, owned by a close friend, the late Don Sieverts. *Snooper* was not ABS certified so Don did not compete with us and we helped each other when needed. *Snooper* was transported up to Crescent City and mobilized on *Cavalier* next to *Delta*. Several dives were made around the reef. Nothing was found except rocks that resembled the side-wheel and the safe. On the last night, a couple of DSR personnel continued running side-scan hoping to discover new targets but most went to bed exhausted and disappointed. Someone suggested looking out on the flat muddy seafloor surrounding the reef. A local fisherman had mentioned he lost his nets when they snagged on something several miles away. The DSR group did not want to leave the reef but after they went to bed several men, who had stayed up, moved the *Cavalier* and located a big target in 250 feet of water. The next morning *Delta* and *Snooper* were launched and discovered the remains of the *Brother Jonathan* sitting upright on the seafloor. The storm and currents had carried it about two miles underwater from the rock it hit.

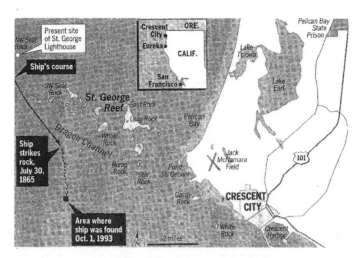

Brother Jonathan wreck site off Crescent City

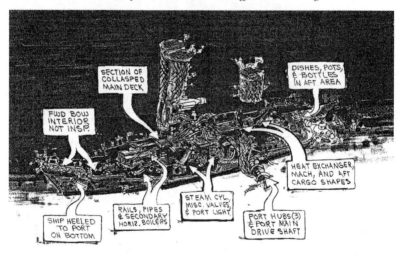

Sketch of Brother Jonathan *wreck by Don Sieverts*

We mapped and photographed the wreck, even though the visibility was less than a few feet. There was crockery, machine parts, a couple of steam boilers, and debris tangled in fishing nets, but no gold. The tangled fishing nets kept the subs from maneuvering close to the wreck. The next day *Delta* dove to collect artifacts to support DSR's legal claim in court.

A month after the discovery, investors and directors of DSR began arguing on how to recover the missing treasure. The directors finally voted to replace the president who wanted to raise $5 million to conduct a detailed search. Most investors wanted to take the wreck apart quickly. Accusations became ugly as DSR's disagreements made the local newspapers and TV news. Before recovery work could start, the California State Lands Commission went to court to prevent DSR from salvaging the *Brother Jonathan* and threatened to arrest anyone near wreck site. They asked the Coast Guard to secure the area. The State claimed that *Brother Jonathan* fell under the Abandoned Shipwreck Act. In order to enforce that act, they had to prove the following in court:

The ship was abandoned. It was not abandoned but was still on the insurance company books and DSR had an agreement with the insurance company that inherited the wreck; the original insurance company no longer existed.

The ship was located on submerged State lands, which are within three miles of shore. The wreck is more than three miles offshore but the State claimed three miles around the rocky reef that is submerged year around except during storms or extremely low tides. The State had never claimed this area until after the wreck was discovered.

The ship was embedded in the seafloor. In geology, the term embedded means surrounded by another medium. Our video proved the shipwreck is still sitting upright on the seafloor and is not buried.

The ship must be listed on the National Register of Historic Places. The State tried to register the wreck eight days before the court hearings.

The judge threw out the State's claim because he felt they had not proved any of the requirements for ownership. The State then appealed to the Ninth Circuit Court of Appeals in San Francisco and lost 3-0 in 1995.

We could now salvage the wreck so we returned to the site in 1996 and on one transect through the wreck *Delta* ran over and broke a small wooden box. Later, when transiting the same path, *Delta* came upon this box again and the observer spotted several gold coins. *Delta* returned to the surface with the sample bag full of gold coins.

Delta *sample bag with first gold coins and David with safe*

With Doug, first coins   Brother Jonathan *plate and* Delta *model*
(Ventura Star *newspaper photo*)

Only two sunken ships have been found containing more than a few American mint condition gold coins, the *Central America* that sank off South Carolina in 1857 and the *Brother Jonathan*. We recovered over 1,200 gold coins, most in mint condition. The broken wooden box, believed to be Wells Fargo's, was carrying newly minted gold $5 (half-eagle), $10 (eagle), and $20 (double eagle) coins. There were only seven 1865-S $20 gold coins in mint condition known to exist before our discovery. We also found the safe, attached a line around it, and hauled it up to the *Cavalier*. It was stored in a San Francisco aquarium to be opened later on live TV. According to ship's records, the purser stored $80,000 in this safe just before sailing but at the safe opening there was only the purser's cap and a small bag of gold dust. Someone had removed the contents before the ship sank.

It looked like my run of zero treasure returns was about to end. However, the State of California had other ideas. They appealed the 1995 court decision to the U.S. Supreme Court. This was costing DSR a lot of money as legal fees piled up. The Supreme Court ruled against the State 9-0 with Sandra Day O'Connor saying DSR took all the chances, spent their own money, the State of California had given them permission to search, and they sued only after the wreck was discovered.

The State of California filed another suit against DSR after the Supreme Court decision knowing that DSR did not have the money to keep fighting. Finally, in 1998, after four years of battling in court, an agreement was reached giving the State of California twenty percent of any treasure we recovered and jurisdiction over the wreck in the future. We recovered many items beside coins, including silverware, plates and cups. Most of this trove, and one gold coin, were given to a Crescent City museum. I ended up with one plate and no gold coin. The Army payroll and Indian treaty money turned out to be paper script and had disintegrated long ago. DSR hired a large diving company to continue searching for coins in 1997. Their divers picked over the wreck but only found a few coins we missed. This million-dollar project cut into the profits.

There was a Los Angeles *Brother Jonathan* coin auction in 1999 that brought in over $5,500,000 dollars. One 1865 $20 coin, with its date mistakenly inverted in the San Francisco Mint, sold for $115,000. I hoped to collect at least $300,000 as our share. DSR expenses totaled over $4 million so our final payment was peanuts (about $60,000) compared to what we recovered. It was exciting to discover an historical shipwreck. However, once something of value is found the worst seems to come out in many people. You attract all kinds of unsavory characters who are willing to rip you off. Years later there was still an ongoing fight between the investors, as more than 100 percent of the wreck had been sold so everyone though they were being short-changed. Some coins have disappeared, we knew exactly how many we picked up. I was glad to receive my share and to leave the treasure-hunting scene to others. (Ten years later I bought one of the double eagle coins we had recovered)

My son David wrote the following story concerning his role as the *Delta* pilot while discovering the *Brother Jonathan*. He called it "Miracle in the Muck." I am including it here as I think it illustrates well what happened that exciting morning off Crescent City.

> I was not happy to be down on the mud flats that morning. We had spent the previous night slowly searching for any trace of the wreck on a section of seafloor far from where we had been searching. All of us would have preferred a night snuggled up in a cove rather than endlessly rolling to and fro in the trough, on what most thought was another pointless exercise to assuage an ego.
>
> We had a boat full of personalities and I wasn't pleased to be on the seafloor with the leader of this group, who was more than convinced that the wreck could not possibly be where we were. We were going through the motions. We were motion sick. We were on our third year of this search, on our sixth day at sea, working twenty-four hours a day, on a small boat full of men; emotions were high. Mine could be called "pissed off". And then I saw a piece of wood.
>
> The visibility down off Crescent City could be described as weak tea with milk. I could scarcely see the seafloor. The ground basically only distinguishable from the water by the deeper saturation of brown, I barely looked out, caring little, knowing that I would run into anything with the submersible before I saw it. I was more concerned with the

digital read-out glowing red in front of me. We were covering a grid. That was my job and I could daydream at will. After all, the ocean is huge and normally offers little but agonizing repetitiveness

Before descending we had agreed to a one-hour dive and both my observer and I were paying the most attention to our watches. When the artifact momentarily entered my consciousness, I pulled the submersible out of gear and called up so that we could mark the spot. I also had some vague feeling that something larger was looming out in the limited expanse of my view, there was a deeper hue of dung brown, but then again that was the nature of skittish submersible pilots who find themselves driving around blindly deep under the water.

"We have something down here," I radioed up while watching the submersible careen broadside with the current. "Time's up," said my observer. "Let's head up." I wasn't opposed but I was too busy trying to return to the site. The reciprocal let's see, 180 degrees, but as I turned I heard, "Dave, get permission to surface." Here was the leader of the expedition, with the first tangible evidence of a target wanting to quit because of an artificial time frame we could ignore. I did as I was told and we returned to the surface.

On the next dive the Brother Jonathon was found by the other submersible using the mark I noted as a center point for the search. I had found only a piece of wood.

I had now been on the wreck enough to recognize exactly where I was at any time despite not seeing much other than a murky haze in front and objects directly below the lower ports. This time was slightly different though. I could clearly see both nets rising from the paddle wheels of the wreck like some weird ethers conjured up from the ghostly ship. They swayed to and fro and I was bored. I then impulsively decided to drift between the nets and attempt to land on a section of the wreck I had not been to before. Intensely staring at a spot past the nets, I began to give both ballast tanks a little air. My heart racing, all puckered up with fear, we started to rise. I put the submersible in gear and through the nets we traveled, all the while ascending toward what were likely massive amounts of submersible catching nets. I panicked and dumped all the ballast air. Better to land hard than to be a skeleton on the web of Neptune's malice. With a thud we landed and the submersible leaned heavy to port. I'm trying to bring my heart out of my throat and the sub into some kind of alignment when I hear a shout below me, "Stop." I had told the observer what I wanted to attempt, knowing full well he would be game. One man's dread is another's thrill shot of adrenaline. He was searching the wreck for a large box, preferably with hinges and a big sign reading "Property of Wells Fargo. Do not open." He could have cared less what I was doing, as long as I remained on the wreck. I peered down through the lowest starboard port and saw what was holding his attention—GOLD.

Later the decision was made that I would carry a line and scuba tanks down to the gold, because I knew where the treasure lay. Great, let's add a line to the surface, and tanks to tangle me up and the job of sitting for hours in the sub waiting for and then watching divers pick up coins. Actually I was thrilled. We were going to scoop up a pile of gold coins off a wreck. How many people ever get to do that? Once I had located the coins, I ballasted down hard and waited for the divers. It is always very strange to be visited on the seafloor, having normally the place to yourself. The two divers seemed to be grinning through their regulators. I could feel the thrill through the steel. Then with a flourish of activity, the oversized divers, appearing huge with all their tanks and gear on so close to the sub, scooped up the coins. A wave, thumbs up, and they were gone.

Directly in front of me, on the submersible deck, the bag of coins awaited the greedy hands of all those on the surface who would consequently be involved in the crude grab for them in the courts. I had the hatch open before the last hooks were placed to secure the submersible on the support vessel.

I suppose all on deck were stunned as I carried the bag over to the center of the ship's deck—its weight reminding me what I had, temporarily, in hand. I recall one participant pushing through the group to grab a coin in a disgusting display of greed. I remember many, temporary smiles from a group that would later be aiming for each other's jugulars.

I retain a sense of pride in having participated in a unique discovery. Many involved might ridicule me for describing a feeling of historical connection to the Gold Rush through actively investigating a preserved timepiece from the era. The gold coins are certainly beautiful but the operation was ugly. Accusations, distrust, and bravado. A few good men were involved; especially some of the investors, but the gold was mired in a different kind of muck, which having tasted, leaves a residual discomfort in my memory. I have never read anybody else's account of what actually happened, though several "memoirs" have been published. My take from the whole affair allowed me to purchase a bicycle. It's gold in color. We have only one coin in the family, whose acquisition is a treasure hunt story in and of itself. I hope that coin gets passed down through the generations, along with a cautionary tale about diving into treasure adventures with buccaneers.

AFTER THE *Brother Jonathan* discovery in 1993, we sailed to Monterey to continue the multi-disciplinary study to assess the importance of small-scale refuges for rockfish species in Soquel Canyon. We evaluated all types of substrate that were potential rockfish habitat. Biologists surgically implanted radio transmitters into several rockfish so we could track them to learn how large a territory an individual fish inhabits and the extent of their movements.

Geologists mapped the seafloor to help biologists identify different substrates. We were now using *Delta's* multi-video camera system to record everything. Observers documented their observations continuously with an externally mounted Hi-8mm video camera while *Delta's* external 35mm camera recorded any specific fish and habitat types for more detailed identification and description. All voice communications were taped with an internal recorder. The two parallel lasers were critical for estimating fish size from *Delta*. It was discovered that rockfish located around deep small rock outcrops were usually protected from fishermen due to their isolation while the similar fish were heavily fished in other more accessible locations. This cruise was a great success with all scientific objectives met. Twenty-four scientists from nine Federal, State, and private research groups participated in the fifty dives over the one week.

THE YEAR 1994 STARTED off with more of the same. We dove on the *Admiral Sampson*, looked at piles of crabs in Kodiak, and ran fish transects for a month off Sitka. Near the end of the season, we dove off Oregon with geologists and biologists, and spent two weeks counting fish off Monterey. I only made twelve dives in 1994, most of them on the *Sampson*.

Brad Stevens developed a theory after studying tanner crab mounds over several seasons. Crab mounds occur coincident with local April and May spring tides. Mounds are built about a month before the peak spring tide and last up to six weeks. Female crabs form mounds when they are ready to release larvae, and leave the mounds immediately after hatching is completed. The large spring tides disburse the larvae.

Between *Brother Jonathan* and the Oregon dives, *Delta* was involved in several other interesting projects. One was off New Jersey with marine biologists from Rutgers University. These scientists were very interested in studying fish nursery habitats in the New York Bight off New York City. We helped compare techniques for estimating densities of fish, which included submersible observations, video sled transects, and trawl collections. Their report concluded:

> The best method for counting and observing juveniles is the utilization of submersible technology where we can identify many more fish than when viewing the videotapes alone, and both of these methods were very superior to beam trawling.

Launching current meter and surface buoy, Santa Barbara Channel

THE LAST *DELTA* project, in 1994, involved search and recovery of three Scripps instrument moorings. Fishing boats located near the western end of the Santa Barbara Channel had damaged these instrument moorings with their trawl gear. Our job was to visually locate each mooring on the seafloor and attach a line connected to the *Cavalier*. The winch on the *Cavalier* then hauled each mooring to the surface. The data on these instruments had been gathered over two years and would cost over $100,000 to replace. The real value of the data is hard to quantify since it is part of a larger data set that is much more valuable when complete. Scripps scientists determined years ago that a manned submersible is the preferred method for locating and inspecting oceanographic equipment on the seafloor. Also, the submersible support ship can recover and replace any equipment, saving the scientists a second trip to sea. *Delta's* pilots found all three-instrument packages in 300 to 500 feet of water. We recovered them during nine dives over three days, and placed each unit back on the seafloor with new release mechanisms. Each unit weighed about 7,000 pounds.

Delta was used for 318 dives in 1994. Only three days were lost to weather and none due to equipment malfunction. Our good reputation continued to grow. We were generating lots of positive publicity with several TV shows featuring *Delta* and newspapers around the United States running articles about our unique business. David and Chris ran the operations at sea while I tended to business back in the office. I had made over 2,200 submersible dives in the past twenty-five years. No one made more, except maybe a driver of a Disneyland submarine.

My wife's cancer returned and I decided it was time to cut back even more and stay closer to home. Being at sea is a young man's game and it was becoming tougher for me to live in the cramped damp sleeping quarters and work around the clock when necessary. I could see the signs and knew it was time to leave the diving to the next generation.

David and Delta *on NURC brochure soliciting proposal*

Chapter Twenty-Two

Edmund Fitzgerald & Carl Bradley

The Captain wired that he had water coming in
and the good ship and crew were in peril,
And later that night when his lights went out of sight
came the wreck of the *Edmund Fitzgerald.*

—Moose Music, Ltd., lyrics by Gordon Lightfoot (1976)

FEDERICK SHANNON contacted me early in 1994 about diving on the wreck of the *Edmund Fitzgerald,* lying on the bottom of Lake Superior in 530 feet of water, after reading about our *Lusitania* dives. Fred lived in Michigan and had spent the last eighteen years studying the *Edmund Fitzgerald.* He conducted hundreds of interviews and collected thousands of records on this ship and now wanted underwater video to highlight his forthcoming lecture tour.

Even though there was no treasure (it was carrying iron ore), I was excited for a chance to view this famous wreck. We ran into many obstacles, including having to obtain permits from both U.S. and Canadian authorities, as the ship rests directly on the international border. And another group, from a local maritime museum, was racing to dive ahead of us.

Fred had trouble obtaining funds and it was not economical for us to dive only two days. We finally reached an agreement and *Delta,* with crew, arrived in July for mobilization aboard a Canadian tug. We made seven dives in two days on the wreck. The rival museum group had dove on the wreck one week earlier. However, they did not make the discovery we did.

T-shirt design for expedition to Michigan

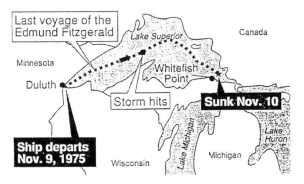

Edmund Fitzgerald's *last voyage*

In 1975, the 729-foot *Edmund Fitzgerald* was hauling 20,000 tons of iron ore from Superior, Wisconsin, east to Detroit, Michigan, when it encountered a fierce November gale on the eastern end of Lake Superior. The ship disappeared from shore radars as it neared safety with the loss of the entire crew. It is now probably the most famous inland shipwreck in the world. (Gordon Lightfoot memorialized it in a song.) It is also a controversial wreck and our dives made it more so.

The wreck consists of two large sections; the forward part is sitting upright and the stern is upside down about 250 feet away. The broken ends of the two sections consist of twisted damaged steel plates with jagged edges. The bow crumbled when the ship plowed into the seafloor but the bridge is in very good shape except all the windows are missing. The water visibility was excellent and the submersible lights illuminated large portions of the wreck.

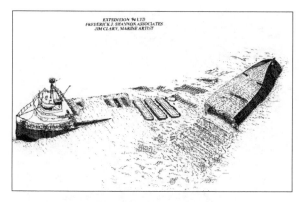

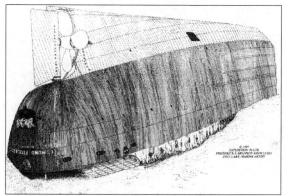

Edmund Fitzgerald *drawings by Jim Clary*

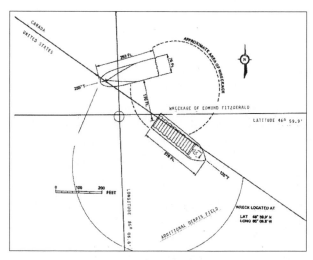

Lake Superior wreck site on the USA/Canada border

Edmund Fitzgerald *with* Delta *(drawings by Jim Clary)*

During one dive, when *Delta* wandered away from the ship's bow, the submersible came across the remains of a body in a life jacket. It is very unusual to find any human remains on a shipwreck after a few years. However, the Great Lakes are fresh water and anaerobic with very low to zero amounts of dissolved oxygen near the bottom. Therefore, there are few animals that can destroy a body. This body was unrecognizable with only a few bones sticking out of a life jacket. When word got out we had photographed the remains, all hell broke loose. The Michigan state legislature immediately passed a bill to ban photographing bodies of any shipwreck victims. Some of the relatives of the *Edmund Fitzgerald's* twenty-nine victims and

Fred's rival at the local museum campaigned for this ban. We could now be thrown in jail for two years and fined up to $5,000 if we photographed a shipwreck victim. Some relatives accused Fred of exploiting the tragedy for money. If Fred made a mistake, it was announcing the discovery of a body to the press and describing the remains in a lecture. The furor caused officials in Canada to consider banning further dives on the wreck. We had started serious international litigation between the United States and Canada. Fred and his rival filed lawsuits against each other.

The reporters now covering *Delta's* dives made our job a lot tougher. They were constantly in the way and never stopped asking questions. There was even a Hollywood screenwriter on hand to assess the project's movie potential. Fred was excited; he was quoted in the press as saying, "I liken this to a moon walk. It is a once-in-a-lifetime opportunity." His feud with the local museum also made the papers. This quarrel had been going on since 1989 when Fred accused the museum director of hoarding video footage from an unmanned camera dive. The museum director was quoted as saying, "Fred treats the shipwreck as his personal preserve. He is obsessed with the *Edmund Fitzgerald* like some people are with the *Titanic.*"

Edmund Fitzgerald *cruise participants*
(Fred Shannon holding plaque, Chris on Delta, *David sitting on left)*

Meeting the Press at night

Local Michigan paper headlines

Delta *and* Edmund Fitzgerald, *magazine cover (1995)*
(drawing by Jim Clary)

Fred was eager to dive again though the lawsuits continued. The Canadian government would not issue another permit so we could not dive on the entire wreck. Fred said he would dive on the U.S. part of the wreck but even those plans were finally canceled. It was decided instead to dive on a similar shipwreck, the *Carl D. Bradley,* a 623-foot limestone carrier that sank in Lake Michigan in 1958 killing thirty-three of the thirty-five-crew members.

Fred found a few other projects for us so it was worth our while to return to the Great Lakes, which we did in August of 1995. This time, we were diving off of a large barge pushed by a tug. It would not be easy, especially when we had to live in a large empty space under the barge deck with thirty-five other people. Everyone slept on an uneven wooden floor covered with outdoor carpeting. Two portable toilets on the deck were the bathroom facilities. Fred placed his pickup truck, with trailer, on the deck so he and his wife had decent quarters. We stayed in our support van most of the voyage when we were not diving or sleeping.

Delta *under the Mackinac Bridge*

Delta *on support barge*

Barge dining room

Delta *and the* Carl Bradley *(drawing by Jim Clary)*

Our first stop was under the Mackinac Bridge, which crosses
the Straits of Mackinac at the north end of Michigan. This
is the third largest suspension bridge in the world and the
biggest in the western hemisphere. It is five miles long
with very strong currents sweeping underneath from water
pouring into Lake Huron from Lake Michigan. Fred and I
made a dive starting at the southern end of the bridge and
inspected the entire crossing, including the bases of the main
bridge towers. The visibility was poor as we bumped our way
along, until we finally reached the northern shore. We are
probably the only people to ever make the entire crossing
underwater.

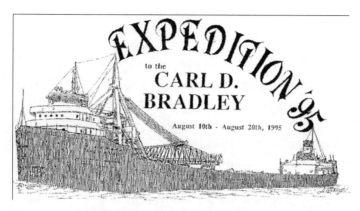

1995 Expedition T-shirt design

Tug pushing Delta *barge across Lake Michigan*

We then steamed about fifty miles into Lake Michigan to dive on the *Carl Bradley*. The weather was terrible and getting worse. Sediment was stirred up so visibility was near zero fifty feet off the bottom making it too dangerous to dive on a shipwreck in those conditions. We turned back to anchor off Beaver Island. This island, with approximately 500 permanent residents, is a popular summer retreat for yachtsmen. We stayed in a dormitory for several nights, while surveying and inspecting power cables during the day from Beaver Island to the mainland.

Beaver Island was once the home of a unique Mormon group. While most Mormon's followed Brigham Young to Utah after the death of Joseph Smith, others followed James Strang. Strang moved his flock to Beaver Island in 1848 to escape persecution and declared himself King of the Island. He continued to practice polygamy until angry mobs arrived from the mainland and drove his several thousand followers off the island. An unhappy husband killed Strang.

The weather improved so we set sail again for the *Bradley* wreck. It was decided to take Frank Mays, the only known living survivor from the *Bradley*, on the first dive. Mays wanted to leave a plaque engraved with the names of the *Bradley* crew, and our expedition members, on the wreck. He was a deck watchman on board the *Bradley* and had survived on a life raft in the icy storm-tossed lake for fifteen hours with another crewmember. The chances of exploring the wreck were slim as water visibility was still very poor. It was decided to make a quick bounce dive and hope Frank could get a glimpse of his ship. We all gathered around the communication center to listen to the observer and pilot talking while *Delta* descended. As it neared the bottom, they reported that the visibility was getting worse and they would probably have to abort the dive. Then we heard Frank Mays say, "There is the name *Carl D. Bradley.*" *Delta* had descended to a spot right next to the name on the stern section. We could have dove for a week in that poor visibility and never saw the wreck. It was an unbelievable moment. They dropped the plaque next to the engine room during their fifteen-minute stay. "We saw it and we were there," Mays said, raising a triumphant fist over his head as he emerged from *Delta.* "It's fantastic, indescribable; I'd love to see more of it." Jim Clary, the well-known ship artist, then went down but his inspection was cut short when *Delta's* pilot lost his bearings in the foggy blanket of silt.

It took several years to get paid for our *Edmund Fitzgerald* and *Carl Bradley* dives and we finally settled for something less than promised.

Chapter Twenty-Three

Shipwrecks, California & Caribbean

As you sink through the water it is like sinking through this thick atmosphere of Mars. You can't see very much and then you land on the bottom and you stir up a little dust cloud and you start looking around through it. There is hazy dirty water layering about two feet off the bottom and soon piles of crab start looming out of the mist. You are looking at these strange creatures and you are saying, what kind of a planet have I landed on? Who lives here?

—Brad Stevens (1995)

DELTA CONTINUED DIVING on a comprehensive work schedule over the next five years. Most dives were for former clients in Alaska, Oregon, and California. Scientists needed more data for their projects. I continued to spend much of my time managing the business while David and Chris were at sea.

Early in 1995, we became involved in a search for a lost shrimp boat off Santa Cruz Island, one of the Santa Barbara Channel Islands. An old, forty-one-foot wooden fishing boat, the *Vil Vana*, disappeared with seven men on board in 1993. Rumors were rampant around the local docks. Did the *Vil Vana* collide with a tanker? Did a UFO take it away? Or did the U.S. Navy's black 160-foot stealth ship *Sea Shadow* run them down? The *Sea Shadow* just happened to be around Santa Cruz Island the day the *Vil Vana* disappeared. The Coast Guard conducted a detailed investigation but found very little evidence. They finally concluded, "All evidence points to the

Vil Vana capsizing and sinking quickly without any prior warning." The ship might have been top heavy with shrimp traps, and rolled over when hit by a big wave. However, no bodies were ever found and if the boat did roll, someone or something should have been thrown off into the water. The victims' relatives demanded further investigation. Some people speculated that because *Vil Vana* was last seen near the Santa Barbara Channel shipping lanes, it was either run over or swamped when a large cargo ship or oil tanker passed close by. The Coast Guard inspected the seven large ships that traveled through the Channel that day and could find no evidence that they hit anything. The Navy said their stealth boat was tied up behind Santa Cruz Island the entire day. The evidence was probably sitting on the seafloor just north of Santa Cruz Island in greater than 700 feet of water.

The mystery continued until January 1995 when U.C. Santa Barbara scientists, aboard the *Jolly Roger*, were attempting to recover a $17,000 current meter array which had broken loose from its mooring off Point Conception. It drifted sixty miles east through the Santa Barbara Channel before tangling into something off Santa Cruz Island, possibly the wreck of the *Vil Vana*. When the surface buoy was pulled on board, scientists found thirty shrimp traps and two *Vil Vana* buoys tangled in the buoy line. The Coast Guard then conducted a detailed search with a ROV around this area. Later a Coast Guard spokesman announced, "The video showed nothing at all, only debris from lobster traps." The oceanographers still had not retrieved their current meter and offered us $3,000 if we could find and recover it. They thought their expensive instruments were probably snarled in the *Vil Vana* wreck, on the seafloor off Santa Cruz Island. Using a small boat echo sounder, a friend and I ran around all day before discovering a likely looking bump on the seafloor. After fixing its location, we then combined *Delta's* ABS annual deep-water certification dive with a day off Santa Cruz looking for the *Vil Vana*. The local newspaper the next day read:

Neither Doug Privitt nor his partner, Rich Slater, was daunted by the Navy's lack of success. Scientists as well as adventurers, they believed that high-tech electronics were no match for their up-close-and-personal sub. They had explored such storied wrecks as the *Lusitania* and *Edmund Fitzgerald* and had discovered wrecks that sonar had missed before. Most notable is the *Brother Jonathan* off northern California. The *Delta* crew, full of confidence, began systematically crisscrossing an area in the southbound shipping lane five miles north of Santa Cruz Island. But they came up empty-handed on the first dive and their enthusiasm began to dissipate. After six dives and a total of six hours of bottom time, they had not found anything but starfish and some sea urchins. The search ended in frustration.

Ventura Star *newspaper article on* Vil Vana *search*

DELTA AND ITS expanded crew then traveled back to Alaska for more Kodiak crab and Sitka fish studies. *Delta* was shipped by ferry to Kodiak where it was loaded onto the 110 foot Alaska Fish and Game research vessel R/V *Medeia*. We used the *Medeia* for several seasons and it was a great support vessel. A reporter dove with us to observe Brad's crab mounds. His write-up in the Kodiak Daily Mirror declared:

It only takes five minutes for the large yellow beer can with windows to drop 500 feet to the muddy floor of Chiniak Bay. A chilly pilot and observer in several layers of clothing peered through the portholes for sea life but the abundance of plankton caused poor visibility. Swarms of arrowworms, krill, sand fleas, and other plankton flock to the subs lights blotting out the observers view. When you turn off the submersible lights, the phosphorescent plankton swim around like fireflies. Poor weather made diving difficult and everyone and everything became very wet from the rain.

This was the fourth straight year for *Delta* diving with Brad Stevens and his NOAA crew of biologists. Every year seemed to provide surprises. In 1995, the researchers concentrated on female crabs and not mating pairs as before. We discovered large numbers of "ghost" crab traps still catching crabs and the usual female crab mounds. There was one enterprising octopus that made his home conveniently close to a crab pile. Occasionally, he would reach out and grab a crab when he became hungry. There were over 40,000 crabs in an area not much larger than a football field.

A local fisherman assisted Brad on this project by setting and recovering their crab traps. He owned the fishing boat *Big Valley* and we became friends with his crew over the years we worked together. Sadly, this boat and crew disappeared at sea a few years later. Fishing in Alaska is a dangerous occupation.

Leaving Kodiak for crab study

Delta *and* R/V Medeia

Working with Big Valley *off Kodiak   Chris and David working in Alaska*

Delta and crew then traveled to Sitka to continue working with Tory O'Connell, now the manager of the ground-fish fishery in southeast Alaska for the Alaska Department of Fish and Game. For over three weeks, we counted rockfish and lingcod. Tory said, as far as she knows, Alaska is the only place where a fishery was being managed using fish counts from a sub for estimating the number of fish in a given area. This was our sixth consecutive year working with Tory and the data she was amassing helped her set fishing seasons, areas to fish, and catch limitations. Tory along with her team of fishery scientists participated in over 500 rockfish survey dives in *Delta* from 1991 to 1995.

Steve Will, a local reporter for the Sitka, Alaska, newspaper, was a *Delta* dive observer on the nearby pinnacle and wrote the following story:

Boarding *Delta* is a little like getting into a mummy bag. You squeeze through the hatch, slither straight down, squirm into the forward section, and then extend your legs between the feet of the pilot after he follows you in. Sharp metallic sounds ring through *Delta's* hull as she is freed from her harness and crane. From the support ship *Cavalier* the *Delta* unbound is an endearing sight. Bright yellow, compact and tiny in the vast blue Pacific, the submersible looks more like a bathtub toy than a high-tech scientific tool as she takes on water ballast and slowly sinks beneath the waves. As she dives, the constant motion of the sea's surface gives way to stillness. The light filters through as a pale, soothing blend of blue and green. *Delta* abruptly drops into a school of thousands of silvergrey rockfish and just as abruptly passes beneath them.

Three minutes after beginning the dive, the sub arrives at the floor of the ocean 340 feet beneath the *Cavalier*. The view through the portals reveals a density of life that easily rivals any counterpart in the neighboring rainforest. In the beam of *Delta's* powerful lights the dominant colors are reds and blues; the blue of the water, the reds of the coral, and large clouds of half-inch long juvenile rockfish. Adult yelloweyes, or red snapper, drift in the current. The surface of the rock outcrop is decked with sponges, hydrocorals, brittle stars, sea strawberries and a forest of pure white anemones that look like stalks of cauliflower waving in the current. To the inexperienced eye there is way too much to absorb. Tory believes that this entire area is a vital nursery, fostering healthy fish population for Sitka Sound.

As *Delta* rises back to the surface the field of anemones fades to blue. *Delta* breaks the surface and the pilot jockeys the sub into position alongside the mother ship. Dings and clangs sound through the smaller craft as the crew clips the crane harness to the sub and she is hoisted back on board. The data Tory was gathering will take months of analyses when she gets back to her office. Her work will pay off in better management of rockfish off Alaska and the results will benefit everyone including rockfish fishermen as more fish were found than once believed existed in this area.

Even though I was not diving much anymore, I was busy dealing with business matters and many prospective clients. In 1995-96 alone I negotiated with over fifty potential clients we would never make a dive with. Some of the more interesting projects that never materialized in 1995 and 1996 included:

- Galapagos Islands TV special for Discovery Channel
- Bass Strait giant crab study off South Australia
- Texas A & M archaeology projects off Turkey and in the Black Sea
- Diving in European lakes searching for Nazi loot
- Finding a Japanese aircraft carrier off Palau and taking surviving family members down to the ship
- *National Geographic* Special on the Battle of Jutland and Scarpia Flow, Scotland
- Three-year study of "turtle ships," Korea
- Searching for an explorer's ship lost off Greenland
- Recovering a jet engine in Santa Monica Bay off the Los Angeles airport
- Diving on the ocean liner *Britannic*, Greece
- Searching for Amelia Earhart in the South Pacific
- Abalone study, Baja California
- Diving in the Black Sea searching for ancient sailing ships and evidence of early man
- Diving on a sunken ferry boat, North Sumatra
- Searching for a lost missile, Crete.
- Various treasure hunts around the world including the mysterious *San Jose* off Columbia
  Searching for a missing Alaska Airlines airplane off Ventura County

None of these projects eventually came through but I spent a lot of time and effort working on them. Most failed due to lack of money or permit problems—we rarely lost a job to a competitor. *Delta* continued to be busy at sea from April to October every year.

IN 1996, DAVID AND CHRIS found the *Montebello*, a 440-foot oil tanker, sunk by a Japanese torpedo in December 1941, two weeks after Pearl Harbor. This wreck lies six miles off central California just north of San Simeon. The ship, built for Union Oil Company in 1921, sank in 900 feet of water but the crew survived, even though the submarine surfaced and fired its deck gun at the lifeboats. In 1943, the Union Oil Company filed a million-dollar claim with the War Damage Corporation for the loss of the *Montebello*. This claim was denied because, for one reason, no one knew exactly where the wreck was. Our mission was to find her and determine if the four million gallons of oil had leaked, was leaking now, or was still in the shipwreck.

 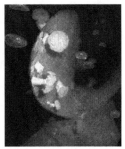

Montebello   Montebello *propeller, 900'*

David took David Doudna, Alaska's NURP representative on the initial dive to find the *Montebello*. Doudna later said;

> "Dave Slater and I made the first dive, vectored to her by the *Cavalier* that was tracking us and the wreck on its echo sounder. Whamo, there she was! We spent about an hour circumnavigating her 450-foot length. The bow was gone. Broke clean off forward from where the torpedo struck. We later found the bow several hundred feet away, buried nose first into the seafloor. It appears that on sinking, the *S/S Montebello* traveled straight down through the 900-foot water column to ram her bow right into the bottom. The aft ninety percent then bounced backward and settled

squarely on her keel, like she was at the dock, just as Rich Slater had predicted. Delta Oceanographics made it all possible, they were great."

Scientists mapped and photographed the wreck in detail. The ship looked ghost-like, draped with tangled fishing nets. There were no obvious oil leaks so the conclusion was that the two forward tanks had ruptured during the attack and that oil was gone. The other eight tanks were intact and possibly still contain some original oil. There was concern for the future. If there is any oil left, it could leak out as the ship continues to corrode. However, the good news was that heavy California crude oil has the consistency of toothpaste in cold water and will not go anywhere.

[Note: A detailed ROV inspection of the *Montebello* was completed in October 2011. It discovered the ship's thirty-two oil storage tanks were filled with seawater. There is no oil now.]

WHILE DIVING OFF Alaska in 1996, we were asked by an insurance company to spend a day with Alaska State Troopers to help investigate a case concerning a local businessman who lost his wife and daughter during a boating accident thirty miles north of Sitka. The businessman said his forty-eight-foot boat filled with smoke after the engine compartment caught fire in the middle of the night. He told his wife and daughter to get into a skiff they were towing, and he ran back into the boat to save his dog. When he returned his wife and daughter were missing. His wife owned fifty-one percent of his business and she was insured as was his daughter for $500,000. Their bodies were never found. The boat was insured for $250,000.

The businessman was not sure of his location when the boat sank and no one thought a boat in deep water somewhere off Alaska would ever be located. Our mission was to find the boat, which we did, in 512 feet of water. We also hoped to locate the bodies but were unsuccessful. As *Delta* circled the wreck we could see evidence of the fire but not much else as the boat was otherwise undamaged. Suddenly my observer, a police arson specialist, said, "It was arson." When I asked how he knew he continued, "There are burned spots on the swim platform where fuel dribbled when someone was splashing it on the boat from behind." Also, the engines were not burned so the fire did not start in the engine room. The husband told police he took his skiff back to Sitka after searching for his wife and daughter. He did not volunteer the information that his wife had recently asked for a divorce and was leaving with her daughter for Montana the next week. Also, he did not call the Coast Guard until the following morning after spending the night with the woman he was having an open affair with. His clothes had diesel fuel on them but no soot, which you would expect if he had walked through a smoky boat. The skiff he took back to Sitka contained splatters of blood from his wife. It looked like an easy case to prove.

He was indicted on two counts of first-degree murder and for scheming to defraud an insurance company. Without any bodies or witnesses, the state had to make a circumstantial case against him. His lawyer argued our dives were not legal because the boat was still his property and he did not agree to the search. He was in a car accident while waiting for trial and became wheelchair bound, paralyzed from the neck down. Then a month before the trial was to start, he apparently committed suicide by wheeling his wheelchair off the end of a Sitka dock. His girlfriend, and later wife, was put on trial for being an accessory to murder—she was found guilty.

IN 1994, MILTON LOVE, a fish ecology professor from the University of California Santa Barbara, started using *Delta* to study the undersea world around Santa Barbara Channel oil platforms. Milton is an expert on rockfish, not known as the most glamorous fish to study. He even has a rockfish tattoo. Milton had discovered that rockfish and other sea life were flourishing under the oil platforms while similar fish were not doing as well on nearby natural rocky reefs. The theory he formulated was that the platforms protected the fish from fishermen who were not allowed near any platform.

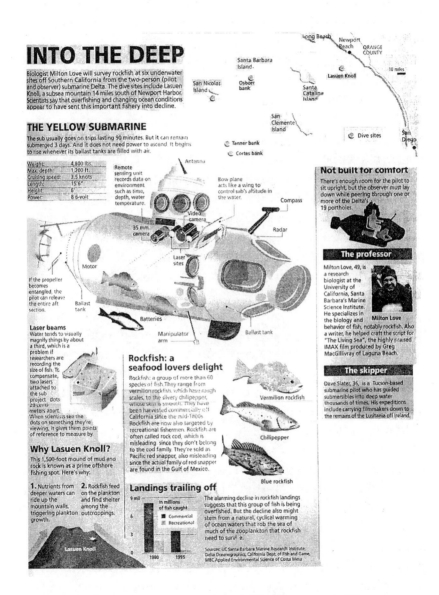

Orange County newspaper article on Milton Love's rockfish project

Rockfish is the generic name for many species of fish of all colors and sizes. They are usually sold in markets as rock cod or red snapper. Many of these fish live over 100 years. One caught recently was over 200 years old. They were over-fished during the 1960s and 1970s along the West Coast and their numbers have dwindled.

Milton and his team, on board my old USC ship *R/V Velero*, dove in *Delta* to survey the legs of each Santa Barbara Channel oil platform and the surrounding seafloor. His studies could help the State of California decide whether the oil platforms will be eventually removed. Some people would like to see the platforms chopped down so their tops would be in about eighty feet of water forming a reef for divers as was done off Florida. Others dislike the platforms and want to see them removed down to the seafloor. Oil companies do not care but they do not want to be left responsible for any accidents if the platforms are just shortened and not completely removed. The decision on whether to pull out the oil platforms still has not been made in Sacramento.

Milton spread his rockfish research to other offshore areas around Southern California where he found populations of rock fish down ten to twenty percent of what they were fifty years ago, and there were very few large rockfish left.

There was a classic onboard scene when Milton was being interviewed on camera comparing old hardhat diving to now working with *Delta*. Milton was unscrewing the faceplate from a hardhat as he was talking. The heavy metal faceplate fell off, hitting his shoe with a heavy thud that nearly broke his foot. Milton went on like nothing happened until the camera was off and then let out a scream and started to jump around. He continued to use *Delta* hoping his funding will last until he has accumulated enough data to predict what and when rockfish population's changes occur. His research has been important in selecting non-fishing zones in the Santa Barbara Channel and other areas off Southern California with the hope that rock fish will return in greater numbers.

DELTA WAS USED to search for white abalone around the Santa Barbara Channel Islands in 1996. I had started my career free diving for abalone off Morro Bay in the late 1940s, and now some fifty years later, I had another opportunity to search for abalone, but this time with a sub. My family had enjoyed many abalone gourmet meals from my diving through the 1950s and 1960s. However, the once plentiful gastropods are now rare and thought to be extinct in many places. It is the first marine invertebrate known to have disappeared due, at least partially, to human interference. There was a withering disease that killed many, and they are the favorite meal of sea otters which devoured abalone off central California. Abalone catches peaked in 1972 but they had virtually disappeared by 1978. The only abalone species thought to have survived around the Channel Islands was the white abalone that lives in water depths from 80 to 200 feet, too deep for recreational divers and too far south for sea otters. Surveys during the late 1970s found about one white abalone per square yard off the Channel Islands. In order to reproduce, they need to be within a few feet of each other.

CALIFORNIA FISH AND GAME received a grant from NOAA to use a manned submersible to help find and count surviving white abalone. During fifteen dives in four days, we found five living white abalone. The problem, white abalone only live about thirty years and the last time they successfully bred was probably in the late 1960s when they were abundant. The animals we found, at depths of 90 to 140 feet, were the last survivors and dying of old age. In 1997 *Delta* went abalone hunting again, this time for sixteen days on an offshore rocky bank seaward of the Santa Barbara Channel Islands. *Delta* was underwater for ninety-seven hours while covering nearly forty miles of rocky reefs where we discovered only 157 live white abalones. Unfortunately, most of the specimens were too far apart to reproduce. It is now illegal to take white abalone and most scientists think the species will soon be extinct

IN 1999, I RECONNECTED with Dr. Robert Ginsburg, one
of the first scientists to use *Nekton* submersibles. He was still at
the University of Miami and was now considered one of the top
coral reef experts in the world. Bob never lost his desire for
adventure and science. He was still calling me occasionally
about future possible projects. This time he wanted to dive near
the Dry Tortugas at the far southwestern end of the Florida
Keys. He wanted to map "Sherwood Forest," a coral encrusted
bank located at the confluence of the Gulf of Mexico, Florida
and the Caribbean. We would collect specimens for age dating
as Bob thought this might be the oldest coral reef in Florida.

Everyone met in Key West and we mobilized *Delta* on an
old Navy landing barge before sailing for the Dry Tortugas.
Our sleeping quarters were a bit tight but the ship proved to
be a decent support vessel. There was a small galley containing
the only toilet and a weird female cook who guarded the toilet
while she cooked. We tied the landing barge to a permanent
buoy anchored over Sherwood Forest but somehow dragged
the buoy anchor a few miles during the first night and it was
with great difficulty that we returned the anchor to its original
site. We were close to Fort Jefferson. This old Dry Tortugas
fort was used as a federal prison after the Civil War. Its most
famous prisoner was the doctor that set John Wilkes Booth's
leg after he shot Lincoln. It was great having some of the old
timers together again for our last submersible dives together.

This was good diving but extremely hot and humid on the
support ship and in *Delta*. The reef was the most luxurious I
had seen off Florida with the top surface a labyrinth of large
mushroom-shaped corals, some so large you could drive the
submersible under them. It looked like something out of Alice
and Wonderland. The scientists thought this reef might be
very old because the up to six-foot-tall, slow-growing coral
mushrooms, located in a 100 feet of water, were not damaged
during hurricanes. Most of Florida's reefs are in shallower
depths where hurricanes can cause lots of damage.

Navy landing barge with Delta   Delta *off Fort Jefferson, Dry Tortugas*

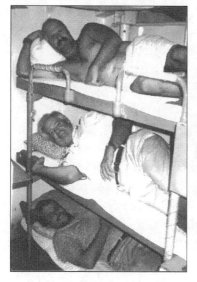

Sleeping quarters on barge   *Bob Ginsburg with mushroom coral*

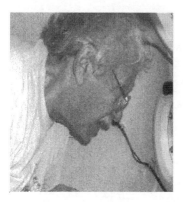

Bob in Delta   *Mushroom coral, ≈90'*

Using *Delta*, I knocked over one small coral mushroom, tied a line to it, and had the crew on the support ship haul it to the surface. It was later determined that one type of coral died out 500 years ago and a different kind of coral grew on the old stumps forming the mushroom heads. The mushroom's stems were old but the caps were modern.

FOLLOWING THE Dry Tortugas dives, we then completed another survey of the south Florida reefs along the Florida Keys for the USGS and the U.S. National Park Service. Gene Shinn, my friend and experienced submersible observer, was the project chief. In ten days, we made forty-seven dives, some as deep as 1,060 feet just offshore Biscayne National Park. One goal was to determine the health of the Florida Keys' reefs. We found many healthy reefs with very few sick corals. Ground water seepage was thought to be stressing several nearby coral reefs but our research verified this was not true for most reefs. Fresh water seeps are easy to see underwater. They cause a shimmering effect that makes the water look out of focus. We mapped several fresh water seeps, so any future artificial reefs would not be placed nearby. Using *Delta* enabled the scientists to accomplish in a few days what would have taken months with scuba. Deep-water artificial reefs, mainly sunken ships, were found to have extensive marine growth on them and they supported hundreds of fish.

One of the most startling observations during this project was the number of untended fish traps along the reefs. Some of these "ghost" traps were continuing to capture fish. Gene observed, "Almost every unmarked trap had a fish in it. One had over thirty lobsters which had grown too big to escape. The worst situation I saw was when one trap contained a queen angelfish with a second angelfish, probably the mate, on the outside. They were repeatedly ramming their heads into the cage and tearing themselves apart, probably in an attempt to mate." We checked out the Miami sewer outfall again where we found more fish than anywhere else, as usual.

AFTER THE FLORIDA dives, we sailed to Lee Stocking Island in the Bahamas. I had been diving off this island for many years and it was one of the most spectacular dive areas I ever saw. There is an exceptional vertical wall below the living reef and a steep lower slope from about 400 to 800 feet. Below 800 feet there are large, white, sand dunes trending vertically down slope that continue beyond 1,200 feet. Some of these steep glistening dunes are nearly a hundred feet high and it was awesome to fly over them. The water visibility at these depths was excellent. With submersible lights we could see over a hundred feet.

Many marine scientists used the Caribbean Marine Research Center's facilities on Lee Stocking, and it was always great to spend evenings ashore drinking beer and swapping sea stories. University of California Santa Barbara marine scientists had received a grant for *Delta* to help their research directed at producing new cost-effective underwater tools to monitor the health of coral reefs. Our mission was to place a few different experiments on the seafloor at various depths and then hope to return to retrieve them. Some of these experiments are probably still there as we never returned to Lee Stocking and the Caribbean Marine Research Center is now closed. We made fifty-two dives in ten days and I enjoyed my last deep reef dives.

We had a little mishap at the end of one dive. I had climbed out of the submersible, after it was secure against the side of the support vessel, when my observer emerged. She was Aileen Morse, a professor from University of California at Santa Barbara, and a keen diver who wanted to observe her experiments up close. She had trouble climbing out of *Delta* on earlier dives so I asked several people to assist her. David was standing on the submersible with his arm around her and I was on the support ship deck reaching up to help when, as she stepped on the submersible deck, her foot slid out from under her and, as she fell, she grabbed the submersible hatch cover slamming it down on her other hand. Men, women, and even children had climbed in and out of Doug's submersibles over 10,000 times and this was the only time anything like this had happened. Aileen flew to Miami and had her broken hand and wrist put into a cast. She returned a few days later and soon was continuing to dive with her cast wrapped in a plastic bag.

During these dives, we placed three different experiments on the seafloor. There were large screens with various corals tied to them; cone-shaped nets placed over living corals to collect any eggs, sperm, or larvae given off; and sediment collecting devices. I hope they eventually were retrieved.

Delta *with collecting net*   *Dan and Aileen Morse*

MY WIFE'S ILLNESS had become very serious and I decided to stay close to home and not participate in any further diving expeditions. However, when a chance came for me to dive in the Dead Sea, Lois insisted that I go. Her daughter came out to California from Colorado to stay with her while I was away.

Chapter Twenty-Four

Israel & Dead Sea

And Lot lifted up his eyes and beheld all the plain of Jordan—
before the Lord destroyed Sodom and Gomorrah.

—Genesis 13:10

IN 1998, AMATEUR ARCHEOLOGIST Mike Sanders, who managed the *Mysteries of the Bible Foundation*, contacted me. He asked if we could dive in the Dead Sea. I replied, we would love to dive in the Red Sea. No, he wanted us to dive in the Dead Sea. The Dead Sea lies in a military zone with the Israeli-Jordanian border running straight down the middle. This would be a difficult project as there were no nearby support systems; plus, the Palestinians and Israelis were in conflict over this area. It was unknown if a submersible could successfully dive in the extremely saline Dead Sea. Mike's objective was to discover the lost Biblical cities of Sodom and Gomorrah.

The Dead Sea, in the Great Rift Valley, is the lowest place on the continental earth's surface. It is 1,385 feet below sea level and it is nearly 1,200 feet deep—the deepest hyper-saline lake in the world. The high salinity results in an extremely harsh environment where little life can flourish. Salt on *Delta* would have to be quickly washed off with fresh water after any Dead Sea dive as salt crystals would immediately start forming once it struck the air or was in the water for any length of time. (We left a rope in the water for two weeks and a two-inch crust of salt crystals appeared—we used an axe to free it).

Dead Sea water is very warm, between seventy and eighty degrees, with occasional surface temperatures in the nineties. The interior of *Delta* during a Dead Sea dive would be hot and uncomfortable for the occupants. The air temperatures can reach over 120 degrees, making it miserable on the support ship as well. This would not be easy diving. In most tropical warm water, we cool down by diving deep—this would not be possible in the Dead Sea.

The Dead Sea is about forty-two miles long and eleven miles across at its widest point. Bottom water is saturated with salt that precipitates as crystals on the seafloor. Salt evaporation pans are located at the south end where both Israel and Jordan produce several types of commercial salt, such as potash (the Dead Sea salinity is around 29% versus 4% for ordinary sea water). Dead Sea water level has been dropping about three feet per year since 1970, when the Jordan River was dammed for Israeli irrigation projects. Only a small trickle of water now enters the Dead Sea. There was speculation that in historical times the Dead Sea water level was even lower, so Mike thought the cities of Sodom and Gomorrah might still exist as ruins under the modern Dead Sea.

> [Note: Israel, Jordan and Palestine ministers signed a deal in December, 2013, to build a desalination plant on the Red Sea and pipe the water 112 miles north to the Dead Sea. No one knows what will happen when seawater mixes with Dead Sea water except it will raise the water level.]

Mike had noticed several strange anomalies on recent NASA satellite Dead Sea photos. He thought they might be the lost cities and wanted to find them. I was skeptical any film could penetrate over 300 feet of water. Also, from a little research of my own, I discovered Dead Sea water level was over 300 feet higher during the time of Sodom and Gomorrah. The cities should be above the Dead Sea, not under it. However, it sounded like a great adventure so I agreed to do it.

Sodom and Gomorrah were two of the five cities located near the Dead Sea mentioned in Genesis. The Bible says these cities were destroyed by "fire and brimstone" but it is more likely that a large earthquake leveled them around 4,340 BC. There are lots of tar pits, gas seeps, and sulfur (brimstone) deposits found around the southern end of the Dead Sea. A large earthquake could easily have started fires and ignited the escaping gas, with brimstone thrown high into the air. The Bible says Lot left with his wife just before God destroyed the cities. Lot's wife looked back and was turned into a pillar of salt. There are many pillars of salt, exposed by erosion, found along the south end of the Dead Sea. Tourist guides usually pick one as Lot's wife. A local guide told me the chosen pillar changes over the years because the occasional rain destroys any exposed pillars while unearthing new ones. Jericho, the only nearby city, lies at the northern end of the Dead Sea and is the lowest and oldest (12,000 years old) city known on earth. Palestinians control the city where they run a gambling casino for Israeli citizens. We needed written permission from the Palestinians (north end), the Jordanians (east side), and the Israelis (west side) to dive in the Dead Sea. Eventually, they all gave us permission so we could proceed.

Mike was raising money for the project and found support from *Channel 4* in England and *NBC* in the USA. There would be two documentary movies, *The Search for Sodom and Gomorrah* and *The Ark of the Covenant*. Mike thought he knew the location of the long lost Ark. I was not involved with that film, but the English film crew was going to shoot both documentaries at the same time.

I needed to visit Israel to locate a decent support vessel and to contact scientists and others who wanted to dive with us. I made the trip six months before we would dive. Arriving at the El Al desk in the Los Angeles Airport, I was asked why I was going to Israel. I told them we were bringing a sub over later in the year. They quickly escorted me to a back room where I spent forty-five minutes being interrogated by several young tough looking Israelis (The next time I flew over I told them I was involved in making a movie). Actually the security was quite impressive and, after checking with someone, they seemed to know about our project. My El Al airplane was not at a boarding gate. I had to take a special bus across the LAX airport to a plane sitting by itself near the beach. This was the tightest security I had ever seen. After I arrived at the Tel Aviv airport, I stood in line for an hour to get through passport control, and another hour to find my baggage and to pass through customs. I finally arrived at the rental car desk where I was told I did not have a reservation and my confirmation number was not proper. I rented another car and drove to my four-star hotel in Tel Aviv. What a dump. My room was very small. I kept hitting my head on the overhead light and I had to stand in the bathtub to close the bathroom door. I needed to find something better for *Delta's* crew. The next morning at the breakfast buffet I discovered you were not allowed to mix dairy products with meat in Israel.

I drove north to the University of Tel Aviv, located on a beautiful campus, where I met Professor Zvi Ben-Avraham, head of the Dead Sea Research Center. He was an important contact and eventually made several dives with us. We had a lot in common. He still taught one semester every year at the University of Cape Town and had spent some time at Woods Hole. Zvi introduced me to Moti Gonen, an ex-Israeli Seal, who owned a boat he "borrowed" and sailed back to Israel from the Suez Canal after the Six Day War. I checked out his boat but it was not suitable for our purposes. Moti also owned a tourist boat, *Lot's Wife*, the only vessel of any size on the Dead Sea. It looked like a Chinese junk and could not support *Delta* operations either. Moti finally came up with a plan to build us a barge out of oil drums and tow it around with *Lot's Wife*. He would put a crane, a trailer, a ton of lead weights, and other equipment we needed on the barge. The *Delta* crew would have to stay on shore in a Jerusalem hotel and commute back and forth each day to the Dead Sea. It was a good plan and I agreed. I then drove several hours north to visit some University of Haifa marine archeologists. They were interested in using *Delta* to dive in the Mediterranean, off Haifa, to search for ancient Greek shipwrecks. Unfortunately, they did not obtain funding and we never made a dive there.

Moti Gonen (with salt encrusted line)   *Mike Sanders*

Dead Sea project, London Times   *On the Dead Sea*

I then drove to Jerusalem to check on the hotel where we would be staying during the project. It would be a thirty-minute drive and a 3,000-foot drop in elevation to the Dead Sea from our hotel. When I checked out of my Tel Aviv hotel and returned my rental car, I discovered the film company had not covered my bills and I had to pay even though I had been told the hotel and rental car were prepaid.

The wheels turn slowly when you apply for a permit in a military zone with several countries involved, especially when they are bitter enemies. I was juggling concerns and contracts with an English film company, two television stations, two foreign Universities, a boat company, a shipping company, an airline, and Mike. A complication occurred when the King of Jordan died a few weeks before we arrived. His Minister of Energy and Mineral Resources had signed our permit and it was no longer valid. The new King had not yet appointed his replacement so there was no one to sign a new permit and the Jordanian personnel were a bit paranoid about our project. Arafat personally signed our Palestinian permit, but now we could not dive on the Jordanian side of the Dead Sea which was not good as that was where some of Mike's important targets were located.

In November 1999, we flew *Delta* to Israel in an El Al 747. Doug had to build a flimsy wooden crate around *Delta* before the airlines would accept it. Moti had finished building our barge. Unknown to us, he rented it to the Israeli Geological Survey a few weeks before we arrived. They used it to lower and set off explosives in the Dead Sea to help calibrate seismic equipment. This was not a problem, except the press found out and was accusing the Israeli government of setting off a nuclear device in the Dead Sea. When *Delta* arrived, there was a crowd of reporters wanting to know why it was here. I told them we were searching for Sodom and Gomorrah and they were completely unconvinced. The next day the local headlines said the CIA had sent over a submersible to help investigate the Israeli nuclear test in the Dead Sea.

With Doug and Delta *crate, Los Angeles*

Unloading Delta *crate, Jerusalem*

Delta *on truck (bottom of photo) passing Gold Dome, Jerusalem*

We had shipped *Delta* and its support gear as laboratory equipment, to Zvi at the University of Tel Aviv. That allowed us to quickly get through customs with the help of University personnel. The speed upset the film crew as they were late setting up and missed filming *Delta's* arrival. Also, the shipping company had placed a large sign advertising their company on the side of our crate so any footage with this sign in it was worthless. We picked up the submersible and moved it by truck to our hotel where we unpacked in the parking lot.

The next day, the film director asked us to drive a truck with *Delta* around Jerusalem so he could obtain background film footage. I accompanied two chain-smoking Israelis in a filthy truck. This was the only time I can remember that absolutely no one paid any attention to us. When we stopped at a red light, pedestrians looked straight ahead and walked right by. On other trips people always stopped and asked questions, but not here. They must have thought we were navy and had learned to ignore any military intrusion. The director obtained good footage of us driving by the old city with the gold dome in the background. When traveling from Jerusalem to the Dead Sea we had to pass through the disputed West Bank. It did not take long, about one hour, even though we needed to pass through several military roadblocks.

A large crane lifted *Delta* aboard Moti's barge after arriving at the Dead Sea. After a few hours of unpacking and setting up equipment, the wind started blowing and we suddenly found ourselves in a raging two-day sandstorm. We could no longer work so we returned to our hotel in Jerusalem. Finally, on the third day, we mobilized the rest of our equipment. It took forever as the film crew kept asking us do takes over and over. When we finally were ready to dive it was 4:00 p.m. and too late to start. We drove straight back to Jerusalem. The next morning we were up at 5:30 a.m., grabbed a bite to eat, and rushed down to the Dead Sea to find our boat and barge gone. They had been moved during the night because of the bad weather and no one could bring them back until almost noon.

Delta *arriving at the Dead Sea*

Delta *barge being towed by* Lot's Wife

Lead bars for Delta

Mike was determined to start diving in the northern part of the Dead Sea as the water is clearer, there is less wind, and several of his targets were located there. I guess it was not important that almost everyone else thought the cities of Sodom and Gomorrah were probably at the south end. We decided to dive along the Israeli/Jordanian border and cross over to Jordan underwater. The Israelis were tough; they flew military jets over us nearly every day. Just to be safe we flew the Israeli, Jordanian, and Palestinian flags above our barge. We needed to obtain daily permission from the Israeli Army to use a beach to shuttle people back and forth to the boat.

The film crew spent the entire next afternoon filming and interviewing Mike, Zvi, and me looking important while we were scanning charts and maps. The following morning, the film crew wanted shots of us driving down to the Dead Sea, which caused another delay. Finally, the weather calmed down and everything was ready.

To dive in this hyper saline water, we placed 1,000 pounds of lead bars inside *Delta*. It was obvious by the way *Delta* sat in the water that we needed even more weight. We kept adding lead bars until there were nearly 1,300 pounds of lead inside the submersible. This resulted in a very tight fit for the pilot and the observer. I made the first test dive—we had finally calculated the weight correctly—and *Delta* landed gently on the Dead Sea seafloor in thirty feet of water. The seafloor was covered with salt crystals and the submersible's lights reflected off the crystals to create a fairyland setting. After surfacing, I drove *Delta* by nearby bathers soaking in the hypersaline water. Not one person looked up or came near us—very strange. Tomorrow, our sixth day in Israel, we would finally be ready to work. Our sleep was interrupted with the Muslim call to prayer at 4:45 a.m.

We arrived at the Dead Sea at 8:00 a.m. and again there was no boat and barge. Moti was bringing the barge up to the north end of the Dead Sea and it was very slow going. We kept calling Moti and he would say, "One more hour." After eating lunch we explored the Dead Sea Scroll Caves, located near where we were waiting. Still no boat, so we finally drove back to Jerusalem and I asked for a meeting with the movie producers. I convinced them to come down to the Dead Sea and get things moving. On the seventh day, after our arrival we finally made our first working dive. One of Mike's prime targets, which he picked off a NASA photograph, was chosen to be first. All we found was a flat seafloor covered with salt crystals. Jokingly I said, "We found Lot's wife spread all over the seafloor." The next few days were more of the same. We only dove a few times each day because the sea surface had to be calm for *Lot's Wife* to tow us. It was extremely hot riding on the barge but nobody wanted to jump into the very salty water to cool off—the salt would stick to our bodies for the rest of the day until we could return to our hotel for a shower.

One day, when we could not work, I decided to visit Jordan with Mike. He knew a girl there and was invited to lunch at her parents' luxurious home. We drove down to Jericho, parked our car, jumped into a cab, and passed through several military checkpoints. There were three sets of gates and many armed soldiers at the border. It took one hour to pass through the Israel/Jordan border area and we had to pay several fees. We finally boarded an Arab bus and crossed over the Jordan River on the 50-foot-long Allenby Bridge. I could have easily jumped across the four-foot wide river. After three more checkpoints we were left waiting on the bus until a Jordanian military officer came aboard and called out my name and then motioned to me to follow him into an adjoining building. The bus left with Mike waving to me through the window.

After much discussion it was pointed out that I did not have a proper visa to visit Jordan. However, if I took an Arab bus on a one-hour ride I might be able to obtain a visa, but it would be expensive. I told them I would just go back to Israel. It was not that easy. The Allenby Bridge had checkpoints on both sides and no one walked across. I finally decided to cross the bridge after waiting a long time for a bus. I climbed over the Jordanian gate, walked fifty feet or so across the bridge, climbed over the Israeli gate, and landed in the arms of Israeli soldiers. The soldiers were very excited; this was not done, no one walks across the bridge. They then accompanied me to an office where I spent an hour explaining why I needed to return to Israel. An officer took my passport and I was not sure if it would be returned. Finally, I was sent to passport control and after waiting for some time my name was called and I got my passport back. I jumped on an old fly-filled bus full of Arabs heading to Jericho. At every military checkpoint, the Israeli soldiers asked me what I was doing on an Arab bus. "Saving money by not taking a taxi," I told them. The bus driver was very nice and dropped me off by my car, while warning me not to walk around in this area of town. I drove back to my Jerusalem hotel; the thirty-mile round trip took over six hours!

The next day was Thanksgiving and we arrived at the boat bright and early. Zvi brought along several scientists to dive with us and this caused a problem. Mike wanted to look for Sodom and Gomorrah while the scientists wanted to study the seafloor geology. However, Mike needed the scientists to give some legitimacy to his project. We made one dive and then the wind blew up—it took us about five hours to run to shelter. Everyone was getting edgy with all of the delays and finally an argument broke out between Mike and Zvi. Mike was getting tired of Zvi pushing to get in his scientific dives and Zvi was tired of constantly hearing about Sodom and Gomorrah being under the Dead Sea.

Finally, *Lot's Wife* was anchored and we used a small boat to run into shore. I jumped out and landed in the mud with my shoes disappearing beneath me. This was not the first time but I was really stuck and when others tried to help me they also became mired in the mud. At last, I scrambled out but lost a shoe and was covered with the stickiest mud I had ever seen. After cleaning up at our hotel, I took my crew to a Jerusalem French restaurant for a wonderful Thanksgiving dinner.

Interview for film

With David, end of a working day

Dead Sea mud

Because of all the problems, it was decided to let the scientists and some of my crew have a day off while Mike worked on his *Ark* movie. When they flew a helicopter to an area close to Bethlehem, where the Ark possibly was, they unexpectedly landed in a Hamas terrorists training camp. This caused a lot of excitement—they got their pictures but didn't find the Ark.

It was peaceful on the boat. David and I searched for the lost cities during a six-hour dive with only a few students on board with us. Again, we found no ruins but I did run into a salt encrusted scarp with about ten feet of relief. Mike later thought this was a city wall but could not get me or the other scientists to agree with him. The next day, I made a dive to 840 feet and David went down to 1,090 feet—at least that is what the sub depth gauge read—but the density of the water gave us false readings. The actual depth David reached was probably closer to 850 feet. The seafloor looked the same everywhere, covered with large salt crystals.

I took the next day off and walked around the old city of Jerusalem, missing a bomb scare at the Dead Sea when the army blew up something on the beach. Later, a large military helicopter kept flying low over the barge taking pictures of our dive operations. *Delta* was launched on the Jordanian side after a navigation error and the Jordanian government immediately protested to the Israeli government. The military radioed *Lot's Wife* and said to move back over to the Israel side. We had started another international incident. The following day, Moti had to appear in front of the military council and got his hand slapped for crossing the border, while I was making several dives with Mike and a cameraman.

Upon returning to our Jerusalem hotel that evening, I found a disturbing e-mail. Lois was failing and her daughter thought I should return home immediately. Mike and the film producers agreed I should leave at once and my crew said they would finish up the diving. I caught a plane home the next day. They kept diving for a few more days, but never did discover anything resembling the ruins of Sodom or Gomorrah.

My crew packed up *Delta* and shipped it to Los Angles on another El Al 747. Mike continued lecturing on his *Mysteries of the Bible* tour and NBC produced two one-hour prime time shows concerning his Israeli projects. NBC first aired *Biblical Mysteries* in which Mike claimed he found where the Ark, with the original Ten Commandments stone tablets, was located. The second show concerned our search for the Biblical cities of Sodom and Gomorrah. This film was very dramatic with pictures of Sodom and Gomorrah being destroyed by flames, superimposed with *Delta* diving in the Dead Sea. They even featured some of the ongoing argument between Mike and Zvi. The TV specials received very high ratings during the fall of 2000, so everyone was happy. We made the front page of many local newspapers.

Mike had persuaded a production company to finance his expedition to the Middle East for over a million dollars. What he did not receive was the respect from professional scientists and other Biblical scholars. One expert said that even if we had found a city there would be no sign saying welcome to Sodom, so how would we know if we had the right village? I enjoyed working with Mike; he told many wonderful stories that made the trip enjoyable. He was serious about his work and kept his nose to the grindstone. Mike was going to locate the Tower of Babel and the Garden of Eden next and he wanted to return to Israel to dig up those stone tablets. He did not need a submersible for those projects.

LOIS HAD PUT UP a fifteen-year struggle but passed away a few weeks after I returned home from Israel. I only dove a few times after our Dead Sea adventure and gave my shares of *Delta Oceanographics* to Dave and Chris. It was time to retire.

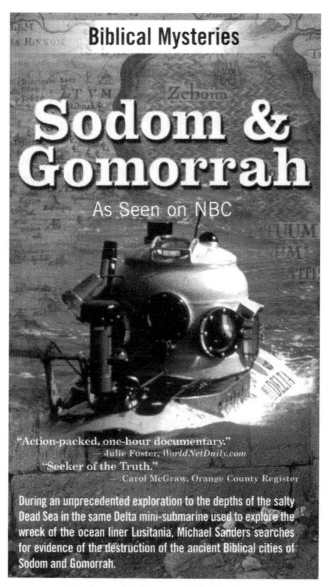

Sodom and Gomorrah VCR *cover*

Chapter Twenty-Five

Waratah & Oceanus

There were many doubts about the submarine operating in the strong current. I considered that the *Delta* crew had operated in the Gulf Stream and were experienced with strong currents. I also hedged my bets on the fact that the sub was an untethered vehicle and free to use the current to its advantage with sufficient ballast to drop down and punch through the current, which is only about fifteen to twenty meters deep. The *Delta* submarine was to operate flawlessly on every dive. The *Delta* crew hardly mentioned the current.

—Emlyn Brown (2000)

I THOUGHT I WAS through with diving, when an intriguing project appeared off South Africa. I could not stay away when this unique opportunity arose. In 1999, just before leaving for Israel, I had read an article about Emlyn Brown, a well-known South African undersea explorer who had been searching for a famous shipwreck, the *Waratah,* off South Africa for the past eighteen years. The *Waratah* is considered the Australian *Titanic* and its story is well known in both Australia and South Africa. She was built in Scotland in 1908, as a 465-foot long, twin-screwed, coal-fired, ocean liner. On outward journeys to Australia from England, she transported emigrants and on the return trips she hauled mainly cargo. In 1909, the *Waratah* sailed from Sydney, bound for London, carrying 211 people and 7,000 tons of cargo when she vanished without a trace off the southeastern coast of South Africa. It is one of the most baffling nautical mysteries of all time.

The ship disappeared after leaving Durban and never arrived in Cape Town. Her last communication was an exchange of signals with a shore station a day after leaving Durban. The loss mystified maritime experts. The ship was thought by some to have been unsteady and top heavy. It was possible a large rogue wave tipped the ship over but it was strange that not one piece of wreckage was ever found. Very rough seas and giant waves form off South Africa when a gale approaches from the southwest and runs into the Agulhas current coming down from the northeast.

Emlyn Brown and the Waratah

Some experts suggested the ship might have lost power and drifted down to the Antarctic but there was no evidence of that. The *Waratah* probably went down very fast. There were séances held in London where Sir Arthur Conan Doyle was involved in talking to the missing passengers for their loved ones. The owners suffered a huge financial loss and eventually sold their fleet to their main competitor, P&O.

I wrote to Emlyn, who lived in Cape Town, and mentioned that *Delta* might be the vehicle he could use to travel down to the wreck if he ever found it. He wrote back saying he had just finished reading Bob Ballard's book on the *Lusitania* and was intrigued with *Delta* as a shipwreck diving vehicle. He was planning a side-scan sonar survey over the area of *Waratah's* last known location and would get back to me if they found anything.

The results of his side-scan survey were excellent. Working with a local University professor, he located a wreck that very likely was the *Waratah*. He accurately identified the ill-fated vessel, lying in 374 feet of water, using diagnostic features found on his side-scan sonar records. These features included the overall dimensions, the "champagne glass" stern shape, rudder shape, davits, air intake funnel positions, and location of the deck derricks. The ship was in an upright position, was not buried, and was broken into several pieces. This discovery generated a lot of media coverage in South Africa. Emlyn was featured in many newspapers and appeared on South African television. He was so convinced the wreck was the *Waratah* that he sent out an international press release supported by expert scientific opinions. There was immediate worldwide publicity. The *London Times* and *Daily Mail* newspapers devoted pages to his discovery.

Emlyn attempted to get a video camera down to the wreck using several different vehicles. He used diving bells, camera sleds, ROVs, mixed gas divers, and a submersible. Nothing could get close to the wreck site due to the strong currents. He attempted to dive in the German submersible *Jago* over a ten-day period but the submersible was never launched because of high seas and the very strong currents.

The Agulhas Current whips around southern Africa from the Indian Ocean typically at four knots with surges up to six knots near the ocean surface in Emlyn's survey area. This strong current made it extremely difficult to use a vehicle, like a ROV, tethered to a surface ship. Because we had experience diving in the Gulf Stream off Florida and New York, I told Emlyn the Agulhas current should not be a problem for *Delta*. I was excited for a chance to return to South Africa and be part of this historical search. I was also confident we could descend to the wreck in this very unfavorable environment.

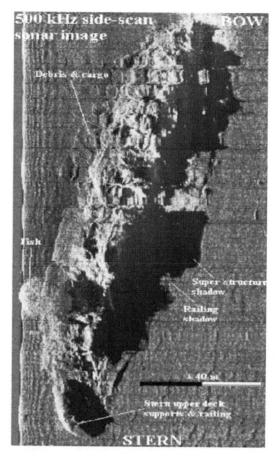

Emlyn's side-scan record of mystery shipwreck

M/V TOTO *at dock in Durban*

I wanted to ship *Delta* down to South Africa from Israel after our Dead Sea dives, but the timing was wrong, as Emlyn was still trying to raise money. He had spent his own money up to this time but now found industrial and television companies interested in helping. He also teamed up with Clive Cussler, the American novelist, who was interested in shipwrecks worldwide. Cussler controls NUMA, the National Underwater and Marine Agency which he funds for shipwreck searches.

I located a shipping agent, as it is important to have a good shipping agent in both the U.S. and in any foreign country where we worked. Agents can grease the skids with officials and make passing through customs much quicker and easier. My major concern, as usual, was locating the right support vessel. Emlyn e-mailed me information on several boats and I finally chose one. I also needed to locate someone who could dive down to rescue us in case *Delta* became entangled. Finally, a dive company in Durban said they would come out for up to to $60,000 per day. Insurance is a problem when shipping equipment overseas. The South African government wanted a $400,000 deposit that would be returned when *Delta* left South Africa. I told them this was unacceptable and they finally dropped that demand. The movie and television companies involved with this project all wanted to push the Conan Doyle connection. Everyone had heard of him and few people in America knew about the *Waratah*. Later it was finally decided to name the TV show *Conan Doyle's Ghost ship*. There was also a treasure angle and Emlyn asked us to retrieve the captain's safe and any other important artifacts. I wanted everything signed and sealed concerning the support ship while we were still in California, and, eventually they agreed.

Meanwhile, Emlyn returned to the wreck site and lowered a heavy video camera with some success. He saw the wreck was in poor condition and the stern section was completely broken off but he could not get any close-up photos. He decided we would need a small ROV to work off *Delta* similar to what Bob Ballard did from *Alvin* on the *Titanic*. I told him this was possible but we would have to work with the ROV Company to make sure it was compatible with *Delta*. He chose a small company in Australia, so now I was corresponding daily with both Australia and South Africa. The Australian ROV was not completed in time.

Our support ship was *M/V TOTO*, a Mozambique Channel supply vessel. It had a large after deck close to the water, and a crane we could use to deploy and recover *Delta*. It was a great support vessel. We still needed a large mat of tires for *Delta* to rest against when it was alongside the ship, a large pole for our navigation transponder to reach below the ships keel, a small tender skiff, 110v 60 cycle and 220v 50 cycle power for our equipment, an articulated crane with a 10,000-pound lifting capacity, four large oxygen bottles, communications from the bridge to our sub shack, a work area on the bridge for our navigation system, a scuba air compressor, and room on the after deck for our container/work station. With Emlyn's help, we found everything we needed.

Delta was trucked, in its container, to New York where it was shipped to Durban, South Africa. We were still using our old yellow shipping container and it had to pass inspection by New York shipping officials. I was a little concerned as our container was becoming quite rusty, but it passed. We also needed a seven-day minimum dive schedule to make the long trip worthwhile. I received a third of our contract money up front, completed all of the detailed paperwork, and we were ready by early 2001. I flew down to South Africa on January 1st with the *Delta* crew. It only took a few days to clear our equipment through customs and another few days to mobilize.

We were anxious to distance ourselves from the press who had been hounding us. At last, we sailed from Durban and headed southwest along the South Africa coast to an area near where I had worked when I was at the University of Cape Town in 1969. Arriving at the appointed area, we ran an echo sounder over the seafloor to locate the wreck site and then prepared to make the first dive. There was still a huge concern that *Delta* could not reach the seafloor through the strong Agulhas Current. We moved the support vessel up-current and launched *Delta,* with David as pilot, letting the current carry the submersible down toward the wreck. When the sub landed on the seafloor, there was a huge roar of approval from all the bystanders. I directed *Delta* to move to the northeast about one hundred yards and they immediately spotted the wreckage. Again, a cry of joy arose from the ship.

I decided to leave the bridge and went down to my room to read and to escape all of the commotion. A few minutes later, someone knocked on my door and said I was needed on the bridge immediately. I raced up to the bridge and contacted *Delta.* David asked, "Were there military tanks in 1908?" The wreck was not the *Waratah* but a cargo ship. There was stunned silence and disbelief. This ship was very similar to the *Waratah* but it had military tanks sitting on deck and fourteen tanks resting on the nearby seafloor. I felt sorry for Emlyn. Not only did his nearly twenty years of searching hit a dead-end but he had to face the press and TV reporters when we returned to Durban. A Durban newspaper later stated:

> The revelation over the weekend that a mini-sub diving on a wreck claimed to be the *Waratah* really found a World War II cargo ship instead, a heartbreaking conclusion to an epic search for the doomed liner that disappeared off the Cape coast in 1909. Clive Cussler said, "We have already searched for the *Waratah* on nine separate expeditions since 1983. I guess she is going to continue to be elusive a while longer, but Emlyn and I refuse to give up."

The mystery ship found was the *Nailsea Meadow,* a British freighter torpedoed in May 1943 by a German U-boat. Two of the crew died and there were 42 survivors. It was carrying over 7,000 tons of war material and mail for troops fighting in North Africa. Emlyn had been so sure and now he had to admit defeat. The liner *Waratah* is still missing. In 2004 Emlyn announced he was giving up his

Waratah search as he had covered all approaches, spent over $1 million, and came up with nothing.

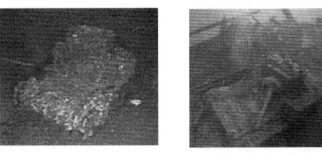

INSIDE STORY 9

Waratah mystery continues

by
DAVID
WILLERS

The whereabouts of a ship that went missing over 90 years ago remains unknown

South Africa newspaper article on the Waratah

Tanks on the Nailsea Meadow, *375' (photos by Emlyn Brown from* Delta)

We only dove one day and decided not to spend another six days diving on an unknown wreck. We moved over to another shipwreck site, only twelve miles away, but no one was very excited about diving there. It was a Greek-owned liner, the *Oceanos* that sank in 300 feet of water in 1991. It is well known because when the ship started to take on water during a storm, the crew panicked. Many of the crew, including the Captain, jumped ship. They seemed to be unconcerned with the safety of the passengers. The South African Navy and Air Force launched a massive seven-hour mission with helicopters airlifting 225 passengers off the deck of the sinking ship. All 571 passengers were saved in one of the most dramatic rescue operations ever witnessed.

Oceanus *sinking, 1991, South Africa*

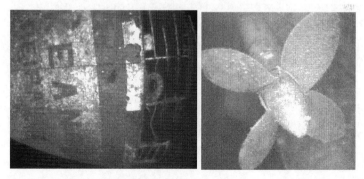

Oceanus, *300' (photos by Emlyn Brown from* Delta)

The Captain later said that he left early in order to coordinate the rescue operations. He lost his license. These dives were great with excellent visibility. I remember observing roulette wheels and lots of poker chips lying on the seafloor. The liner was lying on one side and seemed to be in good condition. After a few dives on the *Oceanos* we sneaked back into Durban during the night to miss being discovered by the press.

Just before we left for South Africa, I received information that two scuba divers recently died while diving off northeast South Africa. They were using mixed gas to dive 300 feet to photograph rare coelacanth fish. Seeing a live coelacanth was one of my dreams. These living fossil fish, whose fossils have been found in rocks ranging from 380 to 70 million years and were assumed to be extinct, were not known to exist until just before World War II. The discovery of a small population of coelacanths off South Africa was stunning. I hoped we would have a chance to go there after wreck diving and be among the first to photograph these large living fossils. Coelacanths are up to five feet long with large hard scales, a wide mouth with big lips, large eyes, and limb-like fins. The coelacanth is closely related to the first fish that ever climbed out of the water and is related closer to us than to other fish (its limbs are similar to our arms and legs).

Because we had finished wreck diving early, professors from the USA and South Africa scrambled to raise money for our coelacanth dives while *TOTO* was still under contract. Our old friends at *Channel 4* in England came through with the money, the professors were ready, and we were available, but the work never materialized. The South African Minister, in charge of the National Park where the coelacanths were located, was on vacation in Switzerland and no one else in her department would sign the permission forms allowing us to dive. What a tragic and great disappointment for me not to be able to dive with a fish that is virtually unchanged for over 300 million years.

[Note: National Geographic, in 2011, published a photo of a South African deep-water coelacanth. Another one made the cover of Nature magazine in April, 2013. There are now six specimens on exhibit in museums around the world.]

Conclusion

Using *Delta* is no longer an unproven concept, but rather an accepted survey tool as demonstrated in more than 85 peer-reviewed publications since 1988.

—*U.S. Fisheries Bulletin* (2008)

IN 2007, DUE IN a large part to our years of diving, there were twenty-nine non-fishing zones established off the central California coast. These zones are now known to support about forty different kinds of rockfish along with various diverse invertebrates. Biologists continually monitor these areas.

Delta's tracks were now being plotted on multibeam sonar maps of the seafloor. It beat dragging a red buoy behind the sub, taking hand-held photographs, and using a sextant for navigation. For over twenty years, we had made visual surveys of rockfish as well as their associated habitats from Alaska to Mexico. Scientists using *Delta* had identified 711 fish species, many photographed for the first time, in water depths of 100 to 1,200 feet. *Delta* was used on over 5,000 scientific dives around the world. I was the pilot on 2,232 of these dives and David was the pilot on over 2,000 of them.

I retired soon after the South Africa trip. David and Chris, continued diving *Delta* for several years, usually from the old USC ship R/V *Velero IV*. After its last dives in 2008, *Delta* sat in Doug's machine shop until he sold it in 2011 to a friend— its future is unknown. David is a RN in Arizona. Doug still works in his machine shop every day. He is currently building a helicopter and plans to fly it soon (he has promised his wife that he will not fly it more than 10 feet off the ground).

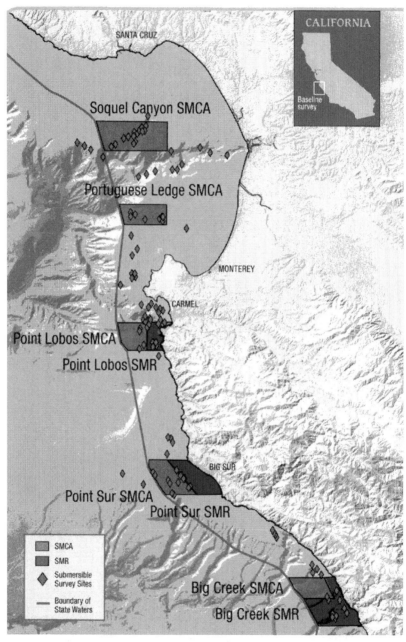

Delta *dive locations and State Marine Reserves off central California coast*
(California Sea Grant, 2007)

Looking back over the past sixty years refreshed many fond memories. I realize how timely it was that I just happened to be in the right place at the right time. I was there near the start of scuba diving and during the short time manned subs were popular before ROVs replaced them for most undersea work. Unknowingly, I was well prepared when my chance came and I took advantage of it. I think often of all the good times we had. The few not so good times are fading from my memory. I remember many of the wonderful people I met along the way. Some are gone now and I have lost contact with others. The ship crews were hard working, great guys who performed well at sea but many, unfortunately, had problems while on shore. Most of the scientists were dedicated and also hard working. A few were not easy to get along with at sea while others were superb companions.

I have always enjoyed exploring new places. My career gave me the opportunity to travel to all of the continents and over 175 countries. How many people spent their lives working at something they love, were paid for something they probably would have done for free, and shared exciting adventures with their friends and son? Not many I would venture to guess—I was one of the fortunate ones.

> Each of us has lived an adventure that most men can only dream about. We have seen the stuff that dreams are made of.
>
> —Robert Marx, *The Search for Sunken Treasure*, 1993

Author, submersible pilot

Doug, submersible pilot

David, submersible pilot

Acknowledgments

I owe a great debt to those who shared my adventures with me and reminded me of many stories I have long forgotten. I want to thank Peter Auster, Kent Barnard, Emlyn Brown, Jim Clary, Richard Cooper, Robert Ginsburg, David Folger, Kim Davidson, Chris Goldfinger, Mark Hixon, Jim Johnson, Chris Kendall, Tom Landis, Tory O'Connell, Jim Owens, Charles Phipps, Jim Prescott, Earl Richmond, Mike Sanders, Gene Shinn, Rick Starr, Brad Stevens, Jim Vernon, John Warme, and Bob Wicklund, among others, for sharing their memories. Jim Vernon, Tom Crawford, Jim Johnston, and Dick Cooper have passed away and they are missed.

I especially want to thank Doug Privitt who made much of my diving career possible with his outstanding submersibles and support.

A very special thanks to my son David who remembered many details from our adventures much better than I.

Most photographs in this book are mine but submersible observers took many of the underwater photographs from *Nekton* and *Delta* submersibles, as I was the pilot on most of the dives discussed. I cannot remember who took some of the photos so I would like to thank all the observers for allowing me to share their photos with the readers of this book.

Many thanks go to Mary Embree for helping to edit and format my original manuscript. Tom Kong made many useful suggestions for the 2nd edition.

Most of all, I want to thank my family for standing by me all these years when I was traveling around the world, gone from home for long stretches.

A special thanks to my wife Pattie who did not have to put up with my absences, thought *Delta* was a boy toy when we first met, and encouraged me to write this book. I express my deepest gratitude to her for keeping after me and seeing that it was finished.

Glossary

Abalone: Marine mollusk with large muscular foot
ABS: American Bureau of Shipping, certifier for submersibles
Adak Island: Alaska Island, western end of the Aleutians
Admiral Sampson: Passenger ship, sank in Puget Sound in 1914
Agulhas Current: Western current, SW Indian Ocean
Alvin: Woods Hole Institute manned deep-ocean submersible
Anacapa Island: Santa Barbara Channel Island, off Ventura
Aquanaut: An individual who lives underwater in a habitat
Bass Strait: Separates Tasmania from Australia mainland
Beaver Island: Largest Island in Lake Michigan
Belize: Central American country, formerly British Honduras
Bering Sea: Body of water between Russia and Alaska
Brother Jonathan: Passenger ship, sank off Crescent City,
    northern California, 1865
Cape Barren Island: Australian Island off NE Tasmania
Carl Bradley: Freighter, sank in Lake Michigan in 1958
Catalina Island: Island, twenty-two miles SW of Los Angeles
Channel Islands: Chain of eight islands along Santa Barbara
    Channel off the coast of Southern California
Chukchi Sea: Arctic Ocean Sea off NW Alaska
Churchill: Town, SW Hudson Bay, Canada
Conning Tower: A raised small observation post with viewports
    on top of a submersible. The pilot usually has a 360-
    degree view of the surrounding seascape. The
    entrance to the interior is through a hatch on top.
Continental Shelf: Part of the continental margin between the
    shoreline and the continental slope
Dawn Star: 65' research vessel owned by General Oceanographics.
Delta: Two-man submersible built by Doug Privitt
Delta Oceanographics: Company that operated *Delta* sub
Discovery Bay: Site of research lab, Jamaica north shore

Dry Tortugas: Small islands, SW end of Florida Keys
DSR: Deep Sea Research Company, found *Brother Jonathan*
Dutch Harbor: Port for Unalaska, Aleutian Islands, Alaska
Eastern Fields: Coral Sea atoll between Australia and
    Papua New Guinea
Edmund Fitzgerald: Freighter, sank in Lake Superior in 1975
Elizabeth Reef: Tasman Sea coral atoll, Australia
Enewetak: Large equatorial Pacific atoll, Marshall Islands
EPA: Environmental Protection Agency of US government
Flinders Island: Large Bass Strait Island, off NE Tasmania
Furneaux Islands: Australian chain of Islands off NE Tasmania
Gastropods: Group of animals commonly called snails and slugs
General Oceanographics: Company, operated *Nekton* subs
GeoCubic: Company, conducted offshore geological surveys
Georges Bank: Large shallow bank off Cape Cod, Massachusetts
GPS: Global Positioning System
Great Barrier Reef: Largest coral reef in the world, Australia
Gulf of Alaska: Large body of water off southern Alaska coast
Guyot: Flat topped undersea volcanic mountain
Habitat: Underwater structures where divers can live for extended
    periods
Helgoland: Large German underwater habitat
Heron Island: Small Island, Great Barrier Reef, Australia
Hudson Bay: Large inland body of water, NE Canada
Hydro-Lab: Small Bahamian underwater habitat
Hydrophone: Underwater listening device, converts changes in
    water pressure into an electrical form
IFREMER: French research institute for Exploring the Sea
Isopach map: Aerial extent showing thickness of a geological unit
Johnson Sea-Link: Harbor Branch submersible, Florida
Kaohsiung: Major port city, southern Taiwan
Lake Malawi: African Great Lake, south end of Rift Valley
Lake Victoria: Largest African Great Lake, borders Kenya
Lee Stocking Island: SE Bahamian Island with Research Center
Lord Howe Island: Tasman Sea Island, Australia
Lusitania: Ocean liner, sank off Ireland in 1915
Montebello: Oil tanker, sank off California in 1941
MMS: Minerals Management Service, US government
MUST: Manned Undersea Science and Technology, NOAA

Mutton Birds: Short-tailed shearwaters

M/V: Motor vessel

Nailsea Meadow: Freighter, sank off South Africa in 1943

Nekton **Submersibles:** Three two-man submersibles *Alpha, Beta* and *Gamma*, built by Doug Privitt in the 1960s and 1970s.

New York Bight: Large gulf along northeastern US, offshore New York City

NMF: National Marine Fisheries, US government

NOAA: National Oceanographic and Atmospheric Administration

Nome: Town, NW Alaska coast just below Arctic Circle

NSF: National Science Foundation

NURP: NOAA's National Undersea Research Program that funded undersea science and technology

OCS: Offshore Continental Shelf

Oil City: Research vessel operated by General Oceanographics

PEACE Project: Research project on nuclear bomb craters, Enewetak Atoll, 1984-85

Pinger: Underwater instrument that emits acoustic signals

Pisces: Manned submersibles built in Vancouver, Canada

Plexiglas: Brand name for man-made acrylic safety glass

PNG: Papua New Guinea

POP: Pacific Ocean Perch, common rockfish on West Coast

Porthole: Small, usually circular window in ship hull

Pueblo Village: Animal habitat that is intensely burrowed, usually found on sides of submarine canyons

Puget Sound: Estuarine system connecting Seattle to Pacific

ROV: Remotely Operated Vehicle, unmanned.

R/V: Research Vessel

Santa Barbara Channel: Between Channel Islands and mainland from Point Conception to Ventura

Sclerosponge: Sponges with calcium carbonate skeleton

Scripps: Oceanographic Institute, La Jolla, California

SCORE: Scientific Cooperative Operational Research Expedition, Bahamas, 1975

Scuba: Self-contained underwater breathing apparatus

Seamark: Research ship operated by General Oceanographics

Side-Scan Sonar: Side looking sonar used to map seabed or to search for underwater objects

Sitka: Small island city, Alaska Panhandle

Slit Shell: Beautiful spiral gastropod shell with deep slit

Sonar: Sound navigation and ranging technique that uses sound underwater for communication or detection

Stromatolite: Layered algal structure

Submarine Canyon: Undersea canyon

Submersible: Small submarine that needs a support vessel **Taipei:** City, Capital of Taiwan

Taiwan: Large Island off SE coast of China

Tar Mounds: Accumulations of tar on seafloor

Tektites: Blobs of glassy substance formed when meteorites hit the ocean

Thursday Island: Small Island in Torres Straits between Papua New Guinea and Australia

TOTO: Tongue of the Ocean, deep-water channel, Bahamas; also name of support vessel, South Africa

Trackpoint II: Commercial computer used for acoustic tracking an underwater vehicle

Transducer: A device that changes one type of energy into another, submersible transducer receives and sends voice messages

Transponder: Electronic device that produces a response after receiving a signal

Turbidity Current: Ocean seafloor current rapidly moving down-slope composed of sediment-laden water

Tundra: Treeless permafrost plain located in far north

UNC: University of Northern Colorado, Greeley, Colorado **UQC:** Underwater telephone

USAID: United States Agency for International Development

USC: University of Southern California, Los Angeles

USGS: United States Geological Survey

Waratah: Steamship, sank off South Africa in 1909

Yakutat: Small Alaskan city, Gulf of Alaska

Selected References

Books

Backus, Richard (1987); *Georges Bank*, (MIT Press)

Ballard, Robert D. (1995); *Exploring the* Lusitania, (Warner Bks.)
    Bowers, Q. David (1999); *The Treasure Ship* Brother
    Jonathan, *Her life and Loss (1850-1865)*, (Bowers & Merean)

California Sea Grant (2007); *Monitoring MPA's in Deep
    Water off Central California, 2007 Submersible
    Baseline Survey*, (California Sea Grant Program)

Clary, James (1994); *Ladies of the Lakes*, (Thunder Bay Press)

Cooper, R.A., P. Valentine, J. Uzmann and R.A. Slater (1987);
    Georges Bank Submarine Canyons, (in Georges Bank,
    ed. Richard Backus, pp. 52-63,The MIT Press)

Folger, D.W., H.D. Palmer and Slater, Richard A., (1978);
    *Submersible Observations of Two Dump Sites along the Continental
    Shelf off the Mid-Atlantic States, (in Geologic Aspects of ocean waste
    Disposal*, Eds. H.D. Palmer and M.G. Grant, (Dowden,
    Hutchinson and Ross, Inc. pp 163-184)

Gentile, Gary (1999); *The Lusitania Controversies*,
    Books 1 & 2, (Gary Gentile Productions)

Halley, R., R.A. Slater, E.A. Shinn, D.W. Folger, et. al.,
    (1986); *Observation of OAK and KOA Craters from a Submersible,
    Chapter F, in Sea-Floor Observations and Subbottom Characteristics
    of OAK and KOA Craters, Enewetak Atoll, Marshall Islands*,
    (U.S. Geological Survey Bull. 1678, 32 pp)

Hellwarth, Ben (2012); Sealab, (Simon & Schuster)

James, N.P. and R.A. Ginsburg (1979); *The Seaward margin of
    Belize Barrier and Atoll Reefs*, (Spec. Pub. No. 3, Int. Assoc.
    of Sed.,191 pp., John Wiley & Sons)

Jenkins, Geoffrey (1971); *Scend of the Sea, the mysterious voyage of
    the* Waratah (Authors Choice Press)

Kinder, Gary (1998); *Ship of Gold in the Deep Blue Sea*, (The Atlantic Monthly Press)

Kolpack, Ronald L. and Dale Straughan (1973); *AAPG Field Trip 3*, 1973 Annual Meeting,

May, J., J.E. Warme and R.A. Slater; *Role of Submarine Canyons on Shelfbreak, Erosion and Sedimentation: Modern and Ancient Examples*, (in SEPM Spec. Pub. No. 33, The Shelfbreak: Critical Interface on Continental Margins, Eds. D.J. Stanley and G.T.Moore)

Maxwell, W.G.H. (1968); *Atlas of the Great Barrier Reef* (Elsevier Publishing Co.)

Menard, H.W. (1969); *Anatomy of an Expedition*, (McGraw-Hill Book Company)

Smith, P.J. (2009); *The Lost Ship* SS Waratah, *Searching for the Titanic of the South*,(The History Press)

Phillips, Carla Rahn (2007); *The Treasure of the* San Jose, (The John Hopkins University Press)

Powers, Dennis M. (2006); *Treasure Ship, The Legend and Legacy of the* Brother Jonathan, (Citadel Press) Prager,

Ellen (2008); *Chasing Science at Sea, Racing Hurricanes, Stalking Sharks, & Living Undersea with Ocean Experts*, (The University of Chicago Press)

Preston, Diana (2002); Lusitania, *an Epic Tragedy*, (Walker & Co., New York)

Shepard, Francis P. (1973); *Submarine Geology*, (Harper and Row, New York)

Simpson, Colin (1972); *The* Lusitania, (Little, Brown & Co)

Slater, Richard A. (1964*); Sedimentary Environments of Suisun Bay*, Master's Thesis, Univ. Southern Cal. Geology Dept.: 108pp.

———— (1970); *Marine Geology of the Banks Strait-Furneaux Islands Area, Tasmania*, PhD Dissertation, University of Sydney Geology Dept.: 347pp

———— J.E. Warme, and R.A. Cooper (1978); *Bioerosion in Submarine Canyons, (in Submarine Canyons and Fan Deposits*, Eds. D.J. Stanley and G. Kelling, (Dowden, Hutchinson and Ross, Inc.)

———— (1987); *Review of the Late Pleistocene Holocene Geologic History of the South and Central California Continental Shelf*, (in Archaeological Resource Study: Morro Bay to Mexican Border, U.S. Dept. of Interior MMS Outer Shelf Study 87-0025, Chap. V: 33-46)

———— (1987); *Isopach Maps of Post-Wisconsin Sediment Thickness, Pt. Estero to the Mexican Border*, in (Archaeological Resource Study: Morro Bay to Mexican Border, U.S. Dept. of Interior MMS Outer Shelf Study 87-0025, Chap. VI: 47-60)

Smith, Patsy A. (1965); *Moonbird People*, (Rigby Limited, Australia)

Tippin, G. Lee and Herbert Humphreys, Jr. (1989); *In Search of the Golden Madonna*, Daring Publishing Co.)

Vernon, James W. (2004); *Deep Six My Heart, a Geologist and the Sea*,(Vernon Press)

Weinberg, Samantha (1999), *A Fish caught in Time, the Search for the Coelacanth*, (Fourth Estate, London)

Articles

Able, K.W, R.A. Cooper and J.R. Uzman (1982); *Burrow construction and behavior of Tilefish in Hudson Submarine Canyon* (Environ. Biol. Fishes 7:199-205)

Auster, Peter J., et. al. (1995*); Patterns of microhabitat utilization by mobile megafauna on the southern New England continental shelf and slope*, (Mar. Eco. Pro. Ser. 127:77-85)

Awramik, Stanley (2006), *Paleontology: Respect for Stromatolites*, Nature 441: 700-701)

Bangert, Randy (1975); *UNC oceanographer to participate in deep Bahamas dive*, (Greeley Tribune April 4)

Belknap, D.F., et. al. (1988); *Sediment dynamics of the nearshore Gulf of Maine: submersible experimentation and remote sensing*, (NURP Res, Rep. 88-3: NOAA)

Betz, Clinton H. (1997); Admiral Sampson–*Part II*, (The Sea Chest, v.30, No. 3:119-137)

Bigelow, Bruce V. (1993); *Doomed liner's wreckage inspected*, (San Diego Tribune, Nov. 23)

Bowie, Laurel (1992); *Navy Sub finds 30-ft. human skull on ocean floor*, Weekly World News, July 21)

Buckley, Mark (1992); *Dumping waste has little impact on ocean floor*, Kodiak Daily Mirror, Jan. 27)

Campbell, Larry (1991); *Amorous Crabs get lots of attention*; (Anchorage Daily News, May 1)

Cooper, R.A., Valentine P., Uzmann J.R. and R.A. Slater (1988); *Submarine Canyons*, In: Georges Bank, p. 53-63, (Massachusetts Institute of Technology Press)

Cordes, Helen (1974); *UNC students explore coast of island in submarine*, (UNC Mirror May)

Freese, J.L., (2001); *Trawl-induced damage to sponges observed from a Research Submersible*, (Mar. Fish. Rev. 63(3): 7-16)

Ginsburg, R.N. and N.P. James (1976); *Submarine botryoidal aragonitein Holocene reef limestone's*, Belize, Geology, Vol. 4:431-436)

Grammer, G.M, R.N. Ginsburg, et. al. (1993); *Rapid Growth Rates of Syndepositional Marine Aragonite Cements in Steep marginal Slope Deposits, Bahamas and Belize*, (Journal of Sed. Pet, V. 63, No. 5:983-989)

———— R.N. Ginsburg, and P. Harris (1993); *Timing of Deposition, Diagenesis, and Failure of Steep Carbonate Slopes* in *Response to a High-Amplitude/High-Frequency Fluctuation in Sea Level, Tongue of the Ocean*, Bahamas, (in Carbonate Sequence Stratigraphy, Recent Developments and Applications, eds. R.G. Loucks and J.F. Sarg, AAPG Memoir 57:107-131)

———— and R.N. Ginsburg (1992); *Highstand versus low stand deposition of carbonate platform margins: insight from the Bahamas*, (Mar. Geol. v. 103:125-136)

Grimes, C.B and K.W. Able (1982); *Direct observation from a submersible vessel of commercial longlines for tilefish*, (Trans. Am. Fish. Soc. 111:94-98)

Gunstrom, Gary (1993); *Undersea Research in a Little Yellow Submarine*, (The Alaskan Southeaster Mag. July Issue: 23-25)

Hall, Andy (1991); *Fisherman and scientists explore the depths of Bay;* (Kodiak Daily Mirror, April 29)

Hancock, Suzanne (1991); *Submarine will help study Tanner crab*, (Kodiak Daily Mirror, Mar. 28)

Hepp, Jeff (1981); *Slater shares sub experience on TV show,*
(UNC Mirror Jan 16)

Hixon, M.A., and B.N. Tissot (2007); *Comparison of trawled vs.
untrawled mud seafloor assemblages of fishes and macroinvertibrates
at coquille Bank, Oregon,* (J. Exp. Mar. Biol. Ecol. 344:23-34)

Hulen, David (1989); *Holy Cow! That was a boving endeadeus!,*
(Santa Barbara News-Press, Sept 4)

Lundberg, Eric (1980); *A crash, a tremendous crash,*
(Empire Mag. April 20)

Kelly, Peter M. (1974); *He specializes in trash from the sea bottoms*
(The Fort Worth Press July 1)

Krieger, K.J. (1992); *Shortraker rockfish observed from a manned
submersible,* Mar. Fish. Rev. 54 (4): 34-36
———— (1993*); Distribution and abundance of rockfish
determined from a Submersible and by bottom trawling,*
(Fish. Bull. U.S. 91:87-96
———— (1997); *Sablefish observed from a manned submersible,*
(NOAA Tech Rep. NMFS AFSC 130, pp.39-43)

Land, L.S. and C.H. Moore (1977); *Deep forefeef and upper island
slope, north Jamaica,* (AAPG Geol. Stud. Vol. 4: 53-65)
———— and C.H. Moore (1980); *Lithification, micritization and
Syndepositional Diagenesis of biolithites on the Jamaican island slope,*
(Jour. Sed. Pet. v. 50:357-370)

Love, M.S. and A. York (2005); *A comparison of the fish
assemblages associated with an oil/gas pipeline and adjacent seafloor
in the Santa Barbara Channel,* (Bull. Mar. Sci. 77:101-117)
————, J.E. Caselle, and L. Snook (2000); *Fish assemblages
around seven oil platforms in the Santa Barbara channel Area,*
(Fish. Bull. U.S. 98:96-117)

Lowe, Missy (1977); *Slater a "doer": scuba diving, sailing, teaching*
(UNC Mirror April)

Mallinson, D. (1992); *20,000 Leagues under the Keys,*
(Earth Magazine 46-53, Nov)

McEntee, Marni (1992); *Scientists immerse selves in research,*
(Ventura Star Free Press, April 13)

McCosh, D. (1996); *Secrets of the Great lakes,*
(Popular Science, Vol. 6:92-96)

Morris, Eric (1996); *The Admiral's Diamo*,
(Discover Diving, Dec. Issue: 25-31)

Myers, Jeff (1994); *Fatal Voyage of the* Vil Vana,
(L.A. Times Aug. 4 1994)

—————— (1994); *Taking the Plunge*, (L.A. Times Nov.10 1994)

O'Connell, V.M. (1993); *Submersible observations on lingcod nesting
below 30 meters off Sitka, Alaska*, (Mar. Fish. Rev. 55(1): 19-24

——————, and D.W. Carlile (1993); *Habitat- specific density of adult
yelloweye rockfish in the eastern Gulf of Alaska*,(Fish. Bull. U.S.
91:304-309)

—————— and D.W. Carlile (1994); *Comparison of a remotely operated
vehicle and a submersible for estimating abundance of demersal shelf
rockfishes in the eastern Gulf of Alaska*, (N. Am. J. Fish. Manag.
14:196-201

Percy, W.G., et. al (1989); *Submersible observations of deep-reef fishes
of Heceta Bank*, (Oregon Fish. Bull. U.S. 878:955-965)

Porter, Patricia (1993); *Oceanographer probes* Lusitania,
(Oxnard Press-Courier)

Revkin, Andrew (1994); *Fathoming the Mysteries of the* Lusitania,
(TV Guide, April 4:29-31)

Sauder, Eric (1995); *Probing the Mysteries of the* Lusitania,
(The Titanic Commentator, Vol. 18, No. 4)

Shannon, Frederick J. (1995); *Does Expedition '94 to the* Edmund
Fitzgerald *solve the mystery of the greatest inland shipwreck?*
(Michigan Natural Resources Mag. Dec. issue: p.22-27)

Shinn, E.A., et. al. (1989); *Impact of exploratory Wells
Offshore South Florida*, (U.S. Dept. Interior MMS,
OCS Report/MMS 89-00220, 111 pp.)

—————— and B. Lidz (1991); *Impact of Exploratory Drilling, Eastern
Gulf of Mexico*; (OTC report 6871)

—————— and R.I. Wicklund (1989); *Artificial Reef observations from a
manned Submersible off southeast Florida*, (Bull. Mar. Sci.
V. 44(2): 1041-1050)

Shipp, R.C., D.F. Belknap, and J.T. Kelley (1991); *Seismic-
Stratigraphic and Geomorphic Evidence for a Post-Glacial Sea-Level
Lowstand in the Northern Gulf of Maine*,
(Jour. of Coastal Research, V. 7, No. 2:341-364)

Sink, George (1994); *Peering through the porthole, scientists study crab
in its seafloor home*, (Kodiak Daily Mirror, April 29 1994)

Sink, George (1994); *Underwater crab research yields some surprises,*
(Kodiak Daily Mirror, May 2 1994)

Slater, R. A. (1970); *Geomorphology and Cainozoic Geology of
The Continental Shelf between Cape Seal and Cape St. Francis,*
(SANCOR Tech. Report No. 2:28-33,
Dept. of Geology, Univ. of Cape Town
———— and R.H. Goodwin (1973); *Tasman Sea Guyots,*
Marine Geol. v.14: 81-99
———— and C.V.G. Phipps (1977); *A Preliminary Report on the
Coral Reefs of Lord Howe Island and Elizabeth Reef,
Australia,* (Proceedings, 3rd Int. Sym. on Coral Reefs, Miami)
———— and C.V.G. Phipps (1978); *Morphology of Elizabeth and
Middleton Reefs, Tasman Sea,*
(Int. Assoc. of Sediment. Meeting Abs, Jerusalem, Israel)
———— et. al. (1979); *Slumps on the Upper Continental
Slope Northeastern United States Observations from a Submersible,*
(Abs. Nat. AAPG- SEPM Meeting, Houston, Texas, and
AAPG Bull. v. 63 No. 2:529)
———— (1980); *Potential Hazard to Exploration and Exploitation of
Petroleum in the United States Atlantic Continental Margin,*
(U.S. Geological Survey Open File Report: 48pp)
———— (1981); *Submersible Observations of the Sea Floor near the
Proposed Georges Bank Lease Sites along the North Atlantic Outer
Continental Shelf and Upper Slope,*
(U.S. Geological Survey Open File Report 81-742: 65pp)
————, D.C. Twitchell, and J.M. Robb (1981);
*Submersible Observations of Potential Geologic Hazards along the
Mid-Atlantic Outer Continental Shelf and Uppermost Slope,*
U.S. Geological Survey Open File Report 81-968: 50pp)
————, D. Schofield, and C.V.G. Phipps (1981);
Geology and Recent history of Elizabeth Reef, Australia,
(Abs. Nat. AAPG-SEPM Meeting, San Francisco,
California, and AAPG Bull. v. 65 No. 3)
————, D. Schofield, and C.V.G. Phipps (1983);
Holocene Erosion of Elizabeth Reef, Tasman Sea, Australia,
(in SEPM Core Workshop Spec. Pub. No. 4:558-577
National AAPG-SEPM Meeting, Dallas, Texas)

————, L.D. Furse, and J.W. Vernon (1972); *Inspecting Pipeline Clusters, Wellheads, Fixed Platforms and Pollution Controls*, (Hydrospace Magazine April, 1972)

———— et. al. (1986); *Submersible Studies: Detailed Observations of the Seafloor of OAK, KOA and MIKE craters, Enewetak Atoll, Marshall Islands*, (U.S. Geological Survey Open File Rep. 86-419, Chapter 13:1-156)

————, R.N. Ginsburg, et. al. (1987); *Reef-Sourced Slope Deposits, Holocene, Bahamas*, (SEPM Carbonate Depositional and Diagenetic Symposium, AAPG-SEPM Nat. Convention, Los Angeles, and AAPG Bul. Abstract

———— and R.B. Halley (1987); *Geologic Reconnaissance of the Natural Fore-Reef Slope and a Large Submarine Rockfall Exposure*, Enewetak Atoll, AAPG-SEPM National Convention, Los Angeles, California, and AAPG Bull. Abstract)

———— (1987); DELTA *Submersible 1986-87 United States East Coast Operations*, (Oceans 87 Abs., Nova Scotia, Canada)

———— and Robert S. Grove (1991*); Sedimentation patterns and bedforms in the nearshore zone off San Onofre, California*, (1991 GSA meeting abstract)

———— et. al. (1991); *Physical processes that affect the siting of artificial habitats for fish off Southern California*, (1991 GSA meeting abstract)

———— (1992); *Commercial Submersibles – Staying Busy with* Delta, (Sea Technology Dec. Issue: 27-31)

————, D.S. Gorsline, R.L. Kolpack, and G.I. Shiller (2002); *Post-glacial sediments of the Californian Shelf from Cape San Martin to the US-Mexico border*, (Quaternary International Vol. 92:45-61)

———— (2004); *Douglas N. Privitt, Submersible Pioneer*, (Historical Diver, V. 12, Issue 4, No. 41: 27-30)

Speer, Larry (1992); *The Deep: Firm gets tiny Sub shipshape for research in the Pacific*, (L.A. Times, April 11)

Stanley, D.J., and G.L. Freeland (1977); *The Erosion-Deposition boundary in the head of Hudson Submarine Canyon defined on the basis of submarine observations*, (Marine Geology, V. 26:37-46)

Starr, R.M., et. al (1996); *Comparison of submersible-survey and hydroacoustic-survey estimates of fish density on a rocky bank,* (Fish. Bull. U.S. 94:113-123)

Stevens, B.G. et. al (1992); *First observations of podding behavior for the Pacific lyre crab (* J. Crust. Biol. 12:193-195)

———— et. al. ((1993); *Morphometry and maturity of paired tanner Crabs from shallow and deepwater environments,* (Canadian Jour. Fish and Aqua Science V. 50:1504-1516)

————, Jan Haaga and William E. Donaldson (1994); *Aggregative mating of Tanner crabs* (Can. Jour. of Fish. and Aqua. Sci. v.51, No. 6: 1273-1280)

———— (1994); *The Mystery of Crab Mountains,* (Ocean Realm: 41-44)

Stone, Dave (1993); *Local ship uncovers* Lusitania, (Ventura Star)

Stoner, A. W., et. al (2008*); Evaluating the role of fish behavior in surveys conducted with underwater vehicles* (Can. J. Fish. Aquatic. Science. 65:1230-1243)

Swagel, Will (1991); *Submarine lets Scientists get close to Fish,* (Sitka Daily Sentinel, May)

Turkel, Tux (1990); *Explorers probe mystery of craters under Belfast Bay* (Maine Sunday Telegram, July 22)

Unknown (1968); *Search for gold off NSW coast;* (Sydney Morning Herald, Mar)

———— (1970); *Depth swim to survival,* (Los Angeles Herald-Examiner, Sept 29)

———— (1974); *Oceanographer could open pawn shop with discoveries,* (The Columbia, South Carolina, State, June 22)

———— (1974); *He spots planes, cars, beer cans and kitchen sink on ocean floor,*(The Miami Herald, June 23)

———— (1975); *Discovery Bay not much like Gunter pool or Carter Lake,* (Greeley Tribune Jan 31)

———— (1975); *UNC Prof to study coral reef-250 feet below surface of Caribbean,*(Rocky Mountain News April 7)

———— (1975); *UNC students spend break in "dives"* (Greeley Tribune, Apr. 9)

———— (1991); *Sub explores offshore reefs,* Delta *makes 115 dives on four reefs,* (The Oregon Scientist, Vo. IV, No. 4)

Uzmann, J.R., and R.A. Cooper (1977); *Synoptic comparison of three sampling techniques for estimating abundance and distribution of selected Megafauna: Submersible vs. camera sled vs. otter trawl,* (Mar. Fish. Rev. 39(12): 11-19)

Vernon, J.W. and R.A. Slater (1963): *Submarine Tar Mounds* Santa Barbara County, California, (AAPG Bull. v.47, No. 8:1924-1927)

Warme, John, R.A. Slater, and R.A. Cooper (1978); *Bioerosion in Submarine Canyons,* in Sedimentation in Submarine Canyons, Eds. D.J. Stanley & G. Kelling, pp. 65-72

Weller, Doug (1976); *Deep-sea research takes UNC Prof to Barrier Reef,* (Greeley Tribune, Feb. 18)

Weyermann, D. (1988); *Ocean is obstacle in the bid to retrieve scientific equipment,* (Santa Barbara News-Press, Nov 20)

Will, Steve (1994); *Experts to Look at Fish in Depth,* (Sitka Daily Sentinel, 13 Apr 1994)
——— (1994); *Fish Scientists Go to Great Depth for Study,* (Sitka Daily Sentinel, 3 June 1994)

Wray, John L. 1972); *Submarine Reef Exploration in British Honduras,* (Mines Magazine, April)

Yoklavich, Mary M., et. al. (1993); *Submersible observations in a submarine canyon,* (Prod. Amer. Acad. of UW Science, Annual Science diving symposium, pp. 173-181)
——— (1997); *Applications of side-scan sonar and in situ submersible survey techniques to marine fisheries habitat research,* (NOAA Tech. Mem. NMFS SWFSC 239, pp. 140-141)
——— and M. Love (2005); *Christmas tree corals: A new species discovered off Southern California,* (J. Mar. Education. 21:27-30)
——— and Victoria O'Connell (2008); *Twenty Years of Research on Demersal Communities using the* Delta *submersible in the Northeast Pacific,* in *Marine Habitat Mapping Technology for Alaska,* J.R. Reynolds and H.G. Greene (eds.), (Alaska Sea Grant College Program)

Zhou, S., and T.C. Shirley (1997); *Distribution of red king crabs and tanner crabs in the summer by habitat and depth in an Alaskan fjord,* (Invest. Mar. Valparaiso 25:59-67)

INDEX

(Illustrations in **bold**)

Made in the USA
San Bernardino, CA
30 December 2015